Victoria Crosses on the Western Front Battle of Albert

21–27 August 1918

Victoria Crosses on the Western Front Battle of Albert

21–27 August 1918

Paul Oldfield

Pen & Sword
MILITARY

First published in Great Britain in 2021 by
Pen & Sword Military
an imprint of
Pen & Sword Books Ltd
47 Church Street
Barnsley
South Yorkshire
S70 2AS

Copyright © Paul Oldfield 2021

ISBN 978 1 52678 799 6

The right of Paul Oldfield to be identified as the Author of this Work has been asserted by him in accordance with the Copyright, Designs and Patents Act 1988.

A CIP catalogue record for this book is available from the British Library

All rights reserved. No part of this book may be reproduced or transmitted in any form or by any means, electronic or mechanical including photocopying, recording or by any information storage and retrieval system, without permission from the Publisher in writing.

Typeset in Ehrhardt by
Mac Style
Printed and bound in the UK by TJ Books Ltd, Padstow, Cornwall

Pen & Sword Books Ltd incorporates the imprints of Pen & Sword Archaeology, Atlas, Aviation, Battleground, Discovery, Family History, History, Maritime, Military, Naval, Politics, Railways, Select, Social History, Transport, True Crime, and Claymore Press, Frontline Books, Leo Cooper, Praetorian Press, Remember When, Seaforth Publishing and Wharncliffe.

For a complete list of Pen & Sword titles please contact

PEN & SWORD BOOKS LIMITED
47 Church Street, Barnsley, South Yorkshire, S70 2AS, England
E-mail: enquiries@pen-and-sword.co.uk
Website: www.pen-and-sword.co.uk

Or

PEN AND SWORD BOOKS
1950 Lawrence Rd, Havertown, PA 19083, USA
E-mail: Uspen-and-sword@casematepublishers.com
Website: www.penandswordbooks.com

Contents

Master Maps *vi*
Abbreviations *viii*
Introduction *x*

Master Maps 1 and 2 1

387. LSgt Edward Smith, 1/5 Lancashire Fusiliers, 21 August 1918, Near Miraumont, France
388. Cdr Daniel Beak, Drake Battalion, RND, 21 & 25 August 1918, Logeast Wood and Loupart Wood, France
389. Lt Col Richard West, North Irish Horse att'd 6 Tank Battalion, 21 August & 2 September 1918, Courcelles and Vaulx-Vraucourt, France
390. LCpl George Onions, 1 Devonshire, 22 August 1918, Achiet-le-Petit, France
391. Lt Lawrence McCarthy, 16 Battalion, AIF, 23 August 1918, Madame Wood, France
392. Lt William Joynt, 8 Battalion, AIF, 23 August 1918, Herleville Wood, France
393. Pte Hugh McIver, 2 Royal Scots, 23 August 1918, Gomiécourt, France
394. Sgt Samuel Forsyth, NZ Engineers att'd 2 Auckland, NZEF, 24 August 1918, Grévillers, France
395. Sgt Harold Colley, 10 Lancashire Fusiliers, 25 August 1918, Martinpuich, France
396. LCpl Bernard Gordon, 41 Battalion, AIF, 26–27 August 1918, Bray, France

Biographies 45
Sources 181
Useful Information 186
Index 190

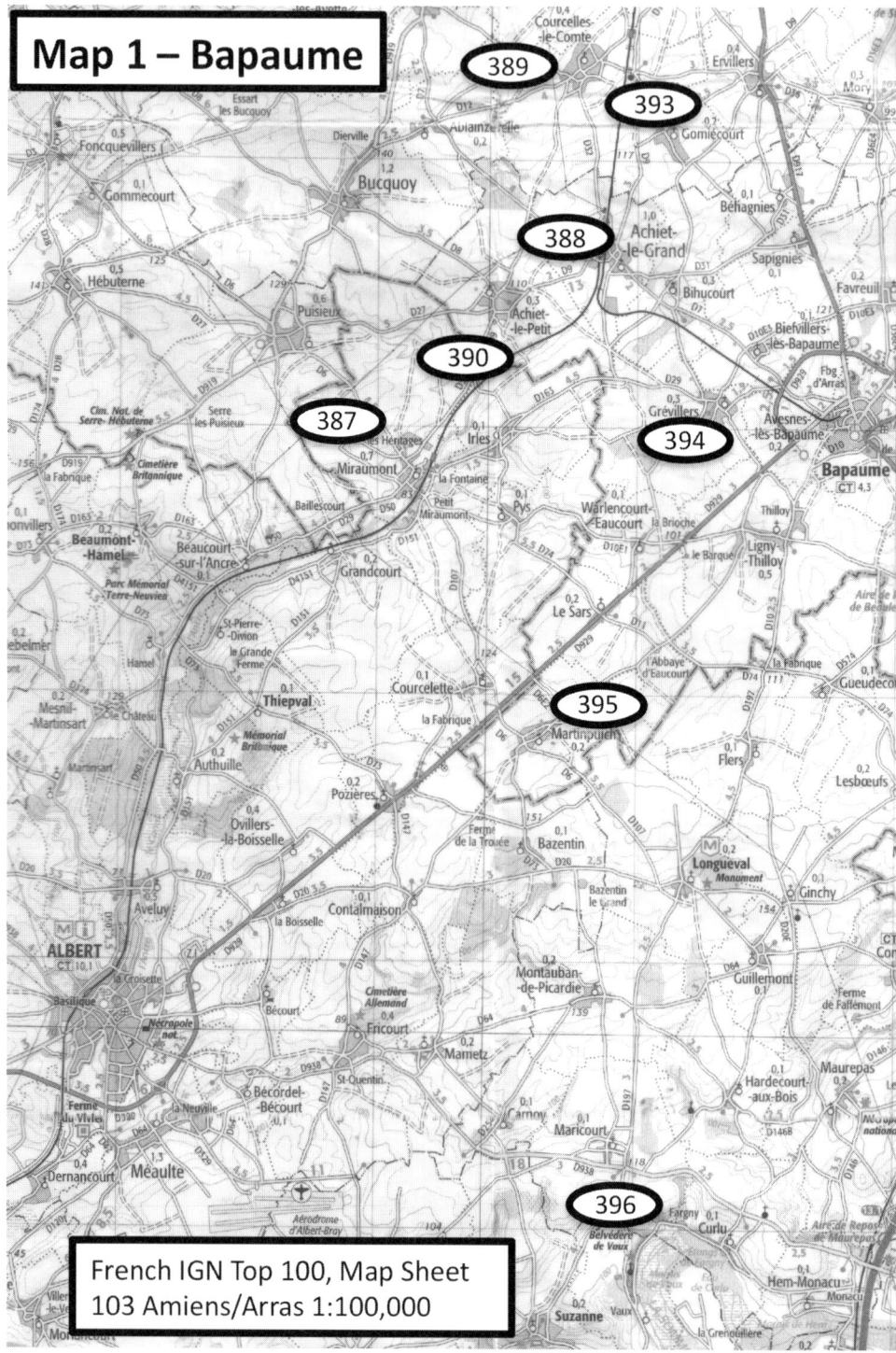

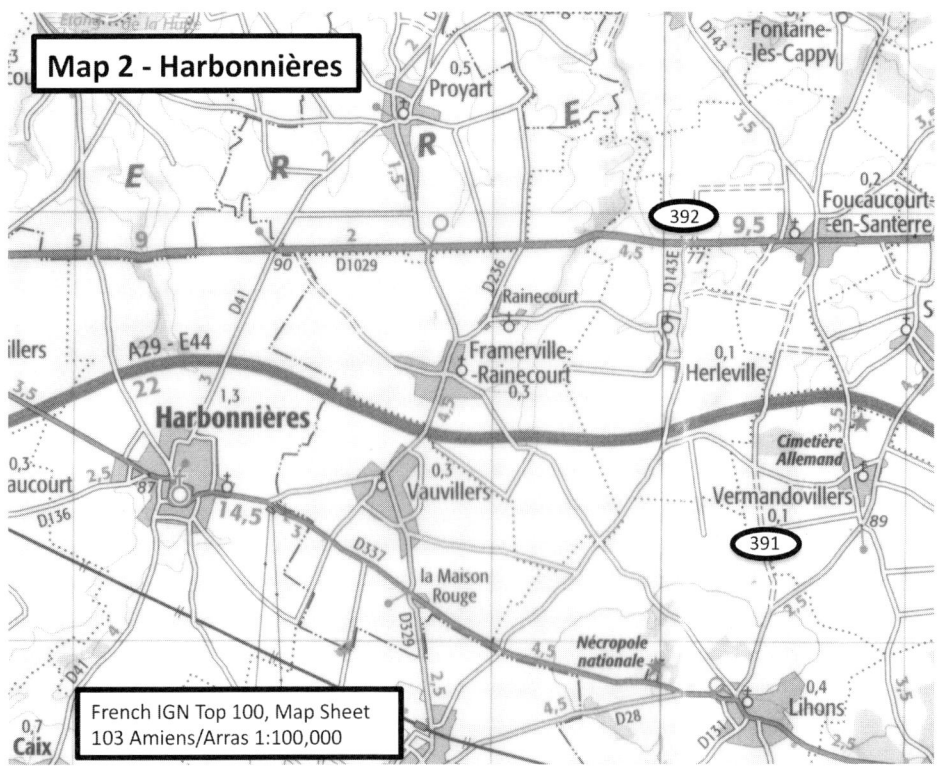

Abbreviations

ADC	Aide-de-Camp
AIF	Australian Imperial Force
ANZAC	Australian & New Zealand Army Corps
Att'd	Attached
BEF	British Expeditionary Force
BM	Brigade Major
Brig Gen	Brigadier General
Bty	Battery (artillery unit of 4–8 guns)
Capt	Captain
CB	Companion of the Order of the Bath
CBE	Commander of the Order of the British Empire
CCS	Casualty Clearing Station
CIGS	Chief of the Imperial General Staff
C-in-C	Commander-in-Chief
CMG	Companion of the Order of St Michael & St George
CMS	Church Missionary Society
Co	County
CO	Commanding Officer
Col	Colonel
Cpl	Corporal
CQMS	Company Quartermaster Sergeant
CSgt	Colour Sergeant
CSM	Company Sergeant Major
Cty	Cemetery
CWGC	Commonwealth War Graves Commission
DCM	Distinguished Conduct Medal
DEMS	Defensively Equipped Merchant Ships
DL	Deputy Lieutenant
DSO	Distinguished Service Order
Dvr	Driver
FM	Field Marshal
FTS	Flying Training School
Gen	General
GHQ	General Headquarters
GOC	General Officer Commanding
HE	High Explosive

HMS	Her/His Majesty's Ship
HMT	Her/His Majesty's Transport/Troopship/Hired Military Transport
Kia	Killed in action
Kms	Kilometres
LCpl	Lance Corporal
LG	London Gazette
Lt	Lieutenant
Lt Col	Lieutenant Colonel
Lt Gen	Lieutenant General
Maj	Major
Maj Gen	Major General
MBE	Member of the Order of the British Empire
MC	Military Cross
MGC	Machine Gun Corps
MID	Mentioned in Despatches
MM	Military Medal
MO	Medical Officer
MSM	Meritorious Service Medal
NCO	Non Commissioned Officer
OBE	Officer of the Order of the British Empire
OC	Officer Commanding
Pte	Private
RAF	Royal Air Force
RCAF	Royal Canadian Air Force
RMLI	Royal Marine Light Infantry
RMO	Regimental Medical Officer
RN	Royal Navy
RND	Royal Naval Division
RNVR	Royal Naval Volunteer Reserve
RQMS	Regimental Quartermaster Sergeant
RSL	Returned and Services League
RSM	Regimental Sergeant Major
RTR	Royal Tank Regiment
Sgt	Sergeant
SNCO	Senior non-commissioned officers
Spr	Sapper
SS	Steam Ship
TA	Territorial Army
TD	Territorial Decoration
TF	Territorial Force
Tr	Trench
USA	United States of America
VC	Victoria Cross
WA	Western Australia
WO1 or 2	Warrant Officer Class 1 or 2

Introduction

The ninth book in this series continues the story of the Hundred Days, the final advance by the Allies leading to the Armistice. The Hundred Days resulted in the award of 119 VCs; almost a quarter of the 492 land forces VCs awarded for the Western Front between 1914 and 1918. This book covers the ten VCs awarded for the Battle of Albert 1918, four of which were to Dominion troops.

As with previous books in the series, it is written for the battlefield visitor as well as the armchair reader. Each account provides background information to explain the broad strategic and tactical situation, before focusing on the VC action in detail. Each is supported by a map to allow a visitor to stand on, or close to, the spot and at least one photograph of the site. Detailed biographies help to understand the man behind the Cross.

The titles of battles, actions and affairs are as decided by the post-war Battle Nomenclature Committee. VCs are numbered chronologically 387, 388, 389 etc from 21st August 1918. Refer to the master maps to find the general area for each VC. If visiting the battlefields it is advisable to purchase maps from the respective French and Belgian 'Institut Géographique National'. The French IGN Top 100 and Belgian IGN Provinciekaart at 1:100,000 scale are ideal for motoring, but 1:50,000, 1:25,000 or 1:20,000 scale maps are necessary for more detailed work, e.g. French IGN Serie Bleue and Belgian IGN Topografische Kaart. They are obtainable from the respective IGN or through reputable map suppliers on-line.

Ranks are as used on the day. Grave references have been shortened, e.g. 'Plot II, Row A, Grave 10' will appear as 'II A 10'. There are some abbreviations, many in common usage, but if unsure refer to the list provided.

I endeavour to include memorials to each VC in their biographies. However, every VC is commemorated in the VC Diary and on memorial panels at the Union Jack Club, Sandell Street, Waterloo, London. To include this in every biography would be unnecessarily repetitive.

Thanks are due to too many people and organisations to mention here. They are acknowledged in 'Sources' and any omissions are my fault and not intentional. The continuing contribution of fellow members of the 'Victoria Cross Database Users Group', Doug and Richard Arman, is fundamental to the completion of these books.

Paul Oldfield
Wiltshire
March 2021

Battle of Albert 1918 and Subsequent Operations

21st August 1918

387 LSgt Edward Smith, 1/5th Lancashire Fusiliers (125th Brigade, 42nd Division), Near Miraumont, France

388 Cdr Daniel Beak, Drake Battalion (189th Brigade, 63rd Division, Logeast Wood and Loupart Wood, France

389 Lt Col Richard West, North Irish Horse att'd 6th Tank Battalion (2nd Tank Brigade), Courcelles and Vaulx-Vraucourt, France

Although the Anglo-French offensive that ended on 12th August had caused considerable damage to the German Army, the Allies had wasted opportunities. Troops had not been handled boldly and the tanks had been disappointing. After years in the trenches, the BEF had little experience of open warfare and a steep learning process was underway.

The Germans fell back to the almost intact trench lines of early 1917 and brought up fourteen reserve divisions. The Allies called a temporary halt while they built up resources for another push. Between 11th and 20th August small scale operations south of the Somme chipped away at the German defences and a general advance of about 1,800m was achieved, following which the Germans pulled back north of the Somme to shorten their line.

The Allied plan was for the Armies on the flanks of the 8th August offensive (French Tenth and Sixth Armies on the right and British Third and First Armies on the left) to envelop the Germans in the centre. Third Army was ordered by Haig to take Bapaume, while First Army to the north was to recover Monchy-le-Preux. At the same time the British Fourth and French First Armies in the centre were to take any opportunity to push forward. Further north, Second Army was to nibble away around Mount Kemmel, to make the Germans believe that an offensive was also threatened in that area.

Third Army's objective was the Albert–Arras railway and preparations were made in utmost secrecy. The first objective (Blue Line), the Ablainzeville–Moyenneville spur, was to be secured by the left of IV Corps and the right of VI Corps. Both Corps were then to advance to the Albert–Arras railway (Green Line). IV Corps was also to capture the remainder of the Serre–Miraumont spur. On the right, V Corps was to be prepared to extend the attack southeast towards Pozières. Half the soldiers taking part were newly arrived youngsters. Consequently tactical handling was concerned

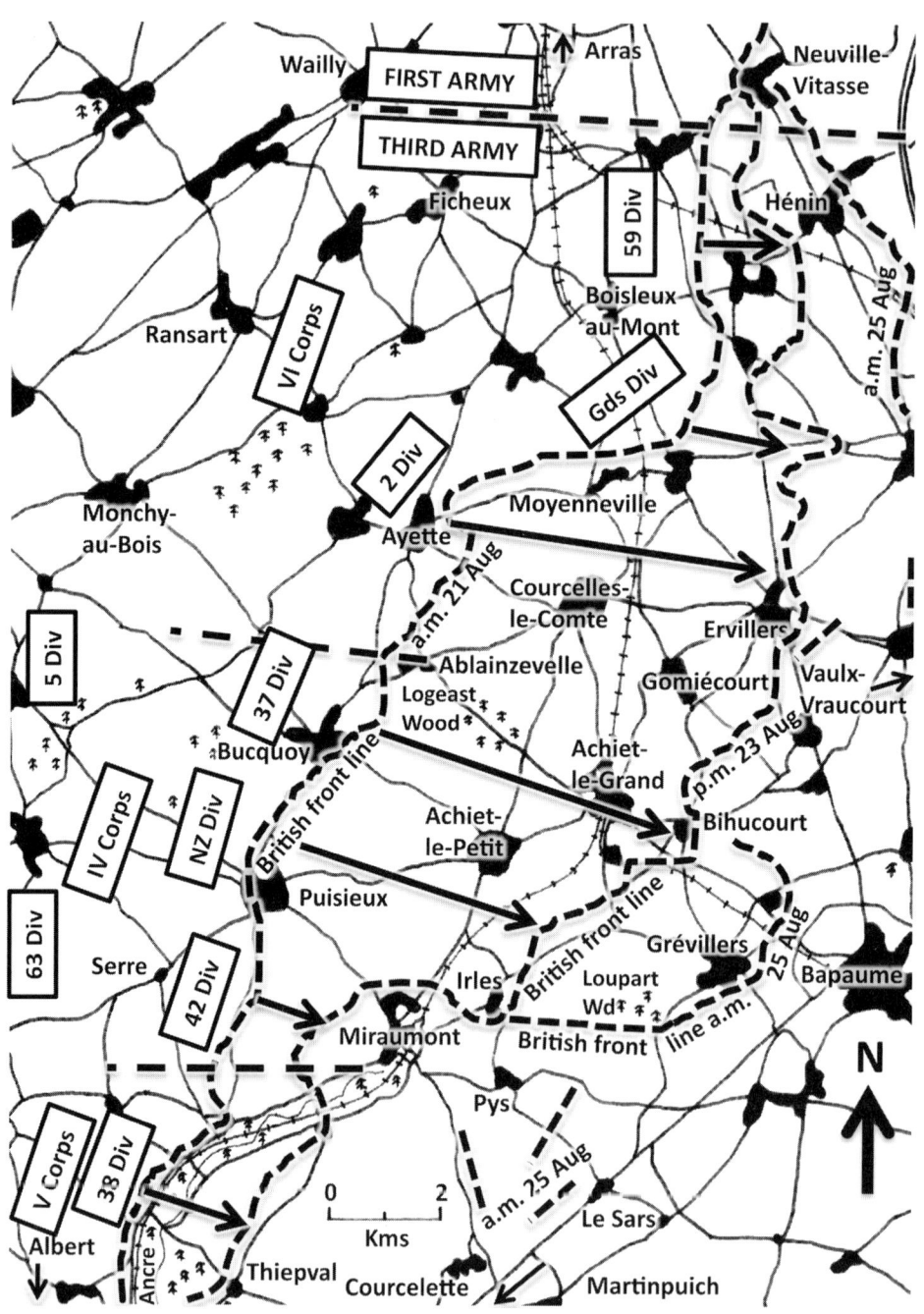

The Third Army area 21st–25th August.

mainly with retaining control in the hands of the few experienced officers. Steady advance was preferred to attempting to rupture the front and infiltrating deep into the enemy's rear areas. Although Third Army faced intact trench systems, the Germans did not occupy them systematically, which allowed for more open manoeuvre than in previous battles.

On the right, V Corps made minor gains but was severely hampered by the flooded Ancre valley. Further operations were suspended there until Albert fell. In the centre of Third Army, IV Corps attacked at 4.55 a.m., with 42nd, New Zealand and 37th Divisions. The first objective was 900m away on high ground. There was an intermediate objective (Brown Line) on the way to the second objective, as this was some 6,400m from the start line. A flank was to be formed on the right to connect with V Corps. At the first objective, 63rd and 5th Divisions, on the right and left respectively, were to pass through and exploit as far as the third objective, east of Bihucourt and Irles. 1st Tank Brigade was in support.

In 42nd Division, 125th Brigade on the left, next to the New Zealanders, was to commence the attack, with 127th Brigade joining in later on the right. 125th Brigade had three objectives. First, 1/5th Lancashire Fusiliers was to seize the Red Line, which included the Lozenge (Hill 140), about 1,600m south of Puisieux. Second, its reserve company was to go on 800m to take the high ground to the east. Finally, 1/7th Lancashire Fusiliers was to take Beauregard Dovecot, a strongpoint at the junction of five roads/tracks, on the high ground northwest of Miraumont. It was then to push patrols forward another kilometre or so. 1/8th Lancashire Fusiliers was in reserve.

Thick mist covered the assembly and at 4.45 a.m. the attackers set off in a series of fighting patrols, covered by most of the Division's artillery and machine guns. D, A and C Companies, 1/5th Lancashire Fusiliers, led, with B Company in support. The fire plan was complicated due to a shortage of guns. The artillery had to cover 125th Brigade onto the first objective, then switch to support 127th Brigade as it made its first moves, before switching back again to support 125th Brigade's advance on the second objective. During this final phase, 1/7th Lancashire Fusiliers was to be supported by the artillery of the New Zealand Division.

42nd Machine Gun Battalion allocated four guns to the Red Line, two on each flank and another four guns to the Brown Line. No.59 Squadron RAF was to fly contact patrols overhead at one, three, five and seven hours after zero hour.

Covered by the mist, the leading companies were soon on the first objective (Red Line) and at 6.55 a.m. B Company set off for the second objective (Blue Line). **Lance Sergeant Edward Smith**, commanding one of the B Company platoons, came upon an intact machine gun post. He rushed the position and the gunners scattered to throw grenades at him. Undeterred he charged and killed six of them. With the way clear, he led his platoon to capture two more machine gun posts and was in the thick of the action again. A little later, he noticed that the neighbouring platoon was held up and took command of both platoons to lead them onto the

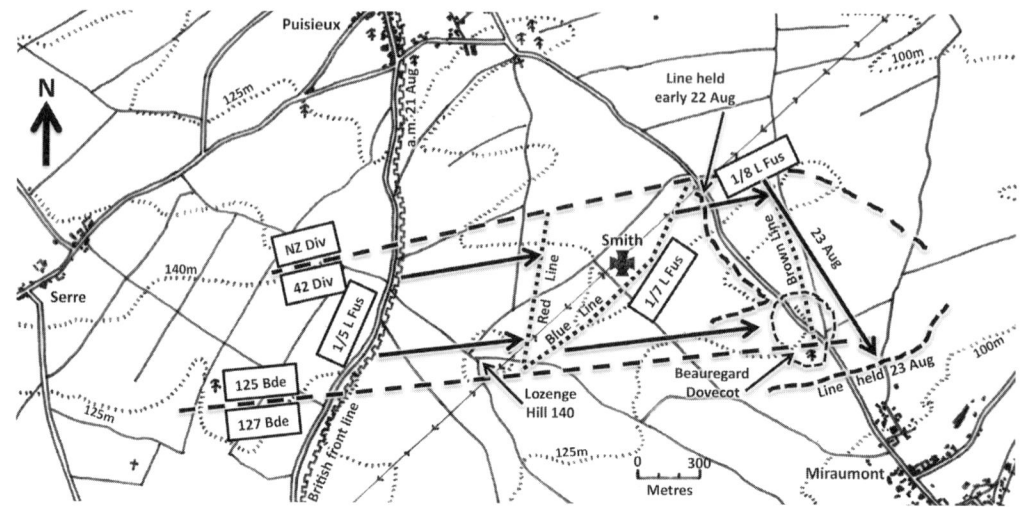

Leave Miraumont northwestwards on the D107 towards Puisieux. After a few hundred metres at the top of the hill is Beauregard Dovecot, marked by the copse to the left of the road. Continue for 900m and, as the road begins to rise after crossing a re-entrant, turn left onto a track. Follow it to the southwest for 650m and stop at the t-junction because the track from here onwards is much rougher. Walk on to the southwest up the slope towards the Lozenge for just over 300m and turn round. This is where the Red Line crossed the track. Look across the re-entrant. The Blue Line ran parallel with the track you are on, about 200m to the southeast. The copse at Beauregard Dovecot is very clear from here.

objective. On the way he killed many of the enemy himself. By 7 a.m. the second objective was held and consolidation was underway.

Touch was established with the New Zealand Division on the left and 127th Brigade on the right. At 8.55 a.m., A and B Companies, 1/7th Lancashire Fusiliers passed through and headed for the third objective (Brown Line), which was taken with the exception of Beauregard Dovecot, which was strongly held. The Battalion was also not in contact with the New Zealanders on the left. The mist lifted around this time and the most advanced troops found themselves under point blank fire from a German battery. They went to ground in shell holes and a

From the Lozenge on the Red Line looking east. The Blue Line ran parallel with and on the far side of the re-entrant that runs across the middle of the picture. Beauregard Dovecot is on the right.

counterattack almost wiped them out. Nevertheless, by 1.25 p.m. 1/7th Lancashire Fusiliers was reporting that an officer patrol had been pushed forward about 900m.

It was not until 2 a.m. on the 22nd that the Dovecot was taken by A Company, 1/7th Lancashire Fusiliers. The Germans counterattacked at 4.45 a.m., putting 1/7th and 1/5th Lancashire Fusiliers under severe pressure. The attack was held, except at the Dovecot, but the enemy suffered very heavy casualties. Smith was once more to the fore, leading a section to restore a portion of line that had been lost. As a result of heavy enemy fire the line was withdrawn to the sunken road running southeast from Puisieux towards Miraumont. His steadiness and skill resolved a potentially dangerous situation. Later in the morning A Company, 1/7th Lancashire Fusiliers, twice asked for a barrage on the Dovecot. At 12.25 p.m. a RAF reconnaissance flight reported no enemy movement in the Dovecot.

Another counterattack at 7 p.m. ran into the German supporting barrage, as well as the British SOS barrage, and faded quickly. In the early hours of the 23rd, A and D Companies, 1/8th Lancashire Fusiliers, attacked from the northern flank and surprised the Germans. They retook the Dovecot in a daring attack, which enabled other formations to take up the battle later in the day. 125th Brigade was eventually relieved on 24th August. By then 1/5th Lancashire Fusiliers had lost twenty-one men killed, sixty-seven wounded and eight missing. In addition to Smith's VC, the Battalion received six other gallantry awards – a Bar to the DCM for CSM J Fisher DCM MM, the DCM to CSM FJ Carless, Sergeant J Lea, Corporal C Greenhalgh and Private F Hewson and the MM to Sergeant H Cawley.

Zero hour for the New Zealand and 37th Divisions was 4.55 a.m. and they took the first objective (Blue Line) with little difficulty. The advance was taken over by 63rd and 5th Divisions at 6.25 a.m., with each division leading with two brigades. In 63rd Division these were 188th on the left and 189th on the right, with 190th Brigade in reserve. Twenty-eight Mark IV tanks were allocated for the intermediate objective and another twenty-four for the second and third objectives, together with twenty-four Whippets. The tanks came from 7th, 10th and 3rd Battalions. 63rd Division had 5th Division on its right and 3rd Division on its left.

189th Brigade, on 63rd Division's right, advanced with the Drake and Hawke Battalions leading on the left and right respectively. Attached were C Company, 63rd Machine Gun Battalion and a section of 248th Field Company RE. The

6 Victoria Crosses on the Western Front Battle of Albert

intermediate objective (Brown Line), just east of Logeast Wood, was to be taken by the leading three companies of the Hawke Battalion and two companies of the Drake Battalion. Three companies of the Hood Battalion in reserve, and the two support companies of the Drake Battalion would then pass through to seize the Red Line (in some documents this is the Green Line), while the Hawke Battalion reformed to create a new Brigade reserve. If the Drake Battalion was held up in Logeast Wood, the Hawke and Hood Battalions were to press on, outflank the Wood and join with 188th Brigade on the Red Line. It was stressed that the capture of the brickfields, west of Achiet-le-Grand, should occur as quickly as possible. Finally 190th Brigade was to pass through to seize the final objective, the Red Dotted Line (Green Dotted Line in some documents).

Drive through Logeast Wood on the D7 southeast towards Achiet-le-Grand. 350m after leaving the Wood there is some hard standing on the left. Park there and look southeast towards the village. The cemetery is off to the left of the road and the brickworks were beyond the copse that surrounds the déchetterie (dump) to the right of the road.

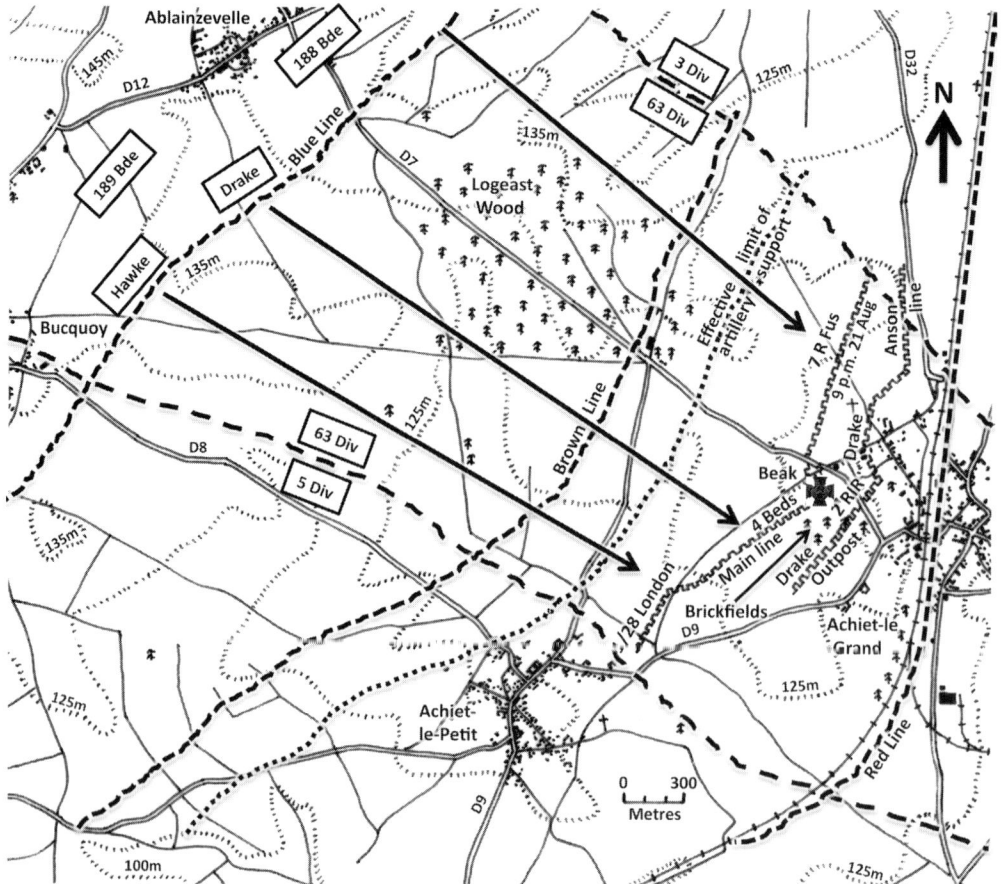

189th Brigade allocated two mortars to each of the assault battalions for the advance to the Brown Line. The two mortars with the Hawke Battalion were to join the Hood Battalion for the advance to the Red Line. Another two mortar teams, with 150 rounds of ammunition, were to move forward with a carrier tank and were to engage any target necessary to assist the infantry to advance. When the advance had been completed these two guns were to be attached to the Drake Battalion. The carrier tank also took forward 240 Mills grenades, 1,500 rounds of small arms ammunition and fifty tins of water. Nine Mark IV tanks of 7th Tank Battalion were to cooperate in the advance to the Brown Line. Mark V tanks of 10th Tank Battalion were to assist with the advance to the Green Line. Whippets of 3rd Tank Battalion were also to cooperate in the final advance, supported by some armoured cars. The Whippets would be about 1,350m ahead of the advancing infantry and two sections of Mark Vs about 900m in advance. A few Mark Vs were to accompany the infantry second wave. A contact patrol of No.59 Squadron RAF was to fly over at zero hour plus three, five and seven hours. The Squadron was also to drop supplies of ammunition into the forward positions.

The Brown Line was reached without major incident at 7.05 a.m., except for navigational difficulties caused by the fog and resistance at Logeast Wood, which was cleared by 7.50 a.m. This delayed 63rd Division and, as a result, 5th Division was on the Brown Line half an hour earlier. By 8.30 a.m. the entire Brown Line within 63rd Division's boundaries had been secured. Although somewhat disorganised, the assault troops were ready to continue and at 9.15 a.m. the advance resumed. Resistance stiffened and 188th Brigade suffered heavily from Achiet-le-Grand. The artillery support weakened as the advance progressed and only B Company, Anson Battalion reached the second objective on the extreme left. The left of 189th Brigade experienced the same problems but, on the right, two companies of the Hood Battalion and a company of the Drake Battalion on their left reached the second objective (Albert–Arras railway) at 11.30 a.m. They joined up with 5th Division on the right flank, which had been assisted by a company of the Hood Battalion and a tank in taking Achiet-le-Petit.

The centre of 63rd Division was held up, including the bulk of the Drake Battalion, in the outskirts of Achiet-le-Grand, around the cemetery, brickfields and some sunken huts. Numerous machine guns and anti-tank guns presented formidable resistance to the attackers. The mist began to clear at about 11 a.m. and had lifted by noon. However, by then the supporting artillery was out of range and the tanks had been knocked out by the anti-tank guns. Without support, the infantry made a gallant but futile effort to capture the position. **Commander Daniel Beak**, commanding the Drake Battalion, led his men with great determination. He captured four enemy positions under heavy fire but was not able to reach the objective on the railway line. This was the first incident for which he was awarded the VC. The second, on 25th August, is described later.

Looking along the axis of advance of the Drake Battalion.

Further advance proved impossible. A counterattack at 12.05 p.m. from Achiet-le-Grand forced the centre of the Division to fall back to the east of Logeast Wood and a line was formed a few hundred metres from it. Outposts were maintained and the Anson Battalion managed a small advance in the afternoon. However, by 6 p.m. all movement had ended and the line was consolidated for the night. By 9.00 p.m. the Anson (188th Brigade) and Drake (189th Brigade) Battalions were forming advanced posts, assisted by two companies of 2nd Royal Irish Regiment (188th Brigade). The main line behind was held by 190th Brigade with, from left to right, 7th Royal Fusiliers, 4th Bedfordshire and 1/28th London, with the Hood and Hawke Battalions (189th Brigade) behind. That night the flanks of 63rd Division fell back from the second objective. Next day between 5.55 a.m. and 1.15 p.m. the enemy came on in three determined counterattacks, which were driven off with the assistance of the artillery and trench mortars.

Meanwhile by 9.30 a.m. on 21st August, 5th Division had two battalions on the third objective. However, other units were not so fortunate and German pressure forced these battalions back to a line between the third objective and Achiet-le-Petit. The New Zealand Division was also unable to make much progress beyond the intermediate line once the fog lifted.

Although IV Corps failed to take its final objective on 21st August, it did succeed in advancing five kilometres and taking 1,400 prisoners. On the left of IV Corps was VI Corps. It attacked at 4.55 a.m. with 2nd and Guards Divisions, each with one brigade. VI Corps was supported by 2nd Tank Brigade, which consisted of 6th (Light) Tank Battalion with Whippets, 12th Tank Battalion with Mark IVs and 15th Tank Battalion with Mark V*s. Attached were four cars from 17th (Armoured Car) Battalion, eleven carrier tanks from No.1 Gun Carrier Company and No.3 Tank Supply Company. 99th and 2nd Guards Brigades made the initial assault, with twenty-six and twelve tanks attached respectively from 12th Tank Battalion. Once

the first objective was taken, 3rd Division was to pass through 2nd Division and take up the advance alongside the Guards Division, both supported by 15th Tank Battalion.

The Guards Division had 5th Brigade (2nd Division) attached for the advance to the second objective (Red Line) on the Albert–Arras railway. As soon as the Red Line was reached, a brigade of 1st Cavalry Division was to exploit in the general direction of Bapaume, supported by 15th Tank Battalion. At the same time, Whippets of 6th (Light) Tank Battalion were to push forward independently towards Ervillers, Behagnies and Sapignies. The 3rd and Guards Divisions were to be prepared to exploit the success of the cavalry and tanks towards the Red Dotted Line. The final objective ran from Moyenneville to the north of Bihucourt.

It was expected that IV Corps on the right would not advance as quickly as VI Corps. Accordingly the latter was to pivot on its right in order to seize Courcelles as quickly as possible on the left. The right was to keep pace with IV Corps as it passed through Logeast Wood.

Many Mark IV tanks (12th Tank Battalion) lost their way in the fog, particularly in the Guards Division's area, but nevertheless the first objective fell with little loss. The advance to the second objective commenced at 5.40 a.m., when 8th and 9th Brigades (3rd Division) passed through 99th Brigade. Although no supporting tanks (Mark V*s of 15th Tank Battalion) arrived in time, many turned up later, with some reaching the objective ahead of the infantry. The mist continued to cause confusion but it also spoiled the enemy's aim. On the left, the Guards reached the Albert–Arras railway at 11.30 a.m. However, 8th Brigade made more rapid progress and was on the second objective by 8.45 a.m. In 9th Brigade on the right, the left battalion reached the railway around 9 a.m., but the right battalion could not reach the objective. Except for this 800m stretch, VI Corps gained the whole of the second

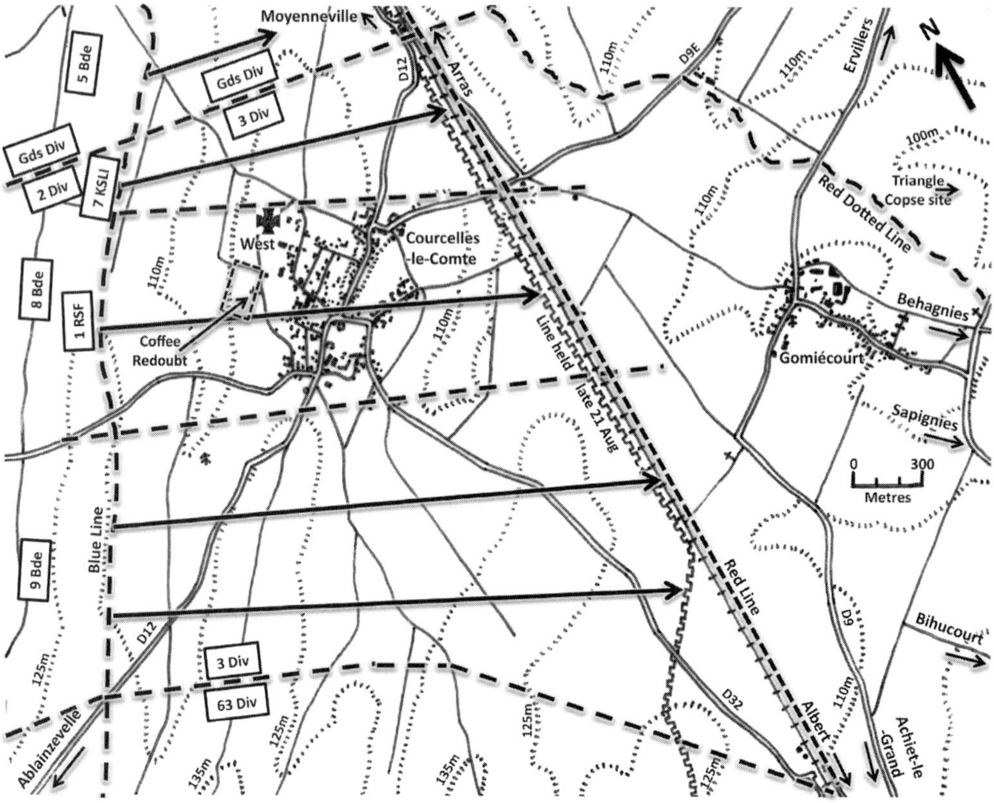

10   Victoria Crosses on the Western Front Battle of Albert

In Moyenneville drive southwest along the D32 from the church. As the D32 turns to the southeast, go straight on along a minor road (Rue d'Ablainzevelle). After 350m turn left onto a track heading directly towards the church in Courcelles-le-Comte and continue for 600m to the track junction. Stop there for a view over the whole of the battlefield in front of Courcelles-le-Comte. The VC location is approximate.

Looking southeast from just left (north) of the inter-battalion boundary in 8th Brigade.

objective. Apart from minor improvements to local positions, the advance came to a halt when the fog lifted.

Major Richard West started the morning as second-in-command of 6th (Light) Tank Battalion (2nd Tank Brigade). In the preceding fortnight he had earned a Bar to his DSO and the MC. The Battalion's role was to follow behind the attacking troops and heavy tanks (12th Battalion's Mark IVs to the Blue Line and 15th Battalion's Mark V*s to the Red Line) in order to exploit success east of the railway. To maintain touch with the Whippets, West advanced on horseback. At first the tanks were able to support the infantry but, by 8 a.m., in front of Courcelles, fog restricted visibility to ten metres and the tanks got ahead of the infantry and were not able to support them closely.

West was aware that the attack was in danger of collapsing. The troops had lost direction in the fog and, under heavy fire, were faltering. Remaining in the saddle, West collected, reorganised and rallied the infantry and led them forward again. He had two horses shot from under him and eventually continued on foot, being the first to reach Courcelles. Despite heavy machine gun fire, the infantry swept into the village and secured it. By 11 a.m. the fog was beginning to lift as the infantry consolidated on the line of the railway east of Courcelles. Tank companies pushed forward into the valley south of Courcelles and 275m west of the railway. However, the opportunity to exploit across the railway in force had passed.

The description of the action indicates that West was most probably supporting 8th Brigade, possibly 1st Royal Scots Fusiliers, but none of the war diaries state this explicitly. 8th Brigade attacked with 7th King's Shropshire Light Infantry on the left and 1st Royal Scots Fusiliers on the right, with 2nd Royal Scots in support. At 5.15 a.m. the leading battalions moved forward behind 2nd Division. Because of the fog, considerable difficulty was experienced in keeping touch. 7th King's Shropshire Light Infantry was delayed and touch was lost between its companies. However, the company commanders pressed on independently and, although they met strong opposition from Coffee Redoubt and the trenches west of Courcelles, they reached

the eastern edge of the village about 7 a.m. The slope down to the railway was also strongly held and the fiercest fighting took place there. The two leading battalions pressed on, supported by two tanks (Lusty and Lucifer), to reach the railway. By 8.45 a.m. both battalions were on the railway and had pushed patrols forward. Two hundred prisoners were taken. At 9.30 a.m. two companies of 2nd Royal Scots reinforced 7th King's Shropshire Light Infantry on the railway embankment and no further moves took place. Despite the disruption caused by the fog, it is unlikely that Courcelles would have been taken with such comparatively light casualties had it been a clear morning. By the time that 8th Brigade was relieved on 24th August, it had suffered 858 casualties. It had captured 591 prisoners, six guns, ten mortars, ninety-nine machine guns and five anti-tank rifles.

Meanwhile in the early afternoon of 21st August it was decided to send Whippet patrols over the railway to prevent the enemy consolidating a new line. A and C Companies, 6th (Light) Tank Battalion had reached the Courcelles area about 8.30 a.m. A section of A Company went to the south of Courcelles and C Company to the north. The CO, Lieutenant Colonel Ronald Beaumont Wood, 12th Lancers attached Tank Corps, was mortally wounded by a shell splinter (Bienvillers Military Cemetery) while giving these instructions. West took command soon afterwards. The Whippets set off at 1 p.m. and reached Gomiécourt and Triangle Copse before returning. Two A Company Whippets received direct hits as they re-crossed the British line. Later in the afternoon the remaining twenty-one Whippets rallied at Ayette, their work for that day done. The action at Courcelles was one of two for which West was awarded the VC. The second is described in the account of the fighting on 2nd September in a subsequent volume.

Overall, Third Army's success was sufficient to allow Fourth Army to continue its advance to the south on the 22nd, with a view to both Armies attacking simultaneously on the 23rd.

22nd August 1918

390 LCpl George Onions, 1st Devonshire (95th Brigade, 5th Division), Achiet-le-Petit, France

At 4.45 a.m. on 22nd August, Fourth Army returned to the offensive with an attack by III Corps north of the Somme. 47th and 12th Divisions attacked on a 6,400m front, while 18th Division protected the left flank and 3rd Australian Division the right. There was no preliminary bombardment. The Australians gained their objectives by 8.15 a.m., but 47th Division halted short of the intermediate objective by mistake. The support units lost the barrage, ran into heavy German artillery fire and progress was halted. 12th Division was on the final objective before 8.30 a.m. and 18th Division forced a way over the flooded Ancre valley and fought through

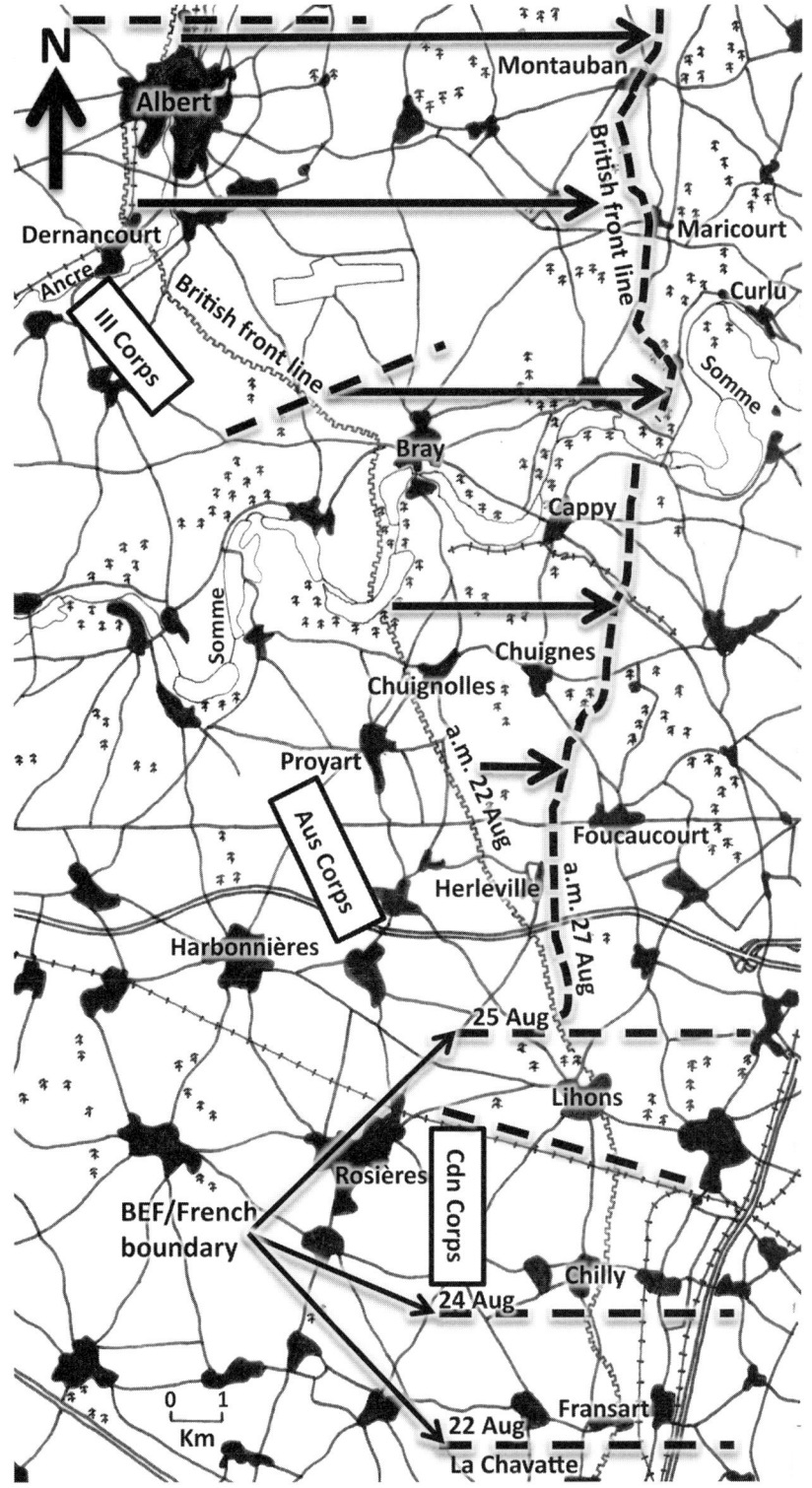

The advance in Fourth Army's area 22nd–27th August.

Albert. Although the final objective was not reached, the troops were close to it and a section was taken in the afternoon.

Once the mist lifted, the Germans dominated the battlefield from the high ground. Counterattacks forced back part of 47th Division to the intermediate line and exposed 12th Division's right flank, which pulled back 550m. Despite Fourth Army's operation not being a complete success, it had removed the dangerous salient between the Somme and Ancre rivers and recaptured Albert.

Third Army stood its ground on the 22nd and prepared to advance the next day. The Germans launched a number of hasty attacks that failed to make any serious impact. One such attack developed against 42nd Division (IV Corps) about 5 a.m. The New Zealand Division on the left was unaffected but 5th Division on its left was bombarded and an attack developed.

5th Division had attacked the previous day as part of the general offensive by Third Army, with 95th Brigade on the right and 15th Brigade on the left. In 95th Brigade the assault was led by 1st Devonshire on the right and 1st East Surrey on the left, with 1st Duke of Cornwall's Light Infantry in support and 12th Gloucestershire in reserve. There had been much confusion and mixing of units due to the thick fog. However, this had reduced the effectiveness of the enemy's fire and casualties had been comparatively light. Although the Red Line (Arras–Albert railway) had been reached in places, it was found that it was not a viable defence line in this area without also holding the high ground to the east. Accordingly a line to the northwest of the railway had been consolidated. About 300 prisoners, fifty machine guns and other material had been captured.

Orders were issued for 12th Gloucestershire to take over the right front and 1st East Surrey the left front. 1st Duke of Cornwall's Light Infantry was to withdraw its two companies in the front line and reorganise the Battalion in a support position. 1st Devonshire, on the right of 95th Brigade, was ordered to withdraw to reserve in the Brown Line, having been relieved by 12th Gloucestershire. Accounts differ

From the embankment of the D8/D50 Achiet-le-Petit–Miraumont road looking southwest. The road is on the extreme left of picture. Just above it, in the middle distance is a hedge, which marks the line of the Albert–Arras railway. Onions and Eades carried out their remarkably audacious action somewhere here in the low ground.

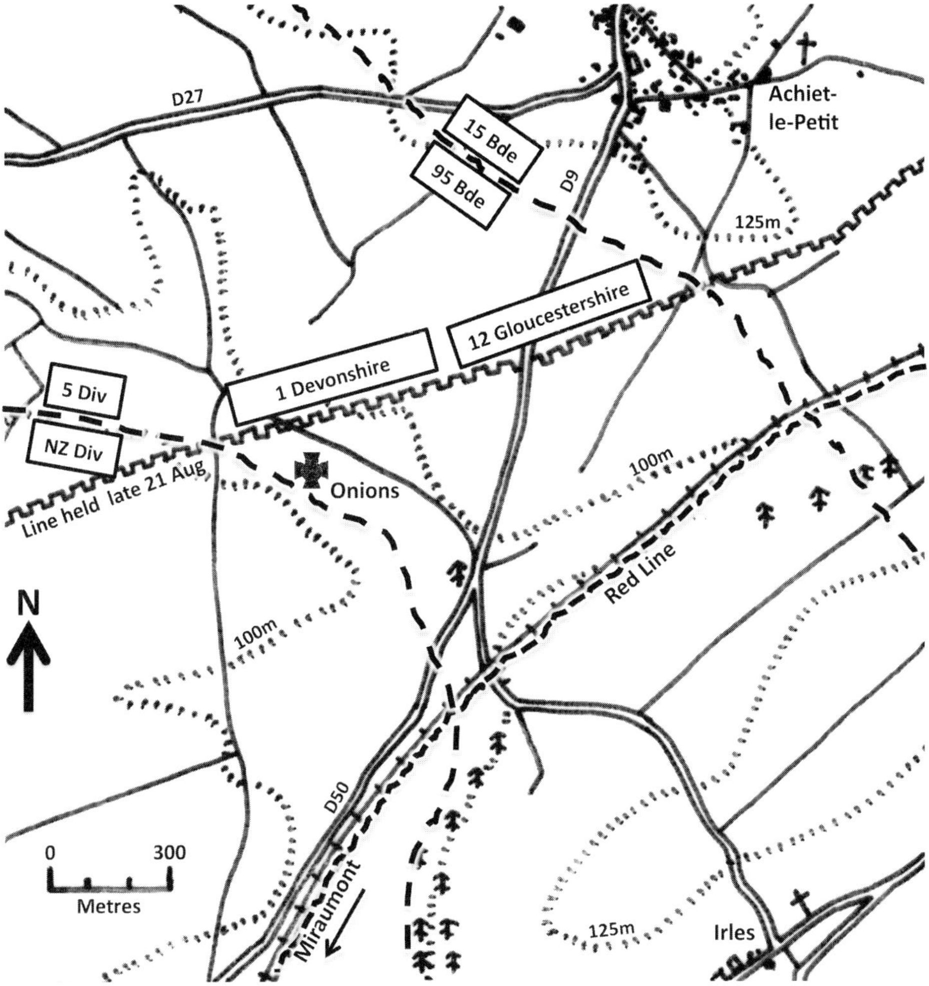

Battle of Albert 1918 and Subsequent Operations   15

Leave Achiet-le-Petit to the southwest on the D9 towards Miraumont. 550m after the last buildings in the village pull over on the right where there are a few entrances to the fields in the embankment. Get well off the road to avoid blocking the traffic. Climb on top of the embankment and look southwest over the low ground, where Onions' VC action took place.

on the precise date and time that 1st Devonshire pulled back into reserve. The Brigade war diary suggests that it occurred on the night of 21st/22nd August, but other accounts indicate that the Battalion did not retire until later on 22nd August. The Battalion's war dairy is also ambiguous. The balance of evidence points to this account being a reasonably accurate version of events.

Before the relief took place SOS rockets went up on the right in 42nd Division's area and 1st Devonshire held fast until the situation became clear. The mist made it impossible to see what was going on. Soon after 7 a.m., No.2 Company on the right sent out a patrol of two scouts, **Lance Corporal George Onions** and 16840 Private Henry James Conway Eades, to investigate. 12th Gloucestershire also sent out a patrol.

Henry Eades' grave in Varennes Military Cemetery.

Onions and Eades approached an old trench and found it unoccupied. While planning their next move a large party of Germans approached and entered the trench, either preparing an attack on the New Zealanders or moving forward to occupy a gap in the line. They became lost in the mist. Onions and Eades would have been congratulated if they had made a clean escape in such circumstances, but instead they took up position to a flank and opened rapid fire. The Germans were convinced that they had run into a superior force and surrendered en masse when about ninety metres away. Onions and Eades would not have survived had the Germans realised how tiny was the force opposing them.

Amazed that their bluff had worked, the two dashed forward, formed their prisoners (all 242 of them) into fours and marched them back to their company commander, Captain Albert John Honywill (MC, LG 7th November 1918), who told Onions to take the prisoners to Battalion HQ. As they approached the HQ, panic broke out as it was thought that the Germans had broken through. Calm was restored when Onions was spotted calmly walking in front with his rifle slung and Eades behind acting as whipper-in. The East Surreys enquired why the Devonshires felt the need to practice ceremonial drill on the battlefield. Eades, formerly a police constable with the Great Western Railway Police, received the DCM for his part in this daring action. He died of wounds on 1st September 1918 (Varennes Military Cemetery, Somme, France – III G 20). The 12th Gloucestershire patrol also came back with some prisoners. 1st Devonshire withdrew after dark as ordered in the early morning. In the meantime 12th Gloucestershire and 1st East Surrey launched an attack, reaching the far side of Irles, and taking almost 500 prisoners and 150 machine guns.

23rd August 1918

> 391 Lt Lawrence McCarthy, 16th Battalion AIF (4th Australian Brigade, 4th Australian Division) Madame Wood, France
> 392 Lt William Joynt, 8th Battalion AIF (2nd Australian Brigade, 1st Australian Division), Herleville Wood, France
> 393 Pte Hugh McIver, 2nd Royal Scots (8th Brigade, 3rd Division), Gomiécourt, France

On 23rd August 1918, four years to the day since the BEF's first clash with the Germans at Mons, the Fourth and Third Armies were ordered to attack in conjunction with the French Tenth Army. Instructions were issued to press on, even if flanks were exposed, as the risk was considered to be worthwhile in view of the state of the enemy. Haig said that… *risks which a month ago would have been criminal to incur ought now to be incurred as a duty*. Success was to be reinforced, rather than persisting where the enemy resisted effectively. Fourth Army extended its attack south of the Somme. However, not all formations north of the river took part due to the disruption caused by German counterattacks the previous day. At the end of the day the enemy had been driven back about three kilometres on a frontage of over six kilometres.

The objective of the Australian Corps was the line Herleville–Chuignes–Froissy Beacon. 32nd and 1st Australian Divisions were to make the attack. The former was already in the line, while the latter was to take over from 5th Australian Division. The assault was to unfold in three phases. The first (main) objective was the line Herleville – Plateau Woods – Arcy Woods – Chuignolles. This had been held by the Germans since 12th August and some resistance was expected, for which the artillery and tanks would have to be used. The second objective, the western side of the Herleville valley between Chuignolles and Chuignes, was not expected to offer much opposition. The final objective was the high ground east of the valley, including Chuignes and Froissy Beacon. On the right flank a small advance was to be made by 4th Australian Brigade (4th Australian Division) to conform with the assault divisions to the north.

During the previous night the Germans opposite 32nd Division were on edge. The RAF bombed the rear areas but this does not appear to be the main cause. The Germans shelled roads and tracks leading to the front, particularly the area between Harbonnières, Vauvillers and Framerville. While 96th Brigade, on the right, and 97th Brigade, on the left, lay out on their start lines the Germans fired numerous red and green flares and bursts of gunfire followed. However, the assault troops were not discovered and most of the fire passed well to their rear. The exception was the left company of 10th Argyll & Sutherland Highlanders on the northern flank of the Division, which lost 70% of its strength and had to be relieved.

There was no preliminary bombardment and the advance was covered by a mixed creeping barrage (10% smoke, 45% shrapnel and 45% HE). 10th Tank Battalion

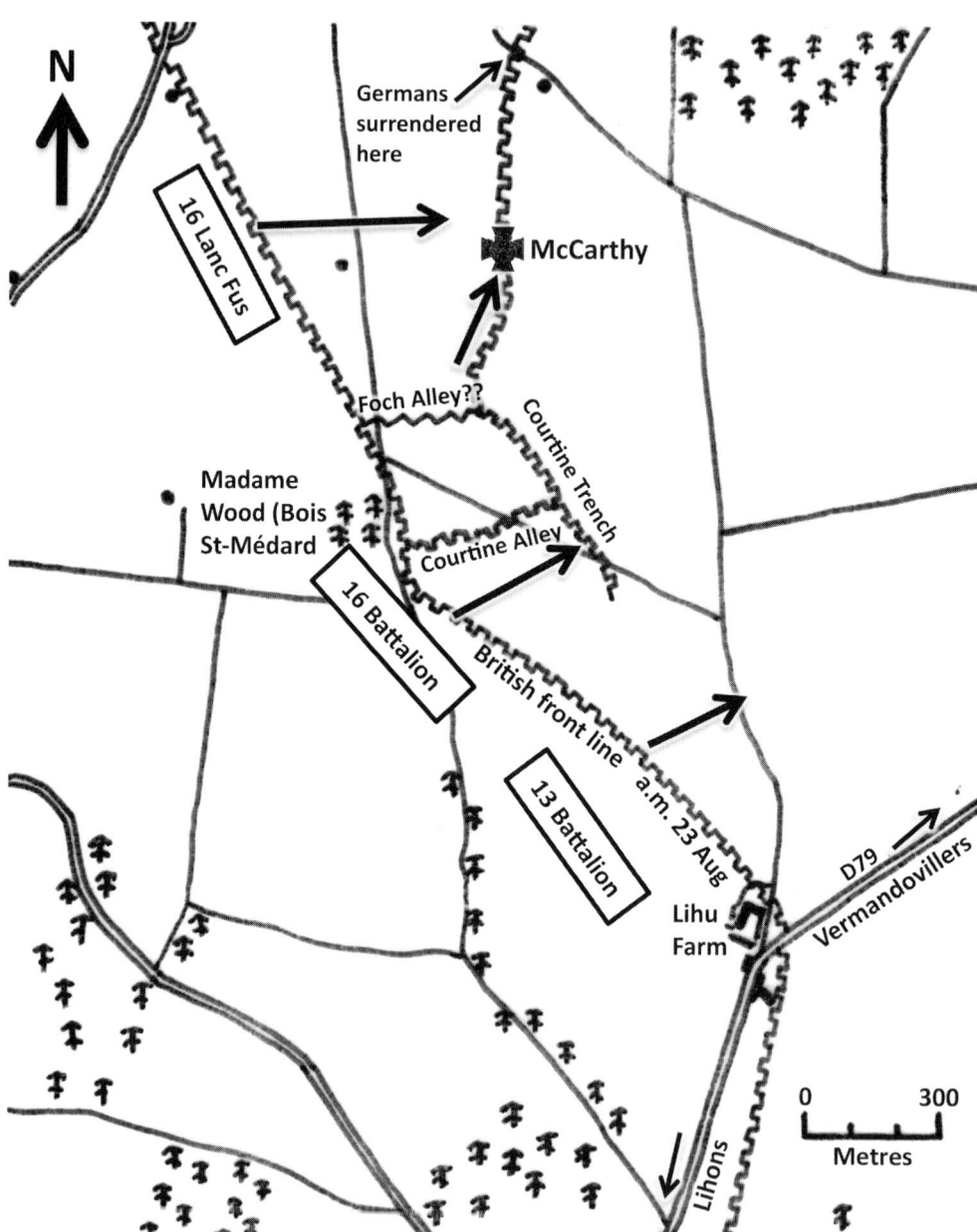

Leave Lihons to the northeast on the D79 towards Vermandovillers. Pass the cemetery on the right and continue for 800m to Lihu Farm. Turn left onto a track that runs north from the farm and after 130m park on the hard standing on the left without blocking access for farm vehicles. Walk north along the track for 600m and turn left onto another track towards Bois St-Médard (Madame Wood) for another 800m. From there look east. Foch Alley and Courtine Alley, left and right respectively ran away from this track to the east about equidistant from this position.

supported 97th Brigade with fourteen machines against Herleville. The RAF was also active above, with No.203 Squadron making low-level attacks on guns and machine guns as they were discovered and also spotting for the supporting artillery.

The attack set off at 4.45 a.m., when it was still dark. On the right, 4th Australian Brigade encountered little opposition on its right and in the centre. However, 16th Battalion on the left ran into some difficulties advancing against Courtine Trench. The barrage, although excellent, fell on trenches behind the objective and did little to assist the assault troops. Despite this C and D Companies, right and left respectively, advanced to the objective and met little opposition in front. There was stiff resistance on both flanks and linking up with both neighbouring battalions was more difficult to achieve. C Company linked up with 13th Battalion on the right but the action on the left was more involved and is described in detail below.

96th Brigade, led by 16th Lancashire Fusiliers, had only a short distance to cover, about 300m. The left seized the objective but the enemy held trench could not be entered on the right, from where there was considerable resistance. A bombing party of 16th Battalion AIF on the right flank, under Lieutenant Charles Clement Garratt DCM & Bar (died of influenza 9th November 1918), worked along Courtine Alley and Trench to join up with 16th Lancashire Fusiliers. At the junction with Foch Alley it was found that Courtine Trench split in two around an island and both branches were blocked with barbed wire. Foch Alley has not been positively identified but an unnamed east-west communications trench joined Courtine Trench northeast of Madame Wood and appears to be in the right place in relation to the narrative. Garratt's party, which included 1807 Sergeant Frederick John Robbins DCM MM, began a long fight with the enemy beyond the wire blocks. The action seesawed back and forth for two hours.

Garrett went back for more bombs and while he was away the commander of D Company, **Lieutenant LD McCarthy**, came forward to see what was causing the hold up. He learned that the bomb supplies of two companies had been expended already in trying to shift the enemy. He concluded that the only solution was to charge the strongpoint. McCarthy observed several posts beyond a German machine gun post that enfiladed the Australian held trench. He and Robbins (some accounts say it was McCarthy's runner) scrambled round the block into the sap beyond, while a British sergeant and a private leapt over into a hole and tunnelled beneath the block to open up communications with the two Australians.

McCarthy and Robbins pressed on and shot a sentry at the next trench junction. Rounding a bend McCarthy came upon the machine gun that was firing at his men further back. He shot the crew and went on to clear another two machine gun posts with bombs and his revolver. By then he was alone. Robbins (or the runner) had been wounded. Undaunted, McCarthy pressed on, picking up supplies of German grenades as he went. Rounding another bend he found a German officer with his back to him, waving his arms at men moving in all directions. There was another officer present and a considerable garrison of enemy troops. McCarthy shot the

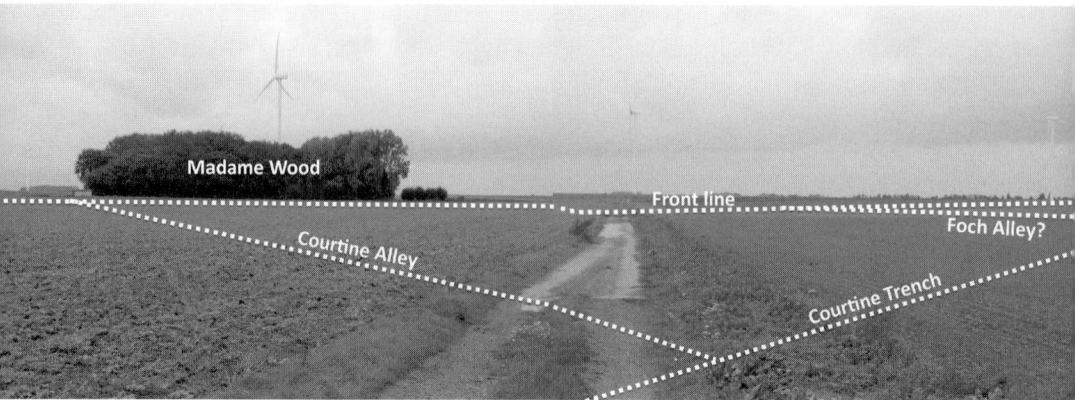

From the track that leads from Lihu Farm behind the camera position.

first German officer dead and seriously wounded the other. Their men bolted into a narrow sap on the right. While their heads were kept down by the Lewis gunners, McCarthy threw in the last of his Mills bombs and followed it with German stick grenades. The two British soldiers joined him about this time, having finished the tunnel. A handkerchief was waved over the top of the sap and forty Germans surrendered, some patting him on the back for his achievement. Others are said to have removed his revolver and grenades to prevent him from killing anyone else. In twenty minutes McCarthy had killed about twenty Germans, taken fifty prisoners and five machine guns and cleared most of the trench that had held up 16th Lancashire Fusiliers. He called forward some scouts and placed them along saps running into the enemy trench as far as Württemberg Trench (not identified but Nuremberg trench ran eastwards from the northern end of Courtine Trench and there may have been a transcription error in the official accounts).

In the Australian Official History, Robbins is reported to have continued along the trench with two Lewis gun teams and set up near some huts in the old no man's land. Lieutenant Garratt then walked across to meet 16th Lancashire Fusiliers as they progressed along trenches from the north. McCarthy had personally cleared 450m of the German held line. A Company came forward to reinforce the gains. Germans continued to throw grenades from the huts and later they were burned down using phosphorus bombs. About noon, 625m of captured trench was handed over to 16th Lancashire Fusiliers by 16th Battalion. A counterattack against 16th Battalion was dealt with by the artillery. The new line was subjected to heavy artillery fire, including gas shells, throughout the remainder of the day. That night 32nd Division took over the fronts held by 16th and 13th Battalions. The following night the remainder of 4th Australian Brigade was relieved by the French.

97th Brigade, with its supporting tanks, which gave valuable assistance, pressed forward through the not very accurate or heavy enemy artillery response. 2nd King's Own Yorkshire Light Infantry was on the right and 10th Argyll & Sutherland Highlanders was on the left. The former reached the objective with few casualties.

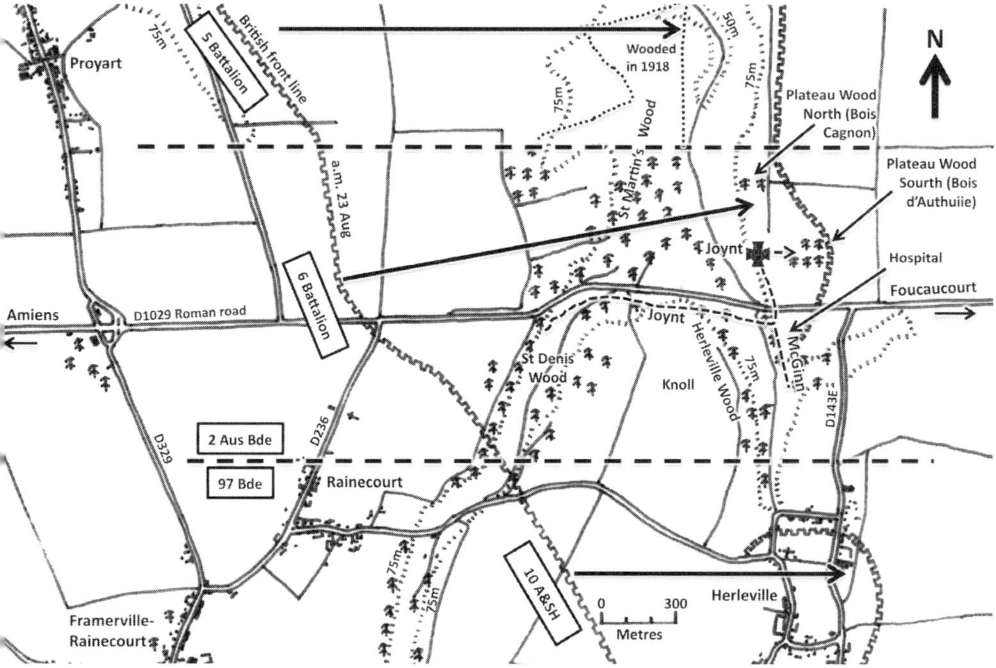

Battle of Albert 1918 and Subsequent Operations 21

Head north from Herleville on the D143E to the junction with the main D1029 Arras–St Quentin road. Turn right and after 150m turn left onto a track. Follow it northwards for 500m and turn left. Continue for 450m to a small copse (Plateau Wood North). Look south to Plateau Wood South and the knoll beyond the Roman road, which is in a dip and cannot be seen from here. Joynt attacked Plateau Wood South from the west up the slope.

However, the latter ran into stubborn resistance in the woods in Herleville gully south of the Roman road. Most of the objective was reached between 8.30 and 9.00 a.m. However, a gap on the left flank was not filled until 9 p.m., with the assistance of 6th Battalion AIF.

The night before the attack, 2nd and 1st Australian Brigades (1st Australian Division) relieved 14th and 15th Australian Brigades (5th Australian Division). The last battalions of the latter division slipped away just thirty minutes before zero hour. On the right, 2nd Australian Brigade advanced with 6th and 5th Battalions leading. On the left, 1st Australian Brigade was led by 4th and 1st Battalions. 14th Australian Brigade remained in support for defensive purposes if required. 3rd Australian Brigade moved up in readiness to advance through 1st Australian Brigade to the final objective.

The advance to the first objective for 2nd Australian Brigade was over ground that was well suited for defence, being intersected by gullies, sunken roads and old trenches. There were also a number of woods and Herleville valley beyond. Smoke was to be used to screen off Froissy Beacon and the high ground north of the Somme. In addition the creeping barrage would have ten percent smoke shells. 5th Battalion on the left faced St Martin's Wood, which was 1,200m wide and up to 1,600m deep. Of the twelve tanks of 13th Tank Battalion attached to the Brigade, four were to go through the Wood, while two tanks on each flank passed around it to cut off the enemy as they withdrew. Three supply tanks were also attached to the Brigade. Once 97th Brigade to the south had gained its objective, the attached tanks were to swing north to assist 2nd Australian Brigade.

The Germans brought down barrages along the plateau between the forward and support battalions several times between 2 a.m. and 4 a.m. These fell behind 5th Battalion on the left but caught the rear of 6th Battalion on the right. It may be that the Germans had heard the noise of tanks moving forward. Both supporting battalions 900m in rear of the assault battalions, 7th on the left and 8th on the right, had to pass through a curtain of shellfire when the attack commenced and about forty casualties were incurred.

At zero hour some of the attached tanks had not arrived but the infantry moved off promptly, following an excellent barrage. The tanks caught up soon afterwards. Several were hit by shellfire and others broke down. The German outpost line did not present many problems but stiff opposition was encountered in the woods beyond.

6th Battalion headed too far north and its right did not clear St Denis Wood, which held about eighty Germans. 6th Battalion also met heavy fire from a series of copses (known collectively as Herleville Woods), from Plateau Woods North and South and from a hutted hospital south of the Roman road. The advance slowed and the barrage was lost. By 5.15 a.m. the Battalion was involved in heavy fighting in St Denis Wood and to the east of it. A tank arrived and circled St Denis Wood. Half an hour later the Wood fell but the enemy held out in the larger St Martin's Wood, where posts continued to resist. Casualties were heavy, particularly amongst the officers.

5th Battalion cleared a number of machine gun posts, in many cases men simply charged straight at them. However, after covering about 800m, St Martin's Wood loomed out of the smoke and resistance stiffened. Here the tanks were invaluable in clearing the way. One alone cleared twenty machine gun posts on a frontage of only one hundred metres. The left company of 5th Battalion entered the northern end of the Wood. The company on the right and some of 6th Battalion's men entered the south. The tanks could not keep up with the infantry inside the Wood and the support battalions rounded up many Germans overlooked by the assault battalions.

At 5.48 a.m. a pause in the artillery programme ended and the barrage moved forward. 2nd Australian Brigade and the right of 1st Australian Brigade advanced again. 5th Battalion and the left of 6th Battalion pressed on to the eastern edge of St Martin's Wood. A piano in a hut in the Wood could be heard being played by a soldier of the 7th Battalion. At the northern end of the Wood a tank was found moving south along the valley, shooting up dugouts with its 6 Pounder. Many Germans were trapped there but were left for the support battalions to mop up. 5th Battalion's left and part of 4th Battalion (1st Australian Brigade) crossed the gully and went straight up the steep slope without encountering any opposition. The right of 5th Battalion cleared some enemy behind the Wood but then came under fire from a machine gun on the reverse slope of the prominent knoll to the south of the Roman road.

Progress slowed as men had to trickle forward in small groups to the shelter of dugouts and trenches on the eastern slope. They advanced again but came under fire from another machine gun in old French trenches near the top and were halted. However, a few communication trenches were found leading up the hill. The troops crept along these, destroyed the machine gun with a rifle grenade and charged into Plateau Wood North. Any attempt to progress to an old French line beyond was hit by fire from trenches just beyond Plateau Wood South, about 200m north of the Roman road.

South of the Roman road, 6th Battalion also lost many officers and men to these machine guns. Two men almost reached the strongpoint at Plateau Wood South before being killed, as was RSM TW Gaston MSM, who had been promoted to lieutenant but never knew it. A tank came from the southern end of St Martin's Wood and climbed the slope but collapsed into a trench at the top. Part of 6th Battalion crossed the gully and reached the hospital huts. However, all the officers in the right company were hit and the troops were held up by the knoll.

8th Battalion advanced in support behind 6th Battalion with A and B companies leading on the right and left respectively, followed by D and C Companies. It formed up about 450m west of and parallel with the Framerville–Proyart road. South of the road in Rainecourt gully was a platoon of D Company, 8th Battalion, commanded by **Lieutenant WD Joynt**. D Company was commanded by Captain George Ernest Johnston, who was hit by a shell fragment in the abdomen and died instantly (Heath Cemetery, Harbonnières, France – IV B 12). Joynt immediately assumed command of the Company.

From the D143E looking north over the D1029 towards the two Plateau Woods, with the southernmost on the right.

Joynt heard the firing in front and saw some men of 5th Battalion north of the road being driven back. Joynt and his batman, 5181 Private Thomas Newman, went forward and found a group of 6th Battalion in a sunken road on the knoll. They had hesitated to cross and Joynt urged them on. Led by a new officer they went forward but Joynt did not see them appear on the next crest. He followed and saw them near the top of the opposite slope held up by the intense fire coming from Plateau Wood South. More Germans were creeping towards the Wood along the main road. Joynt met up with Lieutenant Leslie Clarence McGinn (MC for this action), also 8th Battalion, with a party of fifteen men. McGinn's Lewis gun shot up the German machine gun team and Joynt decided the time was right to seize the Wood. With McGinn's party, he crossed the road, capturing the German hospital on the way. Two German doctors agreed to stay and treat Australian as well as their own wounded. Joynt contacted Lieutenant Harold Francis Darby of 6th Battalion

The opposite view to the previous picture with the two Plateau Woods on the left (South) and right (North) of the view. Between them in the distance is the tree covered knoll. Joynt attacked Plateau Wood South up the slope from right to left.

on the left and asked him to provide covering fire from the sunken road on the knoll. Joynt and McGinn allowed fifteen minutes to get into position, working their way forward along a trench on the plateau. On the way they passed abandoned machine gun posts, enemy dead and some dugouts full of Germans who would not fight. As Joynt was trying to persuade some of them to come out, he heard a party of twenty Germans approaching along the trench. He covered the first man with his revolver and he dropped his rifle and surrendered, as did the rest of the party. They were escorted back by two men.

Meanwhile Joynt lined his men in the trench facing the Wood, which was about fifty metres away. The men were inclined to charge but Joynt realised that a machine gun in the Wood could easily sweep the whole line. Having restrained his men, Joynt found another trench that led directly to the Wood and they crept along it instead. As they closed the Germans broke and ran. The party rushed in after them and captured twelve in a dugout about twenty metres inside the western edge. Joynt went to Plateau Wood North, contacted Captain Eric George de Zemblyn Permezel MC there and they formed a line to the east of both Woods.

By 7.30 a.m. the whole of 2nd Australian Brigade's objective had been seized. However, enemy fire was so intense that further exploitation was not possible and there was a gap on the right between 6th Battalion and 97th Brigade (32nd Division). At 10 a.m., A Company, 8th Battalion was sent to clear Herleville Wood and to close the gap but this was not completed until evening. On the other flank, 5th Battalion encountered little resistance, except near St Martin's Woods and 7th Battalion assisted in overcoming it. 2nd Australian Brigade took over 1,300 prisoners, in addition to eight guns and numerous machine guns. By the time that the Brigade was relieved on the night of 26th/27th August, it had suffered 873 casualties, including 407 gassed.

1st Australian Brigade had its left flank on the Somme Canal. Its task was more difficult than 2nd Australian Brigade's and had to be carried out in three phases. The advance was led by eleven tanks and initially rapid progress was made. British aircraft fired flares to warn of a counterattack by a German company from Lapin Wood, which was held and most of the survivors were captured. Heavy fire was received from a high feature, known as Gibraltar, northwest of Chuignes. The slope was too steep for tanks, except from one direction that was covered by an anti-gun gun. A spur south of Chuignes valley was taken by 7.10 p.m. However, the

most advanced troops came under such heavy fire from two field guns in Garenne Wood, and the anti-gun gun firing grapeshot, that they had to withdraw a short distance, except for a few small posts. Under cover of fire from 16th Brigade RHA, one company reorganised in Arcy Wood. About this time a patrol of 4th Battalion found Chuignes empty.

Further north 1st Battalion also came under heavy fire and a tank assisted in the capture of Long Wood. 10th Battalion, which was to protect the left flank later in the attack on Froissy Beacon, sent two companies to clear the flank. Assisted by a platoon of 59th Battalion and two from 4th Battalion, they succeeded in working through Long Wood by 8.30 a.m. and established posts around it. Field artillery moved forward, engaged the enemy on Froissy heights and in Marly Woods and greatly reduced the German fire. Four platoons of 10th Battalion, covered by Lewis and machine guns, cleared down the spur north of Chuignolles and on the Somme flats.

Just about all of the main objective had been reached and on the left flank the area for immediate exploitation was also taken. A renewed barrage was arranged for 2 p.m. The final objective, including Froissy Beacon, was reached after heavy fighting by 1st and 3rd Australian Brigades, with some assistance from north of the Somme from 3rd Australian Division. 1st Australian Division took 2,000 prisoners, about one quarter of the entire bag for 23rd August.

By nightfall the Australian Corps had gained its main objective everywhere and, with a few exceptions, the ground to be gained by exploitation. However, most of the German gun positions lay east of the line gained and the new positions came under heavy shellfire.

The whole of Third Army took part in the attack on 23rd August. General Byng ordered VI Corps on the left of the Army to extend the attack frontage to the north, with the intention of gaining good positions from which to assault the line Hamelincourt–Héninel Ridge between the Sensée and the Cojeul. VI Corps was a very powerful formation, consisting of seven infantry divisions, with 564 field and 252 heavy guns, supported by two RFA army brigades, three RGA brigades, III Tank Brigade (sixty-three tanks) and squadrons of the RAF.

German positions between Irles and Achiet-le-Grand in IV Corps' area were particularly strong, so it was decided to avoid a frontal assault until the flanks had been secured by V and VI Corps to the south and north respectively. Accordingly V Corps on the right was to push northeast towards Pys and cooperate with Fourth Army on the extreme right. VI Corps on the left was to capture Gomiécourt on high ground dominating Achiet-le-Grand on the night of 22nd/23rd August. Once Gomiécourt was secured, IV Corps could advance against the main Irles–Achiet-le-Grand position.

V Corps' cooperation with Fourth Army, on the right, resulted in the Tara and Usna Hills being secured east of Albert. IV Corps launched a preliminary operation at 2.30 a.m. by the 42nd and New Zealand Divisions (left and right respectively) to secure Beauregard Dovecot, which had been taken and lost again on the 21st. The New Zealand Division's front was 1,100m long and it was intended to complete the operation with two companies of 1st New Zealand Rifle Brigade. The assembly was not detected and under an extremely accurate barrage the assault troops pushed up the slopes and down the valley towards the railway. Little opposition was encountered and the objective was reached, thus securing the Corps' right flank. After the barrage ceased, machine gun fire was received from beyond the railway and the left company suffered. Machine gun teams and light trench mortars were sent forward to assist. At 9.20 a.m. a weak enemy counterattack against the right company lasted over an hour and a half and the survivors were caught in the barrage for the main attack at 11 a.m.

The main IV Corps attack by 5th and 37th Divisions was launched at 11 a.m. The former was to capture Irles and the latter Achiet-le-Grand and Bihucourt. The two companies of 1st New Zealand Rifle Brigade from the preliminary operation advanced on a front of 900m to conform to the movements of 5th Division on the left. The intention was to capture the whole of the Ancre valley north of Miraumont, including the railway. Much opposition was encountered, particularly from machine guns on the wooded slopes before Irles. However, all objectives were seized and the line was pushed 450m forward, with ninety prisoners being taken, in addition to a heavy mortar and seven machine guns. A few enemy machine gun nests, although surrounded, held out until nearly dark. Patrols ventured ahead and maintained contact with 5th Division. The day's fighting cost 1st New Zealand Rifle Brigade seven killed and forty-three wounded. In the evening 42nd Division extended its front northwards to take over the New Zealand Division's area.

5th Division attacked with 95th and 15th Brigades, supported by a barrage of twenty machine guns. Seven tanks of 7th Tank Battalion were not ready in time to take part. The right of 95th Brigade was held up by the deep railway cutting and lost the barrage. It was unable to advance further than the ridge overlooking Irles. However, the left of the Brigade met much less opposition and was on its objective by 11.40 a.m. 15th Brigade also met strong opposition behind three belts of wire before reaching the railway. Two tanks of 10th Tank Battalion knocked out a number of machine guns and this allowed the advance to continue to the objective. With only Irles outstanding, 13th Brigade was brought forward and all three battalions attacked at 7.30 p.m. Elements of 12th Gloucestershire (95th Brigade) joined in and all objectives were taken.

37th Division's first objective was a trench 200m beyond Achiet-le-Grand, the seizure of which required the assault troops to cross the railway and capture the village first. The second objective was the eastern edge of Bihucourt and then southwest towards Irles. Zero hour was at 11 a.m. and five batteries of heavy artillery were available to shell Achiet-le-Grand, Bihucourt and the western exits of Biefvillers and Grévillers. It was the first time that the Division had worked with tanks. They were to make a running start and catch up with the infantry before they reached the railway. 112th and 111th Brigades led the attack. 111th Brigade had secured the first objective by 12.30 p.m. and by 1.20 p.m., the second. 112th Brigade, however, ran into considerable difficulties. The right was held up 350m west of the railway until a tank arrived about 1.40 p.m. and fired along the opposing trench. The railway was reached by 2 p.m. On the left considerable resistance from the brickworks west of Achiet-le-Grand was overcome by a flank attack. The advance continued to the railway, which also proved troublesome. Small parties pressed on, covered by mortars, Lewis guns and rifles, to enfilade the opposition. Four hundred prisoners were taken. The support battalion lost direction and there were delays. As a result only part of the second objective was held. A further attempt in the evening by 112th and 63rd Brigades was met by heavy fire and the barrage started too far forward, which left the enemy untouched. The attack failed.

Although there were frustrations and setbacks, overall IV Corps had advanced about 1,800m. The railway line, which had resisted attempts to take it the previous day, was overrun and three defended villages had been captured, along with large numbers of prisoners. Preparations were in hand to continue the advance next day.

In VI Corps, Gomiécourt was the key to the whole operation and the advance of IV Corps to the south depended upon it being taken early. 3rd Division was to take it supported by seven field and two heavy artillery brigades, forty machine guns and twelve tanks of 7th and 12th Tank Battalions. Having seized Gomiécourt, the advance was to press on eastwards in order to overlook the Sensée valley. 2nd Division was to pass through at 11 a.m. to seize Béhagnies and Ervillers.

The initial assault by 3rd Division was made by 76th Brigade on the right and 8th Brigade on the left, with 3rd Grenadier Guards (2nd Guards Brigade, Guards Division) covering the left flank. 9th Brigade on the far right just had to tidy up a few machine gun posts. There were difficulties occupying the assembly positions due to the presence of enemy parties. However, the attack started on time at 4 a.m., swept forward 900m and, although the tanks were delayed crossing the railway line, it was a resounding success. Gomiécourt fell to 76th Brigade with 300 prisoners at 5 a.m. Eight tanks assisted in mopping up. Despite strong resistance, 8th Brigade was on its objective to the north fifteen minutes earlier. All four supporting tanks were knocked out or otherwise disabled.

In 8th Brigade, 2nd Royal Scots had taken over the front along the Arras–Albert railway from 1st Royal Scots Fusiliers, completing the relief at 11.30 p.m. on 22nd August. It was to be the right assault battalion, with 7th King's Shropshire Light Infantry on the left. The objective was the high ground about 450m east of the railway. All troops taking part wore white armbands. When the attack started the Germans put down a heavy barrage on the line of the railway. 2nd Royal Scots came under machine gun fire after only fifty metres. These machine gun posts were pinned down by Lewis guns, while rifle sections outflanked them. C Company, one of the two leading companies, looked as if it was about to become bogged down. None of the official accounts mention the precise disposition of the companies, just that there were two companies leading.

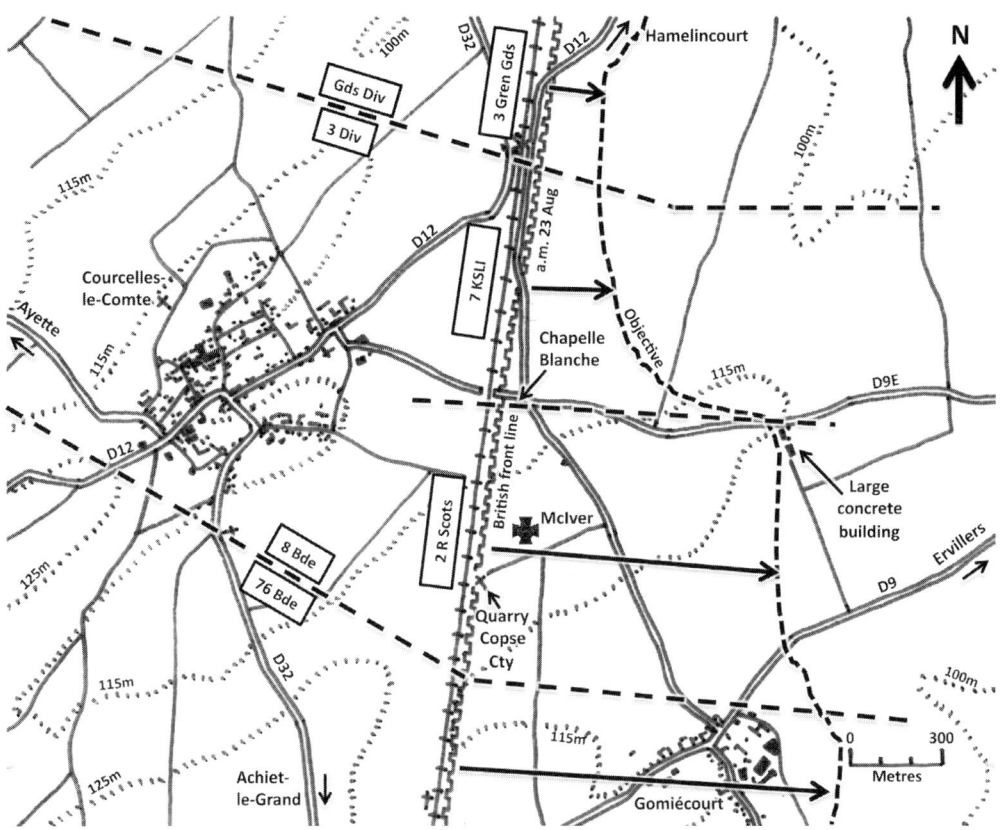

Head northwest from Gomiécourt on a minor road towards the junction with the D9E at Chapelle Blanche. After almost 800m turn left onto a track that leads to Quarry Copse Cemetery, just east of the railway. Park at the cemetery. This point is just south of the middle of 2nd Royal Scots' line. With your back to the railway line, look back along the track to the east. The large concrete building is on the line of the Battalion's objective. Alternatively leave Courcelles-le-Comte south on the D32 towards Achiet-le-Grand. After about 900m pull over safely and look eastwards over the railway. From here the villages on the flanks are easier to see. The railway was the start line for the attack and the large building previously mentioned in the distance is on the objective.

The C Company runner, **Private Hugh McIver**, chased a German for about 150m until he sought refuge in a machine gun post. Thinking nothing of the danger, McIver jumped in after him and bayoneted and shot six of the enemy. This was too much for the rest of the garrison and twenty others surrendered, along with two machine guns. The way was clear for C Company to continue its advance. Later, at great personal risk, he managed to stop a British tank firing on its own troops, thus saving many lives. The Battalion reached the objective at 4.45 a.m. and held this line until 11 a.m. under very heavy artillery, trench mortar and machine gun fire. On the right, contact was made with 76th Brigade, but on the left machine guns prevented a link being made with 7th King's Shropshire Light Infantry, although a tank kept

Looking east from the alternative viewing point over the ground covered by 2nd Royal Scots on 23rd August.

the area clear of enemy. Due to casualties in the assault, the Battalion had reinforced the forward companies with the reserve company. The Battalion took 252 prisoners, together with a formidable haul of weaponry (two guns, two howitzers, two trench mortars, thirty-eight machine guns and an anti-tank rifle). The cost over three days in action was 269 casualties (thirty-one killed, 199 wounded, twenty-eight wounded and missing and eleven missing).

The main attack by VI Corps was by the Guards, 56th and 52nd Divisions, with the latter two passing through 59th Division. The objective was an observation line about 1,100m away. Each assault division had a tank battalion attached to it. 2nd Guards Brigade led the Guards Division attack, with 3rd Grenadier Guards on the right moving forward at 4 a.m. to protect the left flank of 3rd Division to the south. On the left, 1st Scots Guards advanced with the main attack at 4.55 a.m. By 8 a.m. the objective had been reached and a line was established east of Hamelincourt in contact with both flanking formations.

56th Division was led by 168th Brigade, with a battalion of 167th Brigade, artillery, engineers, pioneers, machine guns and two companies of tanks attached. The first objective was Boyelles and Boiry Becquerelle. The Brigade was then to establish a line of posts in a German reserve trench running obliquely from the first objective and 550–1,100m from it. There was no time for the artillery to register targets or for reconnaissance. Indeed the assault troops had an approach march of eighteen kilometres before the attack commenced. In addition respirators had to be worn during gas attacks for two hours. Despite these exertions, the attack commenced at 5.07 a.m. and was a complete success.

52nd Division was to form the left flank from near Boiry Becquerelle back to the front line. 156th Brigade was to make the attack with support from machine guns, nine tanks and a considerable amount of artillery. The assault troops were tasked late in the day and had to move forward in haste by lorry. The tanks caught up during the attack and, fortunately, not much opposition was encountered. By 6 a.m. the objective had been taken.

With the objectives secured, at 9.25 a.m. HQ VI Corps ordered the Guards Division to advance over the Sensée onto the St Léger Ridge. 56th and 52nd Divisions were to conform. The result was that a considerable amount of ground was gained but the line reached was disjointed. The right of 2nd Guards Brigade came under heavy artillery fire but reached the objective at Hally Copse about noon. The centre and left of the Brigade did not cross the Sensée as there were no troops on either flank. On the left 56th Division was held up on the Ervillers–Boyelles road and the gap there was not filled. The gap on the right was filled by sending up four companies from the Brigade, which by 6 p.m. had thrown back a flank to get within 900m of 2nd Division in front of Ervillers.

At 11 a.m., 2nd Division passed through 3rd Division, with the objective being a line 175m beyond the villages of Sapignies, Béhagnies and Ervillers. 2nd Royal Scots' (8th Brigade, 2nd Division) support company followed to mop up. At the same time 9th Brigade (3rd Division) was to complete closing up to the railway line on the right flank. 5th Brigade's attack stalled 900m short of Béhagnies. Lieutenant Colonel WL Brodie VC, CO 2nd Highland Light Infantry, was killed in this action. 6th Brigade overcame fierce opposition with tank support and took Ervillers by 1 p.m. An attempt later to keep up with the Guards Division on the left failed, due to the open ground being covered by numerous machine guns. However, on the right 99th Brigade protected that flank and linked up with 37th Division to the south.

Despite some checks, VI Corps had advanced between 1,800m and 2,750m along a frontage of just over eleven kilometres. Overall Third Army had enjoyed considerable success and took over 5,000 prisoners. However, there was to be no respite as Third and Fourth Armies were ordered to continue the advance next day. The first moves took place before midnight on the 23rd.

24th August 1918

> 394 Sgt Samuel Forsyth, New Zealand Engineers att'd 2nd Auckland (1st New Zealand Brigade, New Zealand Division), Grévillers, France

The relief of the Canadian Corps in Fourth Army was completed on the nights of 23rd/24th and 24th/25th August. The French took over the front that they held prior to 8th August, with the new international boundary running a little north of Lihons. The Canadian Corps transferred to First Army.

By 24th August the hot and dry weather had turned cloudy and cooler with some rain and this hampered air operations. The attacks by formations of Fourth Army started at 1 a.m. In places there was almost universal success. However, some divisions encountered more difficulties and a follow on attack by the Australian and III Corps was cancelled.

In Third Army, all corps were ordered to press on with the advance. V Corps was to head towards Rocquigny and Morval, IV Corps towards Lagnicourt and VI Corps towards Quéant, while 1st and 2nd Cavalry Divisions stood by to take advantage of any opportunities to exploit success. V Corps had a successful day, launching several audacious operations and gaining la Boisselle, Ovillers, Pozières, Thiepval and Grandcourt. There was a gap between 17th and 21st Divisions around Courcelette but the Germans were not able to take advantage of this. On the left flank of the Army, VI Corps' orders were for an advance of about 6,400m. However, only limited gains were made.

In the centre of Third Army, IV Corps' centre and left were already well advanced but the right was blocked by Miraumont. 42nd Division was to take it and the high ground to the east, assisted by a night attack by 64th Brigade on the right flank. The New Zealand Division was to pass through 5th Division to seize Loupart Wood and Grévillers. 5th Division was to advance south-eastwards to cover the right of the New Zealand Division and form a defensive line from Irles to Loupart Wood, where it was to connect with 42nd Division. 37th Division was to advance through Biefvillers and there make contact with 42nd Division, while 63rd Division remained in reserve. Some gun batteries were to be in close support of the infantry.

42nd Division had seized the whole of Miraumont by late afternoon. At 8 p.m. the advance was continued and Pys was taken without much difficulty. However, Warlencourt was too strongly held and a line was occupied about 1,200m from it. Contact was established with both flanking formations.

The New Zealand Division had the additional support of XXVI Army Brigade RFA, all available guns of 5th Division and XC Brigade RGA, plus thirteen Mark IV tanks of 7th Tank Battalion and a company of Whippets. The operation was to be in two phases. First, 1st New Zealand Brigade, supported by two mobile field artillery brigades, eight tanks and three Whippets, was to set off at 4.30 a.m. to capture Loupart Wood and Grévillers and advance 450m beyond. Second, following 2,750m behind, 2nd New Zealand Brigade was to press on to Bapaume and the high ground to the east, assisted by one mobile field artillery brigade, five tanks and a company of Whippets. The brigades assembled to the east and southeast of Bucquoy respectively. The men were in the lightest fighting order, with all heavy gear being dumped. There was some gas shelling and a few heavy guns hit the area but overall it was quiet. It began raining about 10 p.m.

1st Wellington and 2nd Auckland were to lead 1st New Zealand Brigade, on the right and left respectively. However, there was some uncertainty as to where the previous day's advance had halted. As a result there were two scenarios for the advance. If 5th Division had taken the line Loupart Wood–Grévillers–Biefvillers, as was understood to be the situation, the objective was Bapaume. If not, 2nd Auckland was to take Grévillers and 1st Wellington was to secure Loupart Wood. Zero hour was set for 4.15 a.m.

At 2 a.m., while the battalions were moving forward, word was received that the first option was to be followed. However, this information was incorrect. Arriving at Starfish crossroads at 3.40 a.m., 2nd Auckland found itself in no man's land. The Battalion deployed and lay down to await zero hour. 15th Company was on the right and 16th Company on the left, with 3rd Company in support and 6th Company in reserve.

There was no preparatory barrage and, as a result, when the advance began, it was some time before the Germans realised that an attack was underway. However, they offered solid resistance thereafter, although in the early stages the darkness and early morning mist continued to assist the attackers. It was not until midday that 1st Wellington had taken the whole of Loupart Wood, assisted by four tanks. 2nd King's Own Scottish Borderers (13th Brigade, 5th Division) seized a machine gun post at the southwest corner of the Wood and formed a defensive flank along the southern edge as planned.

Before the attack commenced, 2nd Auckland was unable to establish contact with the units on either flank. The location of the enemy positions was also unclear, except in one place where flares were sent up from a post. 2nd Auckland's plan was for 15th Company on the right to split in half, with two platoons passing either side of Grévillers. The platoons on the right were also to make contact with 1st Wellington. 16th Company on the left was to pass north of the village. 3rd Company was to come up between the two halves of 15th Company to clear the village. By the time that the company commanders had been briefed and returned, it was time to move off. Consequently very few men had a clear understanding of what was required. At 5 a.m. the artillery bombarded the northwest edge of Loupart Wood and east of Grévillers.

A belt of wire was encountered and, as the men scrambled through as best they could, machine guns on the left opened fire from the post that had fired the flares, as did a couple in the centre. The platoon on the extreme left was held up

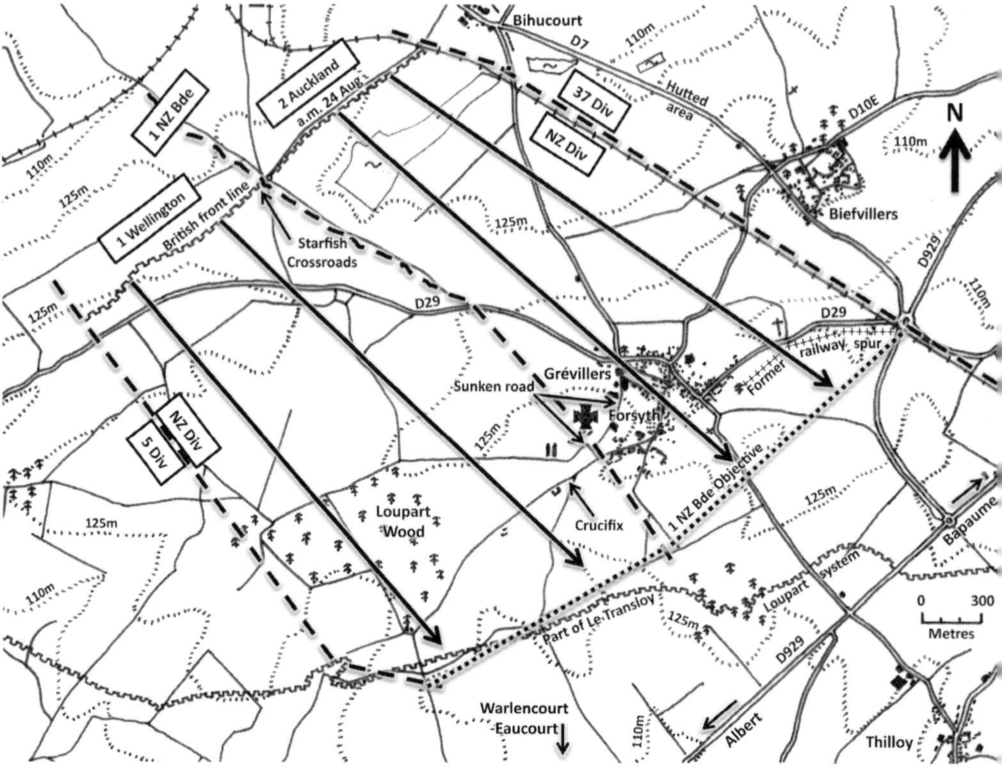

The sunken road is very pitted and full of holes but can be driven with care. New farm buildings and, in summer, standing crops can obscure the view to the west. Instead leave Grévillers on the D29 westwards towards Irles. After about 750m there is a track on the right, which was the boundary between 1st Wellington and 2nd Auckland. Park here and look back towards Grévillers. The sunken road cannot be seen but its line is marked by the series of large barns and other farm buildings on the western edge of the village.

From the boundary between 1st Wellington and 2nd Auckland on the D29 Irles road, looking southeast towards Grévillers. The sunken road is marked by the farm buildings in the centre, although it cannot quite be seen from this position. Forsyth led the tank up the slope towards the sunken road.

and the remainder of 16th Company was badly disorganised. In the centre there was less resistance and the outpost line was broken through quickly, with many machine guns and prisoners being taken. A small party, under Sergeant O'Brien in 3rd Company, was then able to move around and take the machine guns that were causing the delay from the rear. The crews surrendered and the Company was able to press on. Little opposition was met in the village by 3rd Company and one party of Germans was surprised while they ate breakfast. An abandoned dressing station was found in the centre. On the outer edge a large railway gun was towed away just before it could be captured but three 8″ howitzers were seized. Most opposition was encountered on the flanks. On the left there was a great deal of machine gun fire from huts on the Bihucourt–Biefvillers road. 16th Company was assisted by a company of 2nd Wellington in support in overcoming this and many prisoners were taken. Later in the morning a company of 2nd Wellington pushed on over the Bihucourt–Biefvillers road.

On the right, 15th Company was held up due to the opposition encountered by 1st Wellington in front of Loupart Wood. The main part of the Company crossed below the wire belt and found a trench. This was fortunate as it protected the men from a stream of machine gun bullets that caused sparks as they richotted off the wire. Germans were encountered on the right. A challenge was shouted, followed by a rifle shot and a short fierce fight took place. Under two or three SNCOs, including 24040 Sergeant Gerald McMurdo, they extended out and maintained contact with 1st Wellington and 3rd Company as they moved along the southern fringe of Grévillers. Casualties increased as the crest of the ridge between Grévillers and Loupart Wood and the formidable old Le Transloy–Loupart system were neared. Machine guns, snipers and anti-tank guns were encountered.

About thirty metres ahead came a cry of alarm and a machine gun opened fire, soon joined by another half dozen or so. The Company was forced into cover and could not move. Across the valley two tanks were seen and helmets were waved on bayonets to attract their attention. **Sergeant Samuel Forsyth** had by his leadership

and total disregard of danger already rushed three machine gun positions, taking their crews prisoner before they could inflict many casualties. He was scouting ahead and located two of the machine guns holding up the Company, before going back to the nearest tank and explaining the situation. Then, under heavy fire, he led it up the slope toward the sunken road. Two small quick firing guns opened fire on the tank. The shells burst all around but Forsyth never flinched. He was hit in the arm by a splinter and, after having the wound bandaged, again contacted the tank and continued in the face of very heavy fire from machine guns and anti-tank guns. The infantry kept up with the tank until it received a direct hit on its front, slewed half round and stopped.

Forsyth organised the tank crew and his own men into a section and led them in outflanking the machine guns. Under heavy fire, he directed them into positions and forced the machine gun teams to retire. 15th Company then rose up and took the sunken road with the row of machine guns. Pressing on, the Company came under heavy fire but gained the crest. They continued down the slope to gain the cover of old grass covered shell holes from 1916. Forsyth and McMurdo moved around on the bare and exposed slope to organise the new line. Enemy snipers were less than one hundred metres away and one of them shot Forsyth dead. He had been in front throughout the advance, acting with courage and coolness and using his initiative. Forsyth was attached to the Battalion from the New Zealand Engineers, while on probation for a commission.

By 6 a.m. most of Grévillers had been secured and by 9 a.m. it was clear. By 8 a.m., 15th Company had worked forward some way towards Loupart Wood. The right reached a Crucifix on the sunken Warlencourt–Eaucourt road and gained touch with 1st Wellington. With heavy fire still coming from the Wood, the Battalion was unable to advance further. However, with the exception of the open ground in front of 15th Company, 2nd Auckland had gained its objective, with surprisingly light casualties – eighteen killed, ninety-two wounded and three missing. The Battalion seized thirty-five machine guns, the three 8″ howitzers mentioned previously, two 77mm guns, five minenwerfers, three wagons and 386 prisoners. During the afternoon and evening the enemy artillery was very active. About 4 p.m. the Germans appeared to be preparing for a counterattack but were engaged by the artillery and no attack emerged. That night 2nd Auckland was relieved by 1st Auckland and went into reserve.

2nd New Zealand Brigade sent two battalions to the north of Grévillers. 2nd Otago seized a line of trenches 350m east of the village, while one of its companies and 2nd Canterbury with eight tanks, found Biefvillers abandoned and nearly reached Avesnes, close to Bapaume. However, they came under heavy fire there, lost four tanks and were forced to retire to the trenches held by 2nd Otago.

37th Division, led by 63rd Brigade, had little time to organise its part in the attack and artillery support was limited. The left was held up by intense machine gun fire but the right had more success in cooperation with the New Zealand Division.

Biefvillers was entered about 6 a.m. but was subjected to such heavy artillery fire that it had to be abandoned. A position to the west was occupied instead and a battalion was brought up to form a defensive left flank. The New Zealand Division occupied Biefvillers later.

63rd Division was ordered forward just before noon to attack southeast in contact with the New Zealand Division on the left. However, it proved impossible to arrange the attack properly in the face of very stiff enemy resistance and it was cancelled until the following morning. Overall it had been a day of disappointment for IV Corps.

25th August 1918

> 395 Sgt Harold Colley, 10th Battalion, The Lancashire Fusiliers (52nd Brigade, 17th Division)
> Martinpuich, France

On 25th August, Fourth and Third Armies were ordered to continue the advance, while First Army was to be prepared to extend the attack northwards with the aim of breaching the Drocourt–Quéant Line. Cavalry was concentrated in case the enemy front began to fall apart. In Fourth Army's area, north of the Somme, the Germans were demoralised and disorganised. The British artillery was having a serious effect on their rear areas and they pulled back during the night. The situation was similar to that experienced by the British in March, except that British morale had held up.

Fourth Army took advantage of the moonlight and achieved surprise by attacking at 1 a.m. There was some success in places but the enemy frustrated the advance elsewhere. Third Army's corps attacked at various times and also had mixed results. Some corps took advantage of the moonlight and attacked at 2.30 a.m., while others delayed until as late as 9 a.m. V Corps was ordered to advance to the line Flers–Gueudecourt and link up with IV Corps, which was advancing on the line Riencourt-lès-Bapaume – Beugnâtre through Bapaume. VI Corps was to comply with this movement to seize the line Vraucourt – Ecoust-St-Mein.

On the right of Third Army was V Corps. 38th Division on the right was directed towards Flers, 17th Division in the centre towards Gueudecourt, while 21st Division on the left moved on Beaulencourt to gain contact with IV Corps. 38th Division attacked at 2.30 a.m. and the first objective was secured by 5 a.m. However, there was little change in the afternoon. 21st Division started at 6 a.m. and had some problems around Le Sars until the village fell late in the morning. The positions held were not improved much and a strong counterattack was foiled at Eaucourt l'Abbaye.

In the centre, 17th Division had reorganised during the night. 50th Brigade was relieved by 114th Brigade (38th Division) and went into divisional reserve. 51st Brigade, which had been resting on the Ancre, took up position in the line to the left

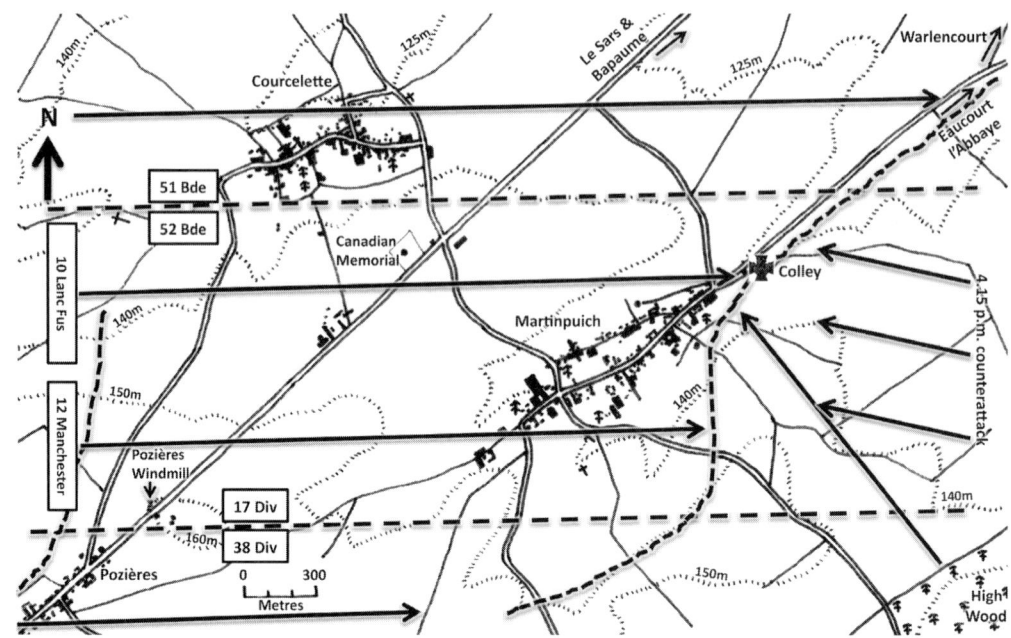

Drive through Martinpuich northeast on the D6E. Where the road swings sharply to the left, turn right and park immediately. Colley's VC action was on the rising ground to the right of the track.

of 52nd Brigade. The two brigades attacked at 4 a.m. with 52nd Brigade's objective being Martinpuich. 12th Manchester advanced on the right and 10th Lancashire Fusiliers on the left, with 9th Duke of Wellington's in support. The plan in outline was to encircle the village from the north (10th Lancashire Fusiliers) and south

From the left bend in the D6E at the northeast end of Martinpuich. The advance on 25th August reached the top of the slope on the right of the track, which leads to Eaucourt l'Abbaye. Harold Colley's VC action was somewhere at the top of the slope above the white signboard on the far side of the road.

(12th Manchester) simultaneously and then mop it up from the flanks and rear. The advance of 10th Lancashire Fusiliers was led by A and C Companies.

The enemy in Martinpuich resisted strongly but the defenders were eventually pushed out, although at first the shelling made it impossible to garrison the village. 10th Lancashire Fusiliers took up a position east of the village astride the Martinpuich–Warlencourt road. Later B and D Companies gained a foothold in a trench north of the village. At 10 a.m. the German artillery shelled Martinpuich, including some gas shells. 12th Manchester managed to make some progress later in the morning but 10th Lancashire Fusiliers was unable to move at that time.

In the afternoon A and C Companies, 10th Lancashire Fusiliers continued the advance but became separated and the reserve companies (B and D) found themselves in the front line again. As he crested a rise half a mile east of Martinpuich, an officer in advance of the main body saw a large German force advancing to counterattack. Positions were hurriedly taken up in nearby trenches and four machine guns of 17th Battalion Machine Gun Corps arrived. The enemy fell determinedly on 10th Lancashire Fusiliers at 4.15 p.m., but did not succeed in reaching Martinpuich.

During the counterattack an advanced trench held by two platoons of B Company suffered very heavy casualties. **Sergeant Harold Colley**, commanding one of B Company's platoons, dashed forward and rallied the survivors. The enemy gained a foothold in the trench and Colley formed a defensive flank to stop their advance, before leading an attack to drive them out. Only three men remained unwounded from the two forward platoons. Colley was so seriously wounded that he died of his wounds that night, but without his swift action the enemy would probably have broken through.

Further advance by 52nd Brigade was halted by machine gun fire from High Wood. The right flank was not in contact with 114th Brigade, as it had been delayed on the Albert–Martinpuich road. Two companies of 9th Duke of Wellington's moved forward to cover the right flank of 10th Manchester. 50th Brigade also moved up in

echelon to the right rear of 10th Manchester. Germans dribbled forward from High Wood in the afternoon. They appeared suddenly at a point in the line where there were no troops near HQ 10th Lancashire Fusiliers. The CO, Lieutenant Colonel RE Cotton, and the HQ staff turned out and, assisted by six Vickers machine guns, stopped the enemy advance. However, the hostile party remained and proved troublesome. That night 9th Duke of Wellington's took over the front from 10th Lancashire Fusiliers.

Meanwhile 51st Brigade had taken Courcelette with little difficulty but, between Martinpuich and Le Sars, it was also hit by machine guns from the southeast. The right halted but the left pressed on and was just short of Eaucourt l'Abbaye at the end of the day. A counterattack in the afternoon from the north from Eaucourt l'Abbaye southwards was repulsed.

Overall V Corps took a considerable amount of ground but other Corps were less successful when they closed up to the strong defences of the Hindenburg Line. IV Corps advanced at 5 a.m. with three divisions in line (63rd, New Zealand and 37th). They were to pass through 42nd Division holding the Corps' front, which was then to form the reserve while 5th Division formed a defensive right flank.

63rd Division had been ordered to advance at short notice. 189th Brigade on the right and 188th Brigade on the left were to lead, with the objective being Riencourt-lès-Bapaume. 21st Division (V Corps) advanced on the right. The evening before the attack, the commander of 189th Brigade cancelled the attack on his own authority, because there was insufficient time for preparations or to brief the troops. He was replaced and, although he was later exonerated, his removal caused considerable disruption prior to and during the attack.

188th Brigade met little opposition at first and le Barque and Thilloy were taken, but the latter was lost almost immediately and a line was established east of le Barque northwards to the Albert–Bapaume road. 189th Brigade was led by the Hood and Hawke Battalions. They were followed closely by the Drake Battalion, which was to clear a communication trench along the divisional right boundary as far as the enemy trenches half way between Loupart Wood and the Albert–Bapume road. The advance through Loupart Wood went well but on the far side the leading battalions were hit by machine guns firing through the mist from the southeast. Both battalion commanders were killed. The machine guns were overcome by Lewis guns with the help of the Drake Battalion and the advance resumed. A ravine (Yellow Cut) was reached east of the Albert–Bapaume road at about 12 a.m. The attack broke down there and the objective of reaching Riencourt had to be abandoned. On the right, 21st Division (V Corps) was behind. On the left, Thilloy remained in German hands after being gained and lost by 188th Brigade, despite a second attempt at 12.30 p.m. 189th Brigade was unsupported on the right or left until 190th Brigade established a flank some way in rear of the right flank. After nightfall 21st Division managed to close up on the right. Counterattacks against le Barque were stopped by concentrated small arms and artillery fire.

During the advance **Commander Daniel Beak**, commanding the Drake Battalion, was dazed by a shell fragment, but continued. When the attack was in danger of breaking down near Loupart Wood, he reorganised the whole brigade line under very heavy fire and led it forward again. At one point the attack was halted by a machine gun. Accompanied by only a runner, Beak overcame the post and returned with nine or ten prisoners. Beak's confidence and initiative inspired all ranks and contributed significantly to the success of the operation. He had already performed outstanding deeds on 21st August, which together with his performance on this day, led to the award of the VC. The New Zealand and 37th Divisions on IV Corps' left enjoyed almost complete success.

In summary, V Corps made a creditable advance on the 25th, although the desired objectives had not been reached. A dangerous gap in the line existed around High Wood, to which the enemy clung tenaciously. IV Corps also made progress, as did VI Corps to a lesser extent, but XVII Corps facing the Hindenburg Line made no progress at all. Since the battle began five days previously, Third Army's thirteen divisions had taken on the original eight German front line divisions and another eleven sent to reinforce the front. Terrible destruction had been inflicted upon them all. Casualties at that rate could not be endured for a protracted period.

26th–27th August 1918

> 396 LCpl Bernard Gordon, 41st Battalion AIF (11th Australian Brigade, 3rd Australian Division)
> Bray, France

A new phase in the Allied offensive was about to open. Haig directed First Army in the north to drive through the northern end of the Hindenburg Line to the east of Arras. The intention was to allow the intact Cavalry Corps to push southeastwards and threaten the rear of the Germans opposing Third and Fourth Armies. This action would continue until Foch brought in the French and Americans to the south and the Belgians to the north. The BEF was, however, under-strength and reinforcements were not keeping up with losses. Haig envisaged having to reduce his force to forty-two active divisions, including ten from the Dominions, and another twelve replacement divisions.

While the main thrust switched to the north, Haig told Rawlinson, commanding Fourth Army, that there was no need to rush the clearance of the enemy in the large bend of the Somme river. These instructions were passed to the Australian Corps. However, Monash was convinced that much more could be achieved, despite his men having been in action for eighteen days continuously and tank support being withdrawn.

South of the Somme the Australian Corps' front was held by 32nd Division and 5th and 2nd Australian Divisions. The former had two brigades in the line and the latter two just one each. 5th and 2nd Australian Divisions were to keep up continuous pressure on the Germans by advancing by infiltration. Hard fighting and heavy losses were to be avoided. 3rd Australian Division north of the Somme was to keep pace.

On the night of 26th/27th August, 8th and 6th Australian Brigades took over the frontages of 5th and 2nd Australian Divisions respectively. They immediately began to probe forward with strong fighting patrols. In places some enemy positions were surprised and fell back but elsewhere they held their posts in strength. To the south, 32nd Division sent out frequent patrols in order to detect any signs that the enemy was withdrawing. At 3.30 a.m., 96th Brigade discovered that the enemy front trenches had been abandoned and occupied them at 5.30 a.m. The Brigade moved forward again at 7.30 a.m. but the French on the right were unwilling to cooperate until the mist dispersed.

14th Brigade came under heavy artillery fire at 3.30 a.m. for two hours, which prevented forward movement until later. It encountered stronger opposition than 96th Brigade. Nevertheless 32nd Division advanced over 1,800m and Vermandovillers was taken, assisted by the progress of the Australians on the left. Prisoners taken by the French indicated that a withdrawal was taking place. After some stiff opposition had been overcome, 5th Australian Division took Foucaucourt.

North of the Somme 3rd Australian Division had forced the Germans out of their front line positions two mornings in succession. On 26th August the Germans still held the Maricourt plateau between the Bray–Montauban gully and the Somme. It was arranged that at dawn on 27th August, 58th Division (III Corps) would drive the Germans out of Maricourt, while 41st Battalion (11th Australian Brigade) seized the Somme bend at Fargny Mill. The right of 3rd Australian Division (10th Australian Brigade and all but the left battalion of 11th Australian Brigade) was to

From the northern edge of Spur Wood looking northeast towards Fargny Wood. 41st Battalion's attack came through Spur Wood, across the re-entrant in the centre to the edge of Fargny Wood, where Gordon was particularly active after the attack. Fargny is hidden amongst the trees in the right middle distance.

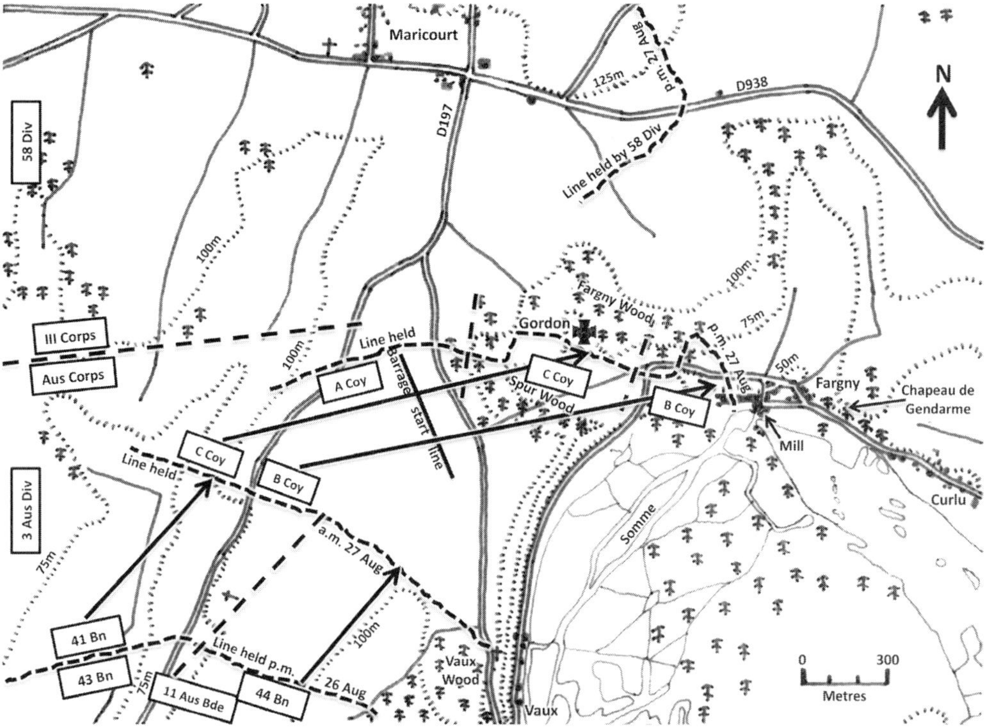

In Curlu drive northwest parallel with the Somme valley. Pass through Fargny. After 450m the road swings sharply to the left. At this point pull over on the right and walk along the track to the southwest for 400m to the edge of Spur Wood. Turn round to look back over the ground across which Gordon attacked towards Fargny Wood on the left of the re-entrant.

stand fast for the time being. 58th Division managed to take Maricourt but was too weak to exploit further and seize the old German line.

On the afternoon of the 26th, 41st Battalion was ordered to relieve 43rd Battalion. However, at 7 p.m. the orders changed to pass through 43rd Battalion and continue

the advance. Accordingly at 9.30 p.m., 41st Battalion moved off and passed through 43rd Battalion at 11 p.m., in touch with 44th Battalion on the right. C Company was on the left, B Company on the right, with D Company in support and A Company in reserve. The advance was conducted in silence to Vaux Wood. The Germans in this area were a collection of exhausted troops belonging to two divisions. They fled as soon as the Australians appeared. Green Very flares indicating success were seen at 2.50 a.m. On the objective, A Company swung over to the left flank and joined the left of C Company.

While the advance was underway at 2 a.m., orders were received for 41st Battalion to attack alone at dawn (4.55 a.m.), in order to protect the right flank of 58th Division. In the dark no reconnaissance could take place and, to complicate the matter, the supporting barrage was fired diagonally to the objective. In addition the troops were very tired after many days of operations. Nevertheless the barrage fell on time and the troops moved off. C Company reached its objective at 6 a.m., having met little opposition. B Company continued and ran into stubborn resistance, which was overcome with the assistance of C Company.

An enemy machine gun post enfiladed the right persistently and accurately. **Lance Corporal Bernard Gordon** MM in C Company, who had led his section through heavy shell fire to the objective, attacked the machine gun post singlehanded. He shot the gunner and captured an officer and ten men. B Company, supported by machine guns and mortars, managed to get forward then despite the opposition.

41st Battalion fought through Spur Wood and reached the river bank south of Fargny Wood. It continued around the river bend to Fargny Mill and a steep scrubby cliff (Chapeau de Gendarme). By 8.05 a.m. the right flank was also on the objective and a series of posts was consolidated along the front by A, C and B Companies.

Enemy machine guns continued to harass the Battalion, making it all but impossible to move about on or close to the objective. This fire gradually died down in the afternoon. Meanwhile Gordon made repeated forays into Fargny Wood. In one he cleared a trench, capturing twenty-nine prisoners and two machine guns. In clearing more trenches he captured another twenty-two prisoners, including an officer, and three machine guns. Almost unaided, during the day he was responsible for capturing a total of two officers, sixty-one other ranks and six machine guns.

41st Battalion remained in this precarious position all day, engaging the enemy with snipers and the accompanying machine guns and mortars. Despite the opposition, the Battalion lost only one man killed and thirty-two wounded over the two days. About one hundred prisoners were taken and twenty machine guns in total, in addition to a German motor ambulance.

That night 11th Australian Brigade was relieved by 9th Australian Brigade. 41st Battalion was relieved by 34th Battalion by 2.30 a.m. on 28th August. 34th Battalion was ordered to continue the advance next day.

Biographies

COMMANDER DANIEL MARCUS WILLIAM BEAK
Royal Naval Volunteer Reserve commanding The Drake Battalion, Royal Naval Division

Marcus Beak, as he preferred to be known, was born on 27th January 1891 at 42 Kent Road, St Denys, South Stoneham, Southampton, Hampshire. His father, William Henry Beak (25th August 1848–1915), was born at Chipping Sodbury, Gloucestershire. He was an assistant surveyor living with his parents in 1871 and married Sarah Anne née Mullins (1846–1919), born at Alvediston, Wiltshire, in 1872 at Tisbury, Wiltshire. By 1891 he was a milk dairyman and in 1901 a master dairyman. The family was living at 42 Kent Road, St Denys at the time of both censuses. By 1911 he was a road surveyor and they had moved to 49 St Paul's Road, Fisherton, Salisbury, Wiltshire. Marcus had seven siblings:

- Ada Mary Caroline Beak (1873–1956), born at Tisbury, was staying with her maternal grandparents in 1881. She was a district nurse in 1911, living at Ivy Bank, Long Cross, Headley, Hampshire, with Alma Thornton, who married her

The paternal side of Marcus Beak's family came from Chipping Sodbury, a Market town in Gloucestershire founded in the 12th century. The town celebrated its 800th anniversary in August 2018. Edward Jenner (1749–1823), who pioneered the smallpox vaccine, started his medical training there. The author JK Rowling was born at the Chipping Sodbury Maternity Hospital and lived in nearby Yate until she was four.

brother, John Walter Beak, later that year. Ada died unmarried at Lothingland, Suffolk.
* William John Beak (1874–76) was born at Donhead St Mary, Wiltshire and died at Williton, Somerset.
* Dora Eleanor Beak (1877–5th September 1962), born at Williton, Somerset, was a spinster living at 80 Durweston, Blandford Forum, Dorset at the time of her death at Portrack General Hospital, Stockton-on-Tees, Co Durham.
* Eva Eliza Beak (31st May 1878–27th March 1972) was a spinster living at Bensham Lodge, Kimberley Road, Croydon at the time of her death.
* George Henry Beak (1880–10th December 1946), born at Aston, Warwickshire, was a boat builder in 1901 and a foreman shipwright in 1911. He married Ellen Chapman (1887–1944), born at Ely, Cambridgeshire, in 1911 at Downham, Norfolk. They were living at 2 Western Esplanade, Southampton, Hampshire in 1911. They had two children:
    ○ Thomas William Beak, born in 1916 at Southwick, Sussex, married Joan Miller (born 1915) in 1939 at Hornchurch, Essex. Joan's father, Sidney Miller (1881–1918), joined the Army on 13th July 1917 and transferred to 1st Royal Marine Battalion RMLI (CH/2464 (S)) on 21st July. He was killed in action on 22nd August 1918 (Vis-en-Artois Memorial, France). Thomas and Joan had four children.
    ○ George Henry Marcus Beak, born in 1920 at Portsmouth, Hampshire, married Norah Lyons (born 1922) in 1943 at Bury, Lancashire. He served during the Second World War in the Royal Hampshire Regiment, Royal Army Ordnance Corps and Corps of Royal Electrical and Mechanical Engineers. They had a daughter in 1949 and moved to Rhodesia in April 1952, where he was general manager of Netherlands Bank of South Africa Ltd, director of Industrial Development Corporation of Rhodesia Ltd and Export Credit Insurance Corporation of Rhodesia Ltd, alternate director of Commercial Bank Zambia Ltd and was also a member of the Scottish Rhodesian Finance Council of Rhodesia. They lived at Crouchmoor, Midvale Road, Highlands, Salisbury, Rhodesia.
George senior married Vera Gertrude Hodges in 1946 at Lothingland, Suffolk. They lived at 84 Bridge Road, Oulton Broad, Lowestoft. He died at The County Hospital, Lowestoft.
* Nora Rose Beak (7th January 1883–31st October 1979) was an assistant matron at a workhouse in 1911, living at West End, Southampton, Hampshire. She married William Milburn Worth (1874–1st May 1951), born at Stockton-on-Tees, Co Durham, in 1928 at Kensington, London. They were living at 4 Queensland Grove, Hartburn, Stockton-on-Tees at the time of his death there. She was living at 5 Green Lane, Newtown, Stockton-on-Tees at the time of her death there.
* John Walter Beak (16th November 1884–1976), born in Birmingham, Warwickshire, was a merchant's clerk in 1901. He was boarding with the Brown family at 15 The

Hundred, Romsey, Hampshire in 1911. He married Alma Mary Hollon Thornton (1st April 1885–18th June 1971) later in 1911 at Alton, Hampshire, where she was born. They were living at Broadwater, Romsey, Hampshire in 1919. They both died at Croydon, Surrey. They had two children born at Romsey:
  ○ Donald John Thornton Beak (1912–2004) married Winifred Lucy Harding (1912–90), born at Wilton, Wiltshire, in 1936 in Salisbury, Wiltshire. She died at Croydon, Surrey and he at Eastbourne, Sussex. They had two children.
  ○ Dora Lorraine Maisie Beak (1916–95) married Arthur Richard Napper (1910–90), born at Marylebone, London, in 1938 at Croydon. They had two children. They both died in Surrey.

Marcus' paternal grandfather, John Beak (August 1823–29th July 1890), married Elizabeth Caroline née Bradbury (February 1817–1896), in Bristol, Gloucestershire on 16th October 1847. They were both born at Chipping Sodbury, Gloucestershire. He was a farmer of twenty-seven acres at Warrens Farm, Yate, Gloucestershire in 1861. By 1871 he was District Surveyor of Roads and they were living in West End Lane, Donhead St Mary, Wiltshire. John died at Rawcliffe, Yorkshire and Elizabeth in Bristol. In addition to William Henry they had five other children born at Yate, Gloucestershire:

- Theodosia Eliza Beak (1850–25th September 1923), a twin with Annie, was a governess in 1871. She died unmarried at Hanwell, Middlesex.
- Annie Clementina Beak (1850–4th September 1927), a twin with Theodosia, was a spinster living at 20 Bristol Road, Weston-super-Mare, Somerset at the time of her death.
- George James Beak (born 1854).
- John Beak (26th January 1857–3rd June 1934) married Rosa Emily Cawthorn (1857–1906), born at Bermondsey, London, in 1883 at Camberwell, London. They had six children – Dorothy May Beak 1885, Reginald Cawthorn Beak 1887, Herbert Stuart B Beak 1889, John Stanley Beak 1892, Basil Charles Beak (1894–1918) and Walter Hugh Beak 1896. Rosa died at Hertford. John married Jessie Lyndsell (1868–13th March 1927), born at Ware, Hertfordshire, in 1912 at Edmonton, Middlesex. They were living at Easthorpe, 145 Ware Road, Hertford in 1917 and at the time of their deaths there. Two of John and Rosas's sons served in the Great War:
  ○ Herbert Stuart Bradbury Beak enlisted in the Army Service Corps on 23rd February 1915 (S4/064848), described as a clerk, 5′ 7½″ tall, weighing 127 lbs and his religious denomination was Church of England. He was posted to A Depot Company ASC, Aldershot next day and to 24th Divisional Train, Lancing, Sussex on 8th April. Appointed acting corporal on 21st May and moved with 24th Divisional Train (73rd Brigade Supply Section)

to West Heath Camp, Pirbright on 1st July. Appointed acting sergeant on 12th August. On 31st August he embarked with 4th Company, 24th Divisional Train at Southampton aboard PS *La Marguerite*, disembarking at Le Havre on 1st September. He was treated for scabies at No.50 Casualty Clearing Station 18th October–24th November and was sent to the Rest Area, St Omer on 27th November. On 22nd February 1916 he was admitted to 74th Field Ambulance with defective vision. Posted to the Base Horse Transport Depot, Le Havre on 27th May and reverted to private on transfer. Posted to the ASC Section, Rouen on 26th June and was appointed acting corporal on 20th July. Next day he was attached to Deputy Director Veterinary Services, Third Army, St Pol and was promoted corporal on 22nd December. He was granted leave 23rd December–2nd January 1917 and applied for a commission on 22nd February. On 25th April he was admitted to 12th Stationary Hospital with debility, transferred to 2nd Canadian General Hospital with anaemia on 29th April and to No.3 Convalescent Depot on 6th May. He transferred to the Base on 14th May and returned to Base Horse Transport Depot, Le Havre next day. Posted to HQ Lines of Communications Area, Abbeville on 30th May and was granted leave 1st–11th August. Herbert returned to Britain on 24th September and was attached to A Depot Supply Company, Southport, Lancashire on probation for a temporary commission. He transferred to Bath on 1st November and the Receiving Depot, Wareham on 7th December. He was posted to No.24 Tank Corps Officer Cadet Battalion, Winchester on 5th April and was granted a temporary commission in the Tank Corps on 23rd October 1918. Posted to the Reserve Unit Tank Corps, Swanage on 4th November and was attached to No.1 Dispersal Unit, Fovant, Wiltshire for duty on 22nd January 1919. Leave was granted 18th–22nd April and 1st–5th July. Herbert was released on 16th September 1919 and relinquished his commission on 15th December 1920, retaining the rank of second lieutenant.

- Basil Charles Beak joined No.1 Company, 1st Hertfordshire Regiment TF on 27th March 1912 (1873 later 265178), described as 5′ 9″ tall. He was embodied on 5th August 1914 and went to France from Southampton on 5th November. Appointed acting paid lance corporal on 24th April 1915 and was granted leave to England 27th July–2nd August. Appointed acting corporal on 25th October and was promoted corporal on 28th November. Appointed acting lance sergeant 29th December and was promoted lance sergeant on 14th January 1916. Basil was granted leave 3rd–10th April. Appointed acting sergeant (later substantive) on 12th April. He applied for a commission on 24th November and returned to Britain on 21st January 1917 as a candidate. He joined No.1 Cadet Battalion, Bisley on 1st March and was commissioned in the Machine Gun Corps (Infantry) on 26th June. He returned to France on 25th August and joined the Base Depot next day

at Camiers. Posted to 22nd Company, 7th Battalion MGC on 28th August and joined on 3rd September. He attended a machine gun course at Camiers 28th September–30th October. 7th Division moved to Italy in November. He attended a horsemanship course 28th January–3rd February 1918 and was granted leave to Britain from 24th March, returning to the unit on 19th April. He was admitted to hospital 21st–23rd May and was granted leave in Rome 17th–20th September. On 28th October he was admitted to 21st Field Ambulance and No.39 Casualty Clearing Station, where he died on 4th November 1918 of broncho-pneumonia following influenza. He was buried in Mirano Communal Cemetery Extension and his remains were moved later to Giavera British Cemetery (6 F 2).
- Elizabeth Caroline Beak (10th October 1860–11th August 1937) was a spinster living at Coombe Down, Bath, Somerset at the time of her death at Wells Mental Hospital, Somerset.

His maternal grandfather, William Mullins (c.1821–1913), born at Alvediston, Wiltshire, married Mary Ann née Jeans (c.1823–98), born at Odstock, Wiltshire, in 1845 at Alderbury, Wiltshire. He was a carrier in 1851, living with his widowed mother and wife at Alvediston. By 1861 he was a grocer and carrier and they were living at The Street, Alvediston. By 1871 he was a farmer and the family was living at Church Street, Berwick St John, Wiltshire. William was also the licensed victualler at the Crown Inn, Alvediston. By 1881 the family was living at the Crown Inn and by 1891 William was a carrier living with his wife in Alvediston. Both their deaths were registered at Tisbury, Wiltshire. In addition to Sarah they had three other children, all registered at Tisbury:

Alderbury, a few miles southeast of Salisbury, is where Marcus' maternal grandparents married in 1845. A church was recorded there in the Domesday Book. A new parish church of St Mary was built on the same foundations in 1857–58. Alderbury was on the short-lived Salisbury–Southampton Canal, which never reached the former before it closed in 1806.

William Mullins was landlord of the Crown Inn at Alvediston for many years. It dates back to the 15th century.

Marcus' maternal grandparents both died at Tisbury, on Cranbourne Chase, about thirteen miles west of Salisbury. There were Stone, Bronze and Iron Age settlements in the area, including Castle Ditches hill fort. A monastery may have been founded as early as 705. The monastic grange, now Abbey Grange Place Farm, has a tithe barn dating back to at least 1279. It has the largest thatched roof in England. In the 13th century, Tisbury quarries provided stone for the building of Salisbury Cathedral. The other main industry was wool and the cloth industry. The village suffered in the Black Death in the mid 14th century but eventually recovered. A station on the Salisbury & Yeovil Railway opened in 1859. In 1885 a brewery was built and improvements to the village included a new road, High Street, seen here. Thomas Mayhew (1593–1682), who established the first English settlement at Martha's Vineyard in North America, was born in Tisbury. Sir Matthew Arundell of nearby Wardour Castle was a cousin of Elizabeth I. He is buried in the churchyard, as are the parents of Rudyard Kipling. He visited them while working on Kim. His father, also his illustrator, used a pupil from Tisbury Boys' School as the model for the main character. The second oldest tree in Britain is also in the churchyard, carbon dated to c.4,000 years old.

- Eleanor Mullins (registered as Mullens) (1848–1917) married Henry William Henly (24th February 1826–1895), a farmer born at Calne, Wiltshire, in 1882 at Tisbury. He farmed Cadly Farm. Henry had married Ellen Rooke (c.1825–78), born at Charford, Hampshire, in 1850 at Amesbury, Wiltshire, registered as Henley. They had six children – Robert Henly 1851, Ellen Henly 1853, Harry Henly 1855, John Henly 1856, Bessie Henly 1858 and Frank Henly 1864. Henry was farming 930 acres at Cholderton, Wiltshire in 1861, employing twenty men and boys. By 1871 he was 'out of business' living with his family at Warminster Road, Wilton. In 1881 he was a farm bailiff living with his daughter at The Street, Alvediston. Eleanor married James Phillip Rendel on 15th December 1909 at Chute, Wiltshire. She died at Salisbury, Wiltshire.
- John Mullins (1851–71) died at Tisbury.
- George William Mullins (1853–23rd December 1910) was an assistant to his father in 1881. He married Sarah Wilkins (1850–1926) in 1881 at Wilton, Wiltshire. She was born at Bower Chalke, Wiltshire. They were living at Alvediston in 1891. By 1901 he was a farm bailiff and they were living at Crook Hill, Alvediston. Sarah was still living there in 1911. They had four children – John William Mullins 1881, Eva Mary Mullins 1884, William Wilkins Mullins 1886 and Walter George Mullins 1890.

Marcus was educated at St Denys School 1897–1904 and Taunton's School, Highfield Road, 1904–10, both in Southampton. He became a pupil teacher at St Mary's School, Southampton but felt that he was *not too good at it* and became a private secretary to a parson in Bristol.

A wintery view of St Denys School, attended by Marcus 1897–1904 (schoolswire).

Marcus enlisted as an ordinary seaman in the Royal Naval Volunteer Reserve at the Crystal Palace, London on 26th January (February in some sources) 1915 (ZP/1061), described as 5′ 7″ tall, with fair hair, hazel eyes and his religious denomination was Church of England. He joined the Benbow Battalion on 17th April and A Company, 1st Battalion on 27th April. He was drafted to the Crystal Palace on 30th April, was promoted petty officer on 8th May and, on the same day, was commissioned as a sub lieutenant RNVR for duty in the Royal Naval Division. Transferred to 1st Reserve on 22nd June. He served at Gallipoli with the Anson Battalion from 9th September and was attached to the Cyclist Company RMLI on 26th September and to the Divisional Bombing School for instruction on 28th September. Marcus was ordered to report to the Divisional Cyclist Company on 3rd November 1915 but this was changed next day to the Drake Battalion. He received orders to report to the Howe Battalion on

Taunton's School, founded in 1760 by Richard Taunton, a wine merchant, privateer and former Mayor of Southampton, to provide education for a career at sea, started with just twenty pupils. It was located in various places over the years, including Grove Street, High Street, Windsor Terrace and the junction of Liverpool Street (later Everton Street) and Kingsfield Road. In 1864 it moved to a specially built site on New Road. In 1875 it became an endowed school named Taunton's Trade School and later Taunton's School. It moved to Highfield Road in 1926 and during the Second World War was evacuated with Bournemouth School. In 1969 it became a sixth form college and was renamed Richard Taunton College. From 1978 girls were admitted. In 1858 Southampton College and High School for Girls was founded. It moved to Hill Lane in 1936 and became a sixth form college in 1967, named Southampton College for Girls. From 1979 it admitted boys and was renamed Hill College. In 1989 the two colleges merged as Taunton's College and in 1993 moved into the refurbished Hill Lane site. In 2012 the name changed to Richard Taunton Sixth Form College. Amongst its famous alumni are:

- Chris Packham, naturalist and television presenter.
- Benny Hill, comedian.
- John Stonehouse (1925–88), government minister who was spying for the Czechs during the Cold War and who faked his own death in 1974.
- Jack Mantle VC (1917–40).

52 Victoria Crosses on the Western Front Battle of Albert

The Crystal Palace was a revolutionary construction of cast-iron and plate-glass built in Hyde Park, London for the Great Exhibition of 1st May–15th October 1851. It attracted more than 14,000 exhibitors from around the world in 92,000m² of exhibition space. It was designed by Joseph Paxton and was three times the size of St Paul's Cathedral, measuring 564m long and thirty-nine metres high internally. After the Exhibition it was moved to Penge Peak, next to Sydenham Hill in South London, where it stood until it was destroyed by fire in November 1936. The surrounding area was renamed Crystal Palace, including Crystal Palace National Sports Centre, previously a football stadium that hosted the FA Cup Final from 1895 until 1914. Crystal Palace FC was founded on the site in 1905. During the Great War, the Crystal Palace was used as a naval training establishment named HMS *Victory VI*. More than 125,000 men of the RNVR, RNAS and RND trained there. Following the war, the Crystal Palace was the first site of the Imperial War Museum until it moved to South Kensington and, in the 1930s, to its present site in Lambeth.

30th December but this was also cancelled and he remained with the Drake Battalion. He served at Gallipoli until the evacuation.

On 15th May 1916 he embarked on HMT *Minnewaska* at Mudros and disembarked at Marseille, France on 20th May. **Awarded the MC for his actions at Beaucourt-sur-Ancre, France on 13th/14th November 1916 in which he led an attack with great courage and initiative and materially assisted in the capture of the enemy line, LG 26th January 1917.** Lieutenant Colonel Bernard Freyberg was awarded the VC for his part in this action. Marcus was granted leave to England 30th November–13th December. On 14th December (November in some sources) he was appointed Adjutant, Drake Battalion. He was appointed acting

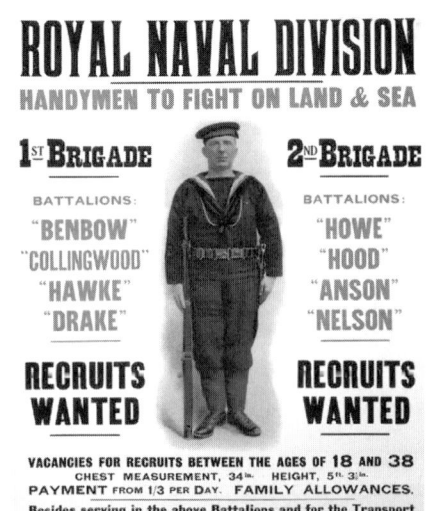

Recruiting poster for the Royal Naval Division.

SS *Minnewaska* (14,317 tons) was constructed for the Atlantic Transport Line in 1908 by Harland & Wolff in Belfast. Her career was short but eventful. In April 1911 a seaman fell overboard and had to swim away desperately to avoid being drawn into the screws. Within a few seconds *Minnewaska* had turned about and a boat was lowered. In just thirteen minutes the seaman was rescued but had lost his sea boots. A year later *Minnewaska* was one of the ships that assisted RMS *Carpathia* in sending the names of survivors following the sinking of RMS *Titanic*. In October 1914 a fire broke out in a consignment of sugar in a hold in New York. It was extinguished by flooding. The sugar was worth $120,000 but *Minnewaska* was not damaged and sailed on schedule. On 28th April she took part in the Gallipoli landings and had a minor collision with SS *Derfflinger* off ANZAC Cove. By the time that she was requisitioned by the British Government in January 1915, *Minnewaska* had made sixty-six voyages from London to New York. Initially she operated on the Avonmouth–Alexandria route and made five journeys to Gallipoli. She had a few narrow escapes involving submarines but on 29th November 1916 her luck finally ran out. On the way to Salonika from Alexandria with 1,600 troops aboard, she struck a mine laid by UC-23 a few miles southeast of Dentero Point, Suda Bay, Crete. A large hole was blasted in the hull and she listed rapidly and threatened to capsize. However, Captain Gates managed to keep control and steamed at full speed for the nearby shore. *Minnewaska* was run aground on the west of Cape Deutero at the entrance to Suda Bay. All crewmen and passengers were rescued without loss. Captain Gates was awarded the OBE. Minnewaska was abandoned and in 1918 was sold to Italian shipbreakers for scrap. However, parts of the wreck still remain on the site, which is popular with divers (Australian War Memorial).

commander on 19th March 1917 to command the Drake Battalion temporarily but reverted to sub lieutenant on 3rd April 1917 and was appointed temporary lieutenant commander and Second-in-Command, Drake Battalion. Appointed acting lieutenant commander 4th April and was promoted lieutenant commander on 18th April.

Awarded a Bar to the MC for his actions at Gavrelle, France on 23rd/24th April 1917, in which he continually dashed forward to reorganise the men and led them with great bravery through the enemy barrage and machine gun fire, LG 18th July 1917. Relinquished the appointment of Adjutant on 8th May. He was granted leave in England 13th–24th May, which included the MC investiture. Marcus attended the Senior Officers' Course at Aldershot on 8th October and was granted leave in England 16th–29th December. He rejoined the Battalion on 31st December and was appointed temporary commander the same day to command the Howe Battalion until it disbanded in February 1918. Appointed

The Distinguished Service Order, instituted by Queen Victoria on 6th September 1886, is usually awarded to majors (or equivalent) or above but in the past was occasionally awarded to valorous junior officers. There were 8,981 awards in the Great War. The order recognised meritorious or distinguished service in war. Prior to 1943 the order could only be given to someone mentioned in despatches. Since 1993 the order has been restricted solely to distinguished service and not for gallantry. Although the DSO is now open to all ranks it has yet to be awarded to a non-commissioned rank.

acting commander on 14th January 1918. He joined the Anson Battalion on 1st March and commanded it until 6th March. He returned to the Drake Battalion on 13th March as the CO, an appointment he held until June 1919.

Awarded the DSO for his actions on the Ypres-Bus (Dickebusch) road on 24th March 1918 during a night attack by the enemy. The right of the Division was dangerously exposed and he arranged for a flank to be formed in that direction. Subsequently he covered the retirement of two brigades with a composite rearguard, based on the Drake Battalion, which he organised and commanded. His initiative and presence of mind greatly assisted in extricating these brigades from a very difficult situation. Throughout he handled his Battalion particularly skilfully, LG 26th July 1918. Mentioned in Field Marshal Sir Douglas Haig's Despatch dated 7th April 1918, LG 20th May 1918.

Marcus was admitted to a field ambulance with influenza 4th–8th July and was granted leave to England 8th–22nd August but returned on 10th August. **Awarded the VC for his actions at Achiet-le-Grand, France on 21st and 25th August 1918, LG 15th November 1918. Mentioned in Field Marshal Sir Douglas Haig's Despatch dated 8th November 1918, LG 20th December 1918.** The VC was presented by the King at Vincent Barracks, Valenciennes, France on 6th December 1918. It was the first time that a naval VC had been presented with the crimson ribbon. He was

Marcus Beak receives the VC from the King at Vincent Barracks, Valenciennes on 6th December 1918.

Marcus was based at The Barracks, Ayr when he married Matilda Wallace there in September 1923. The barracks were built on the south side of the harbour and in response to the French Revolution, in 1795. Under the Cardwell Reforms in 1873, the barracks became the Depot of 21st (Royal Scots Fusiliers) Regiment of Foot and, following the Childers Reforms, the Depot for the Royal Scots Fusiliers in 1881. The facility was named Churchill Barracks in 1942 in honour of the wartime Prime Minister, who was a CO of 6th Royal Scots Fusiliers in the Great War. The Regiment amalgamated with the Highland Light Infantry in 1969 to form the Royal Highland Fusiliers in Edinburgh. Churchill Barracks was demolished in 1967 and the site became The Citadel Leisure Centre. The picture shows a rather forlorn section of Churchill Barracks just prior to it being knocked down.

granted leave to England 7th–13th December 1918, 12th–26th January and 25th March–16th April 1919. The Freedom of the County Borough of Southampton was conferred on him on 2nd April 1919. On 22nd May he embarked at Dunkirk and reported to the Dispersal Unit Crystal Palace, London on 12th June 1919 for demobilisation the same day.

Marcus went into business in Bristol but he did not settle to civilian life. He resigned his RNVR commission on 11th March 1921 and was commissioned the next day into 1st Royal Scots Fusiliers as a captain with seniority backdated to 1st January 1918. He was serving at The Barracks, Ayr, Scotland when he married.

Marcus Beak married Matilda Catherine Frances Ritchie Wallace (24th November 1891–3rd June 1930), born at Cloncaird Castle, Kirkmichael, Ayrshire, at the Old Parish Church, Kirkport, Ayr, Ayrshire, Scotland on 5th September 1923. They

The Auld Kirk in Ayr, where Marcus and Matilda married on 5th September 1923.

Cloncaird Castle, where Matilda Wallace was born, dates partly from the 16th century, with later additions, including an entirely new front in 1814.

lived at Sheep Drove Lodge, Lambourn, Berkshire and at Scotland House, Hawkley, Liss, Hampshire. Matilda died at 17 Auckland Road East, Southsea, Hampshire and is buried in Ayr Cemetery, Holmston Road, Ayrshire. They had two sons born at Portsmouth, Hampshire:

* Marcus Malcolm Vivian Wallace Beak (20th February 1927–7th January 2000) enlisted as an officer cadet (14485810) and was granted an Emergency Commission in the King's Royal Rifle Corps on 30th November 1946 (373477). He was promoted lieutenant on 29th May 1948, with seniority from 20th February 1948, and captain on 20th February 1954. He attended the Staff College. Promoted major 20th February 1961 and was on active service in Borneo 1962–66. Appointed GSO2 Army Strategic Command, Wilton, Wiltshire on 21st September 1967. He retired from the Royal Green Jackets on 24th April 1970. Marcus was married but had no children.
* Peter Charles Victor Beak (1929–14th April 2008) was living at Flat 13B, 55 Queensborough Terrace, London at the time of his father's death in May 1967. He married Barbara Ida Paddic McKay (born 1923), born at Rochford, Essex, on 15th November 1971 at Westcliffe-on-Sea, Essex. There were no children. Barbara predeceased him.

Matilda's father, Lieutenant Colonel Hugh Robert Wallace DSO JP DL (31st August 1861–2nd May 1924), was born in Dugshai, India, son of Captain Henry Ritchie Wallace (1835–73), 92nd Regiment, and Fanny Parker. Hugh was educated at Cheltenham and was a member of the Carlton Club, Pall Mall, London. He also served as a captain and honorary major in 4th Argyll & Sutherland Highlanders (late Renfrew Militia) February 1879–1898. One of Hugh's ancestors was William Wallace (1270–1305) and he was Head of the Wallace Clan. Hugh married Matilda Marion Christie Campbell (11th May 1860–9th February 1905), born at 1 Lynedoch Place, Edinburgh, Midlothian, on 14th October 1886 at Calcutta, India. They lived at Cloncaird Castle, Maybole, Ayrshire and at 2 Netherwood Road, Ayr. Matilda died at Cranston Lodge, Ayr. Hugh joined 10th Gordon Highlanders on 5th October 1914 and was appointed temporary lieutenant colonel to command the Battalion 22nd February 1915–3rd March 1916, including at the Battle of Loos. Hugh embarked at Boulogne and disembarked at Folkestone on 5th November. He was granted leave 6th–19th November 1915 extended to 10th December. He saw a specialist at Grosvenor Square, London for deep-seated rheumatism in his shoulders and arms and a flat foot. After a course of treatment at Bath, a medical board at 2nd Southern General Hospital, Bristol on 4th December found him unfit for General Service for three months but fit for Home Service. A medical board at the Military Hospital, Inverness on 9th February 1916 found him unfit for General Service permanently as far as marching was concerned but fit for Home Service. He commanded 1st (Reserve) Garrison Battalion, Suffolk Regiment from 7th May.

Awarded the DSO, LG 3rd June 1916. He was appointed staff lieutenant 2nd class at HQ VII Corps on 12th June. Hugh was granted leave in Britain 25th August–4th September 1917. He was appointed Commandant VII Corps Reinforcement Camp 17th October 1917–10th February 1918 as a lieutenant colonel. He requested to be relieved, as he did not feel active enough for the appointment or have recent trench experience. He was granted leave until 24th February and relinquished his commission on 19th March 1918. Hugh contested South Ayrshire as an Independent Conservative in the 14th December 1918 General Election but was defeated by James Brown. He appears to have been granted another appointment as he was admitted to 56th General Hospital on 21st October 1919, was discharged to Calais on 16th November and returned to Britain on 21st November. Hugh was MID twice. He was appointed DL Ayrshire and for three years was Convener of the County of Ayr. He was also appointed Honorary Sheriff Substitute for the County. Hugh was an authority on heraldry, a prominent Freemason and a staunch Orangeman. In addition to Matilda, Hugh and Matilda had three other children:

- Hugh Harry Ritchie Wallace (14th July 1887–15th December 1938), born at Tigh-na-ghrian, Millon Road, Ayr, was educated at Cheltenham and Loretto. He never married. He received an order relating to the Bankruptcy Acts 1914–26 that appeared in the London Gazette in December 1927.
- Archibald Malcolm Wallace (23rd October 1888–5th July 1948), born at Cloncaird Castle, Ayrshire, was educated at Charterhouse and was a portioner of Busbie, Ayrshire. He was commissioned in 3rd Gordon Highlanders on 30th January 1907, transferred to 8th Gordon Highlanders and was appointed temporary captain on 18th October 1914. He appears in the Army List under Gordon Highlanders until April 1917 and then just in the index. He was in the Indian Army Reserve as a lieutenant 10th November 1916 and captain 14th October 1917. He had been released by the time of the 1920 Indian Army List. Archibald married Frances Honore French-Brewster née Clover (14th April 1901–3rd July 1963) on 24th June 1931 at Petersfield, Hampshire. She was the daughter of Henry Alfred Clover (1866–1933) and Fannie Papin (1870–1920) of St Louis, Missouri, USA and widow of Arthur Ord French-Brewster (1882–1928). She married Arthur on 26th March 1928 at Montreux, Switzerland and he died sixteen days later at Baveno, Italy. Arthur served in the Royal Flying Corps during the Great War and his older brother, Major Robert Abraham French-Brewster, 1st Irish Guards, died in service on 17th February 1917 (Kensal Green (All Souls') Cemetery, London). Archibald and Frances were living at Field House Farm, Churt, Surrey at the time of his death there. She was living at Redhearn Cottage, Churt at the time of her death at 44 Hale Road, Farnham, Surrey. There were no children.
- Charles John Wallace (6th February 1890–20th December 1943), born at Newfield, 1 Racecourse Road, Ayr, was educated at Charterhouse 1903–07 and was a portioner of Busbie. He was commissioned from the Royal Military

College, Sandhurst into 2nd Highland Light Infantry on 5th October 1910. He was promoted lieutenant on 19th March 1913 and was appointed temporary captain 1st February–9th March 1915 and again on 1st April 1915. Promoted captain 17th May 1915, later revised to 1st April. Awarded the MC (LG 23rd June 1915). Appointed Brigade Major 68th Brigade on 13th June 1916 and brevet major 1st January 1917. Awarded the DSO (LG 1st January 1918). Appointed temporary major and GSO2 Irish Division 13th July 1917. Appointed GSO2 Third Army. MID six times. Awarded the OBE (Edinburgh Gazette 2nd January 1919) and the French Croix de Guerre (LG 14th July 1919). Appointed GSO2 Highland Division, Army of the Rhine until 19th November 1919. Appointed adjutant 20th November 1919. Attended Staff College from 22nd January 1921. Restored to the establishment 22nd December 1922. Appointed deputy assistant adjutant general 1st April 1923–1st April 1925. Appointed GSO2 Royal Military College, Canada 17th April 1925–25th April 1927. Promoted major 1st June 1927 and appointed brevet lieutenant colonel 1st July 1927. Appointed Chief Instructor, Military History and Tactics, Royal Military Academy, Woolwich 1st January 1931 and GSO2 War Office 22nd August 1932. Charles married Helen Elizabeth Swinnerton MacDonald née Dyer (1889–1966) on 20th January 1932, daughter of Sir Thomas Swinnerton Dyer. There were no children. Helen had married Captain the Hon Ronald Ian MacDonald (1884–1918), 3rd (Reserve) Battalion, Cameron Highlanders, youngest son of 6th Baron MacDonald, on 5th May 1915 at Petersfield, Hampshire. He served on the staff at the Infantry Base, Cherbourg, France, was awarded the French Legion d'Honneur and died on 17th January 1918 (Tourlaville Communal Cemetery & Extension, near Cherbourg). Helen was living at Frilsham Home Farm, Yattendon, Berkshire at the time. Charles was promoted colonel on 4th October 1935 with seniority from 1st July 1930, and was appointed Assistant Adjutant & Quartermaster General, 1st Division until 15th December 1938. Appointed ADC to King George VI 16th October 1938–6th March 1940. Appointed temporary brigadier to command a brigade in India 2nd January 1939. Appointed Director Personnel Services, Adjutant General's Department, War Office and acting major general on 6th March 1940, later substantive from the same date with seniority backdated to 19th April 1938. Awarded the CB (1941). Appointed Commander East Central Area, Eastern Command 23rd February 1943. He died in service at Luton Hospital, Bedfordshire on 20th December 1943 and is buried in Ayr Cemetery, Holmston Road, Ayr. Helen was living at Little Orchard, Frilsham at the time of her death.

Hugh married Isobel McRae Dubs née Arthur (died 1947) on 30th January 1908, widow of Charles Ralph Dubs, a manufacturer, of Glasgow, Lanarkshire and daughter of William Raer Arthur and Margaret Boyd. Hugh died at Cloncaird Castle, leaving his estate to his younger sons and daughter jointly as heirs portioner of Busbie.

The camp at Landi Kotal in North-West Frontier Province.

Khyber Pass.

Marcus was appointed brevet major on 1st January 1929. He transferred to the King's (Liverpool) Regiment on 17th February 1932 and served in India for seven years with the 1st Battalion at Jubbulpore, Landi Kotal, Kyber Pass and on the volatile North-West Frontier. He was appointed brevet lieutenant colonel on 1st July 1935 and was promoted lieutenant colonel on 29th December 1938. He served as CO 1st South Lancashire until 1940, including on operations in France. He was promoted colonel on 20th July 1940, backdated to 1st July 1938, and was appointed acting brigadier 14th June–13th December 1940. **Mentioned in War Office Despatches dated 26th July 1940 and 20th December 1940, LG 26th July 1940 and 20th December 1940 respectively.** Marcus was appointed temporary brigadier 14th December 1940–13th July 1942 and commanded 12th Brigade 14th December 1940–29th December 1941. He was GOC Troops Malta as an acting major general 30th December 1941–13th July 1942. His house in Malta was hit by a bomb during a Luftwaffe air raid just a week after he arrived. While he was GOC Malta, King George VI awarded the Island the George Cross on 16th April 1942.

On 3rd August 1942 Marcus was appointed local major general for employment at GHQ Middle East. He begged to be given an active command and reverted to brigadier on 7th November 1942 to command 151st Brigade (50th Division) in the Western Desert. He led an attack against the Mareth Line and later discovered that it had been a feint. The GOC knew this but had not informed Beak, who was furious when he found out, being particularly concerned about the loss of life. He made his views known to the GOC and was relieved of command for his indiscretion. He served as Senior British Liaison Officer with the Canadian First Army prior to, and during, the Normandy landings. From 30th June 1944 he was supernumerary to the establishment as a colonel/local brigadier. He transferred to the Retired List on 19th February 1945 as an honorary major general.

Memorial tablet to Matilda and Marcus in Ayr Cemetery (Memorials to Valour).

Marcus Beak's unmarked grave is in this area of Brookwood Cemetery (Memorials to Valour).

Following his retirement, Marcus served for many years as a county councillor for Lambourn, Berkshire, including a number of years as chairman of the Finance Committee. He lived at Sheepdrove Lodge, Lambourn and served as President of the Drake Battalion Society and the Royal Naval Division Association. He was living at Greengates, Newbury, Berkshire in 1955. He attended a number of VC Reunions – the VC Garden Party at Buckingham Palace on 26th June 1920, the VC Dinner at the Royal Gallery of the House of Lords, London on 9th November 1929, the VC Centenary Celebrations at Hyde Park, London on 26th June 1956 and the first VC Association Reunion at the Café Royal, London on 24th July 1958. In 1955 he was living at Greengates, Newbury, Berkshire.

Commemorative paving stone dedicated at Southampton Cenotaph, Watts (West) Park, Southampton in December 2018.

Marcus died of chronic renal failure and prostatic hypertrophy at Princess Margaret Hospital, Swindon, Wiltshire on 3rd May 1967. He is buried in an unmarked grave (No.222960) on St Gabriel's Avenue, Brookwood Cemetery, Woking, Surrey. He is commemorated in a number of other places:

- Memorial tablet to his wife at Ayr Cemetery, Holmston Road, Ayr (Wall Section, Lair 52).
- Memorial plaque unveiled at Cheltenham War Memorial on the Promenade on 27th September 2006.

- A Department for Communities and Local Government commemorative paving stone was dedicated at Southampton Cenotaph, Watts (West) Park, Southampton, Hampshire on 6th December 2018.

In addition to the VC, DSO and MC & Bar he was awarded the 1914–15 Star, British War Medal 1914–20, Victory Medal 1914–19 with Mentioned-in-Despatches oakleaf, 1939–45 Star, Africa Star with 8th Army clasp, War Medal 1939–45 with Mentioned-in-Despatches oakleaf, George V Jubilee Medal 1935, George VI Coronation Medal 1937 and Elizabeth II Coronation Medal 1953. The medals were bequeathed to one of his sons and were held by the Royal Navy Museum, but on the son's death the widow offered the group for sale. The medals were sold at auction by Spink & Sons on 5th November 2003 for a world record sum at that time of £178,250 (£155,000 hammer price) to Lord Ashcroft. The VC is held by the Michael Ashcroft Trust, the holding institution for the Lord Ashcroft Victoria Cross Collection in the Imperial War Museum.

The 1939–1945 Star was instituted on 8th July 1943 (originally as the 1939–1943 Star) for award to British and Commonwealth forces. There are two clasps – Battle of Britain and Bomber Command. It and the Africa Star were the first two campaign stars instituted for the Second World War. By May 1945 there were eight stars and nine clasps. In 2013 the Arctic Star and the Bomber Command Clasp were added. No one could be awarded more than six stars and five clasps. Only one clasp could be worn on any star. Medal ribbons were issued from August 1943 but no medals until after the cessation of hostilities. The 1939–1945 Star was awarded for operational service between 3rd September 1939 and 2nd September 1945, the only campaign star that covered the full duration of the Second World War. Qualification was 180 days service afloat or in an operational theatre for naval, merchant marine and army personnel. Airborne troops qualified if they participated in any airborne operation and completed sixty days service in an operational unit. Aircrew qualified after sixty days in an operational unit, including at least one operational sortie. Aircrew of fighter aircraft engaged in the Battle of Britain were also awarded the Battle of Britain Clasp and aircrew of bomber aircraft, who participated in at least one operational sortie in a Bomber Command operational unit, were awarded the Bomber Command Clasp in 2013. Ground crew qualified after 180 days in an area of operational army command. The award of a gallantry medal or MID qualified the recipient for the 1939–1945 Star regardless of service, as did death or disability due to service. Special criteria applied when just one day's service was required. Examples include the campaign in France and Belgium 10th May–19th June 1940, Raid on St Nazaire 22nd–28th March 1942, Dieppe Raid 19th August 1942, Anglo-Iraq War 10th April–25th May 1941, Japanese conquest of Burma 22nd February–15th May 1942 and Battle of Madagascar 5th May–5th November 1942.

Left: The Africa Star was instituted on 8th July 1943 for award to British and Commonwealth forces who served in North Africa between 10th June 1940 and 12th May 1943. There were three clasps – North Africa 1942–43, 8th Army and 1st Army – but only one could be worn, the first qualified for.
Right: The War Medal 1939–1945 was instituted on 16th August 1945 to be awarded to those who served full-time in the armed forces or Merchant Navy for at least twenty-eight days between 3rd September 1939 and 2nd September 1945.

Left: The King George V Silver Jubilee Medal commemorated the 25th anniversary of the coronation. 85,235 medals were issued, a proportion to each Commonwealth country, including 6,500 to Australia. The medals were awarded at the discretion of the local government, but in general went to members of the Royal Family and household, ministers, government and local government officials and members of the armed forces.
Right: The Queen Elizabeth II Coronation Medal 1953 was awarded immediately after the coronation on 2nd June 1953 as a personal souvenir from the Queen to members of the Royal Family, selected officers of state, members of the Royal Household, government and local government officials, mayors, public servants, members of the armed forces and police in Britain, the colonies and Dominions. It was also awarded to members of the Mount Everest expedition, two of whom reached the summit for the first time four days before the coronation. A total of 129,051 medals were awarded, including 11,561 to Australians.

40684 SERGEANT HAROLD JOHN COLLEY
10th Battalion, The Lancashire Fusiliers

Harold Colley was born on 26th May 1895 at 60 Winson Street, Dudley Road, Smethwick, Birmingham, Warwickshire. His father, John Colley (6th November 1857–24th August 1934), was a pattern maker (iron) in 1881 living with his parents. He married Hannah Elizabeth née Hadley (26th January 1862–8th November 1930), born at Park Street, Oldbury, Staffordshire, on 10th March 1884 at St John, Wolverhampton, Staffordshire. She was a milliner living with her mother in 1881. John was a pattern maker journeyman and worked at Tangyes Ltd, Cornwall Works and Henry Pooley's, Brook Street, both in Smethwick. In 1891 they were living at 15 Cape Street, Birmingham. By 1895 they were living at 64 Winson Street, Smethwick and had moved to No.60 by 1901. By 1911 they had moved to 74 Cheshire Road, Smethwick, by when John

The Tangye brothers (James, Joseph, Edward, Richard and George) founded the company in 1856. They came from a humble farming background in Cornwall and their first customers were Cornish mine-owners. In March 1857, Richard, James and Joseph started James Tangye & Bros in Mount Street to manufacture hydraulic appliances, particularly lifting jacks. On 31st January 1858, their jacks launched Brunel's SS *Great Eastern*. Richard Tangye said, *we launched the Great Eastern and she launched us*. Cornwall Works in Smethwick opened in 1864 to produce a large range of products. The company designed the hydraulic systems for Britain's first funicular railway in Scarborough in 1869 and its machinery installed Cleopatra's Needle in London in 1878. In 1881 Tangyes Ltd was formed to acquire Tangye Bros, hydraulic engineers, and Robert Price & Co, malleable ironfounders, of Winson Green, Birmingham. The company developed, with offices in Johannesburg and Sydney. Richard and George Tangye were founding benefactors of Birmingham Museum & Art Gallery in 1885. In 1919 the company started production of large-scale industrial diesel engines, pumps and hydraulic equipment. Engine production ceased after the Second World War and the company concentrated on hydraulic pumps and valves. Its machinery helped construct Sydney Harbour Bridge, Australia in 1932, sections of Birmingham's 'Spaghetti Junction' motorway interchange in 1972 and London's Thames Barrier 1974–84, plus many more high profile projects. The trade name is still in use.

was an engineering pattern maker. He was a trades unionist and a delegate of the patternmaker's to the Trades Council. John and Hannah both died at Quinton, Birmingham. Harold had four siblings:

- Elizabeth Beatrice 'Beat' Colley (22nd October 1885–23rd May 1973), born at Heath Town, Staffordshire, was a tailoress in 1901 and a dressmaker in 1911. She married Albert Victor West (3rd July 1885–14th August 1970) in 1911 in Birmingham. He was a director of a non-ferrous metal works in 1939 and they were living at 222 Streetsbrook Road, Solihull, Warwickshire. They were living at 34 Bridge Street, Barford, Warwickshire at the time of his death there. She was living at Furrows End, Barford Hill, Warwick at the time of her death there. They had three children:
    - Albert Raymond West (1913–99), also seen as Raymond Albert West, was a non-ferrous metal worker in 1939, living with his parents. He married Joan Lily Shepherd (1917–2018), born at Aston, Warwickshire, in 1943 at Solihull. The marriage ended in divorce. Joan married John Charles Cow (1914–86), born at Croydon, Surrey, in 1969 at Solihull. He was an electrical engineer and a member of the Auxiliary Fire Service, boarding at 24 Canterbury Road, Farnborough, Hampshire in 1939. They were living at 18 Waverley Road, Farnborough at the time of his death there. Joan was a resident at Gracewell of Church Crookham Nursing Home, 2 Bourley Road, Church Crookham, Hampshire at the time of her death there. Albert married Eileen Mary Spencer West (née Hodgetts) (1917–97), born on the Isle of Wight, in 1970 at Bromsgrove, Worcestershire. She had married Ronald Bernard Wood (1917–75), born at Horsham, Sussex, in Birmingham in 1940. The marriage ended in divorce. Eileen was living at 1 Back of 25 Weston Street, Aston, Warwickshire at the time. Two children appear to have been born to this marriage. Eileen changed her surname from Wood to West in 1950, although she and Albert Raymond West are understood to have had a daughter with surname Wood in 1956. Eileen died at Feckenham, Redditch, Worcestershire.
    - Donald Harold West (born 1916) was a rolling mill manager in 1939, living with his parents. He married Mary N Yost (born 1915) in 1941 at Solihull, Warwickshire. They had four children.
    - Alan Alfred West (born 1918) was a non-ferrous metal roller in 1939, living with his parents. He married Edith E Cork (born 1921), born at Aston, in 1947 at Solihull. They had four children.
- Dora Colley (24th August 1888–22nd November 1962) was a ladies outfitter in 1911. She married Robert Cecil Best (13th April 1890–28th September 1956) in 1915 at King's Norton. He was a stockbroker's clerk in 1911, living with his parents at 76 Laxey Road, Birmingham. They were living at 21 Hannon Road, Birmingham in 1939 and were still there at the time of his death at Queen Elizabeth Hospital, Selly Oak, Birmingham. She was still living there at the

time of her death at 48 Meadowbrook Road, Northfield, Birmingham. They had twins:

- Ivy Dora Best (1915–97) was a statistical clerk in 1939. She married Leslie John Newey (1907–54) in 1941 in Birmingham. Leslie's father, Albert Eaton Newey (1867–1917), served in the Rifle Brigade (6240), enlisting in Birmingham on 1st October 1883. He was later a fitter staff sergeant in 242nd Brigade RFA (835009) and in the RGA (314808). He died on active service with 242nd Brigade RFA on 10th October 1917 (La Clytte Military Cemetery, Belgium). Ivy and Leslie had a daughter.
- Norman Harold Kelsey Best (14th September 1915–9th January 2010) served in the RAF during the Second World War as a leading aircraftman and later as a sergeant air gunner (1041081) flying numerous missions in Wellington bombers (MID, LG 3rd June 1943). He married Beryl J Dudley (born 1920) in 1945 in Birmingham and they had two daughters. He was a company director in 1962 and married Mary E Best at Bridgnorth in 1972. He married Maxine C Davis née Cohn (1928–2015), born in Chicago. Illinois, USA, in 2002 at Pershore, Worcestershire. They met in Sarasota, Florida, USA. She had married previously as Rose and had at least two sons. Maxine was a horse stable manager, real estate agent, interior designer, merchandise display artist and coordinator of the Tumor Board at Chicago's Children's Memorial Hospital. She was also an accomplished sculptor. She authored the book, *Automatic Writing, Communicating with Spirit through the Written Word*. Norman died in Sarasota Co, Florida and Maxine at Tidewell Hospice, Sarasota.

• Frances 'Fanny' May Colley (26th October 1892–14th November 1927) was a clerk in 1911. She married Richard Thomas Pritchard (born 1892) in 1918 at King's Norton. His birth was registered as Richard Thomas Pritchett in Birmingham. They were living at 114 Clevedon Road, Birmingham in 1925. Frances died at Coventry, Warwickshire. Frances and Richard are understood to have had two children, born at West Bromwich:

- Olive G Pritchard (born 1919) married Henry Lloyd in 1943 and they had a daughter.
- Rita Pritchard (born 1920) married Horace Evans in 1941.

• Albert Henry 'Jimmie' Colley (11th August 1896–15th November 1968) served in the Royal Warwickshire Regiment during the Great War (451). He was gassed and buried by debris after a shell explosion at Messines in August 1916. This resulted in a permanent injury and he was discharged. He lived at 684 Hagley Road West, Quinton, Birmingham. After the war Albert tried to contact Harold through a number of mediums. He is reported to have approached the author, Arthur Conan-Doyle, who told him to see an old lady at a terraced house in Crewe, Staffordshire and to take a camera. This he did, purchasing new plates that morning from Boots in the town. On arrival the father and son of the house were called inside by the old lady. They said prayers and Albert was sat in a chair with a warning that he may go numb on one side of his body. The son took the camera, while the father, who had the 'power', pointed his thumb at Albert. Albert's side became numb and the son took a picture. Albert's side was charged with ectoplasm, which showed the name John in vivid blue fire. When the plate was developed Harold Colley was standing by Albert's chair in full fighting order, a Webley pistol stuck in his greatcoat belt, wearing a flat cap rather than a steel helmet, and covered in mud. Albert was terrified and refused to proceed further. The plate was taken by the Society for Physical Research and, together with letters from Conan-Doyle, were lent by Albert to his bank manager, who died shortly afterwards and the plate was never recovered. Albert married Doris Hunt (26th November 1896–2nd July 1987), born at Smethwick, in 1922 at West Bromwich, Warwickshire. They were living at 684 Hagley Road West, Quinton, Birmingham in 1939, when he was Midland Counties Organising Superintendent (travelling) in the Wholesale Bakery Department of J Lyons & Co. His wife was not with him at the time.

Harold's paternal grandfather, Charles Colley (c.1828–5th August 1905) married Frances 'Fanny' née Lloyd (born 1826), born at Bilston, Staffordshire, in 1846 at Dudley, Staffordshire. Charles was a stone miner in 1851 and they were living at Wolverhampton Street, Bilston. By 1861 they had moved to Stafford Street, Willenhall, Wolverhampton and to Market Street, Bilston by 1871. By 1881 he was a coal miner and they were living at 15 Oxford Street, Bilston. He was living at 107 Temple Street, Bilston at the time of his death there. In addition to John they had eight other children:

- Mary Colley (born 1847) probably died in infancy as she was not with the family in 1851.
- William Thomas Colley (1849–77) was a stone miner, living with his parents in 1871.
- Enoch Colley (25th February 1852–1893) was an engine fitter, living with his parents in 1871. He married Mary Blaney (1853–1932), born at Bilston, on 18th June 1872 at Dudley. They were living at Court 6, 112 Wolverhampton Street, Bilston in 1891. Mary married James William Jones (23rd December 1848–25th January 1907), born at Wellington, Shropshire, in 1896. Mary was living with her son, William Thomas Colley, and family at 42 Beckett Street, Bilston in 1911. James had married Mary Ann Owen (born 1853), born at Ketley, Shropshire, on 5th February 1872 at Wellington. Mary Ann died at Bilston in the early to mid-1890s. James was a commission agent in 1901 and they were living at 6 Broad Street, Bilston. James died at 33 Broad Street, Bilston. Enoch and Mary had four children:
    - William Thomas Colley (1877–1940).
    - Abraham Colley (1880–1938) enlisted in 1/6th South Staffordshire (3458) on 20th October 1914 and went to France on 25th June 1915. He was discharged due to wounds on 7th April 1916 and was issued War Service Badge No.86078.

- Mary Elizabeth Colley (born 1883).
    - Joseph Colley (1892–1955).
- James and Mary Ann had six children:
    - Albert Edward Jones (born 1872), a gardener, married Lydia Jane Davies (1887–1940), born at Codsall, Staffordshire, on 15th October 1898. He was a hospital porter in 1911 and they were living at 55 Green Lanes, Bilston. They had four children but none survived infancy. He was a gardener when he enlisted in 1/6th South Staffordshire (15673) at Wolverhampton on 9th November 1914, declaring previous service in 1st Volunteer Battalion, South Staffordshire Regiment. He went to France on 17th March 1915, returned to Britain on 6th June and was discharged on 4th September 1915 no longer physically fit for war service. He was a cemetery superintendent after the war. They were living at 82 The Ferns, Green Lanes, Bilston in 1939, by which time he had retired.
    - William James Jones (1873–1942).
    - Charles Ernest Jones (1878–1929).
    - John Henry Jones (1883–1947).
    - Percy Jones (born 1885).
    - George Victor Jones (1887–1962).
- Charles Colley (1854–1924) was an engine fitter living with his parents in 1871 and 1881. He married Mary Elizabeth Pearson (born 1870), born at Brierley Hill, Staffordshire, in 1898 at Wolverhampton. They were living at Court 6, Wolverhampton Street, Bilston in 1891, at 6 Cambridge Street, Bilston in 1901 and at 14 Dudley Street, Bilston in 1911. They had two children – Charles Colley 1898 and Leslie Colley 1900. Charles Colley junior enlisted on 16th October 1916 (61731).
- James Colley (1855–1914) was living with his parents as a colliery clerk in 1871 and as a corn dealer in 1881. He married Elizabeth Cadman (1858–1937) on 19th August 1883 at Wolverhampton. James was a colliery manager in 1891 and they were living at 56 Temple Street, Bilston. By 1901 he was a colliery office clerk and they were living at 107 Temple Street. By 1911 he was a labourer in an iron works and they were living at 80 Temple Street. They had seven children including – Herbert Charles Colley 1883, William James Colley 1885, Frances Mary Colley 1887, Maud Elizabeth Colley 1888, Joseph Arthur Colley 1890 and Ethel Jane Colley 1891.
- Thomas Colley (born 1859) was a solicitor's general clerk, living with his parents in 1881. He married Mary Elizabeth Nash (born 1858), born at Bilston, on 12th December 1882 at St Thomas, Bath Row, Birmingham. Thomas was a clerk and they were living at 78 Birmingham Street, Wednesbury, Staffordshire in 1891. They had three children – Frances Maud Colley 1884, Charles W Colley 1888 and Pollie Mildred Colley 1890.
- Fanny Colley (born 1861).

- Joseph Henry Colley (born 1865) was a colliery manager in 1891. He was living with Emily Cooper (1863–97), his housekeeper, born at Ettingshall, Wolverhampton, and their children at 1 Bradley Street, Bilston. Both were recorded as single. They had four children – William Charles C Colley 1887, Sidney Josiah C Colley 1889, Gertrude Elizabeth C Colley 1890 and Gladys Elsie C Colley 1893. Her death, unmarried, was registered at Wolverhampton. Joseph was recorded as a widower in the 1901 Census, boarding at 101 & 102 Rushall Street, Walsall, Staffordshire, while the children were residing at Cottage Homes for Children of the Poor Law Union of Wolverhampton at Willenhall, Staffordshire.

His maternal grandfather, William Hadley (1832–80), born at Whiteheath, Staffordshire, was a farmer living with his mother on her farm at Birchfield Lane, Oldbury, Worcestershire in 1851. She was also a grocer and iron dealer. William married Selina née Pearce (c.1830–27th December 1909), born at Harborne, Birmingham, on 21st November 1852 at St Peter's Parish Church, Harborne. He was a general dealer in 1861 and they were living at Park Lane, Oldbury, Worcestershire. By 1871 he was a scrap iron dealer and they were living at Cranford Street, Smethwick. Selina was a fancy dealer living at Winson Street, Birmingham in 1881. She was living at 119 Winson Street, Birmingham and had moved to 37 Winson Street by 1901, where she ran a shop. Her death was registered at Stourbridge, Worcestershire. In addition to Hannah they had seven other children:

William Hadley married Selina Pearce at St Peter's Parish Church, Harborne in November 1852. There has been a church there since Saxon times and it is believed that St Chad preached there. The current church dates from the 1860s but the tower is probably 14th century. Anne Chamberlain, wife of Prime Minister Neville Chamberlain, is buried there.

- William Hadley (born 1852), a scrap iron dealer, married Ellen Cox (1852–27th April 1914), born in Birmingham, in 1876 at King's Norton, Warwickshire. They were living at 218 Heath Street, Birmingham in 1891, at 277 Heath Street in 1901 and at 42 Cranford Street, Smethwick in 1911. Their son Herbert, a hotel waiter, was living with them in 1901 and 1911. They had seven children, only one of whom was still living by the time of the 1911 Census, including Herbert Hadley 1880 and Florence Selina Hadley 1889.
- Samuel Hadley (born 1855).
- Charles Albert Hadley (born 1857).
- Thomas Hadley (born 1860) was a gas fitter in 1881, living with his mother.

- John Hadley (1864–1915) was a jeweller in 1881 and a fitter in 1891, living with his mother.
- Emma Selina Hadley (born 1866) was a housemaid in 1881, living with her mother. She married Herbert Farmer (10th September 1862–1939) on 16th March 1890 at St Thomas Parish Church, Dudley, Worcester, where he was born.
- Edwin Hadley (1868–1937) was a fitter, living with his mother in 1891. By 1901 he was a cycle maker, still living with his mother, and was recorded as Edmund. He married Mary Ann Williamson (born 1874), born at West Bromwich, in 1903 in Birmingham. He was a motorcar fitter in 1911 and they were living at 29 Hill Street, Netherton, Worcestershire. His death was registered at Smethwick, Staffordshire. They had at least two children – Sidney Hadley 1905, Alice Hadley 1907 and possibly Albert S Hadley 1919.

Harold was educated at Dudley Road Council School, Smethwick, Staffordshire. He was a proficient sportsman, winning a gymnastics championship medal, wicket-keeping for the Mission XI cricket team and was a member of Smethwick Crescent Wheelers Cycling Club, as was Thomas Turrall VC (see the third book in this series – Somme 1916). Harold was also a member of Smethwick Baptist Church on Regent Street. In 1911 he was a silversmith's errand boy and later became a silver spinner with J & R Griffin Ltd, Link Works, Soho Hill, Smethwick.

Harold enlisted in the Duke of Cornwall's Light Infantry on 1st September 1914 (13684). He went to France on 10th September 1915, where he served as a cyclist despatch rider in the Army Cyclist Corps (5615). He was wounded on 30th March 1917, when he was buried by debris following a shell explosion while attempting to rescue a comrade. He was evacuated to England. **Mentioned in Sir Douglas Haig's Despatch dated 9th April 1917, LG 25th May 1917.**

Harold Colley, sitting front row centre, with other members of the Bearwood Baptist Men's Gymnasium (Norman Best).

On returning to France, Harold transferred to 10th Lancashire Fusiliers (40684). In his first engagement with the new unit, he again rescued two men who had been buried by a trench mortar bomb while under heavy machine gun and mortar fire. For this action he was awarded a Special Certificate of Merit by the Divisional Commander. On another occasion, while clearing a trench, he was hit by a bullet in the chest. He feared that he had been mortally wounded but the bullet hit a steel mirror in his breast pocket, leaving him badly bruised.

Awarded the MM for his actions south of Beaumont Hamel, France in the early hours of 4th June 1918, when the enemy launched a heavy raid. The garrison was overcome on the left but the enemy was met by vigorous Lewis gun fire on the right. Harold Colley and two others bombed along the trench and recaptured an outpost after the sergeant had been wounded. They killed five Germans, captured eight more and drove off the remainder, LG 7th October 1918. Harold was appointed acting sergeant the same day. **Awarded the VC for his actions at Martinpuich, France on 25th August 1918, LG 22nd October 1918.** He died of wounds at Martinpuich later the same day and is buried in Mailly Wood Cemetery (Il Q 4). There was no investiture and the VC was sent to his brother, Albert, by post.

Harold is commemorated in a number of other places:

- The Colley Memorial Cup, presented by Mitchell and Butler's in 1920 to Smethwick Crescent Wheelers Cycling Club, was later used by the British Cyclo-Cross Association for the best improved junior rider. The original cup was lost and in 1989 Harold's nephew, Norman Best, presented a replacement to the North Birmingham Section of the Vintage Motor Cycle Club to be awarded in the annual Levis Cup Trial (100-mile route in Worcestershire and Shropshire) for the best rider on a former War Department machine.

Private Thomas George Turrall, 10th Battalion, The Worcestershire Regiment, was awarded the VC for his actions at La Boisselle, France on 3rd July 1916, in the opening days of the Somme offensive. Thomas was about eight years older than Harold. His story is related in the third volume in this series, *Victoria Crosses on the Western Front: The Somme 1916.*

Harold's grave in Mailly Wood Cemetery.

Biographies 71

War Memorial outside St Mary's Church, Bearwood (Memorials to Valour).

Harold's memorial plaque in Smethwick Council Building.

- A Department for Communities and Local Government commemorative paving stone was dedicated at Victoria Park, 35 Suffrage Street, Smethwick, West Midlands on 25th August 2018.
- War Memorial outside St Mary's Church, Bearwood Road, Bearwood, Birmingham.
- War Memorial, Baptist Church, Bearwood Road, Bearwood, West Midlands.
- Memorial Plaque, Council Building, High Street, Smethwick, Birmingham.
- Illuminated address in the Fusiliers Museum Lancashire, Bury.
- Named on his parent's grave in Quinton Cemetery, Halesowen Road, Birmingham (Section 5).

Harold never married but was engaged to Miss May Bell, whom it is understood never married. Harold's parents unveiled Smethwick War Memorial in 1925. The names of those commemorated do not appear on the memorial. They also attended the opening of the Hall of Memory in Birmingham on 4th July 1925.

In addition to the VC and MM Harold was awarded the 1914–15 Star, British War Medal 1914–20 and Victory Medal 1914–19 with Mentioned-in-Despatches Oakleaf. The VC is held by the Fusiliers' Museum Lancashire, Moss Street, Bury, Lancashire.

4/400 SERGEANT SAMUEL FORSYTH
No.3 Field Company, New Zealand Engineers attached 2nd Battalion, Auckland Regiment

Samuel Forsyth was born on 3rd April 1891 at Newtown, Wellington, New Zealand. His father, Thomas Forsyth (c.1858–21st September 1919), is believed to have been born in Lanarkshire, Scotland. His mother, Grace Dalgleish (4th January

1855–29th April 1943), was born at Craigshinnie, Dalmellington, Ayrshire and married Alexander Brown (25th December 1848–6th February 1877) at Dalmellington in 1876. Alexander died in Liverpool, Lancashire and she emigrated to New Zealand. Thomas Forsyth married Grace Brown there in 1889. He was a master mariner and the family lived at 26 Cottleville Terrace, Thorndon, Wellington. Samuel had four siblings from his mother's two marriages:

Samuel was born in the Newtown district of Wellington.

* Mary Brown (20th April 1877–24th March 1896), born at Dalmellington and died at Hawera, Taranaki, New Zealand.
* Mary Hope Forsyth (18th March 1890–19th September 1922) married William Arthur Thomas (24th March 1887–14th July 1937) on 24th December 1912. They had at least three children:
    ○ Ellen Grace Thomas (born 1913) married Bedlington William Frank Twort (1910–42) in 1935. He was a compositor and they were living at 12 Carlisle Street, Wellington in 1938. He was living at 9 Balfour Street, Mornington, Wellington at the time of his death there.
    ○ Mary Margaret Thomas (born 1915) married Bernard Joseph Watson in 1937.
    ○ Frederick Thomas (born 1917).
* Robert Dalgleish Forsyth (2nd February 1894–6th March 1933) was a battery hand at Wakamarina gold mine, Marlborough, New Zealand. His year of birth has also been seen as 1892. He married Ruby Jane Boyd (1892 or 94–1975) on

Cottleville Terrace, Thorndon, Wellington, where the family lived for some years.

14th October 1914 at Ronga Valley. She married James Brown in 1939. Robert and Ruby had five children:
- Samuel Forsyth (1915–68), born at Canvastown, married Mary Miller.
- Grace Emily Forsyth (1916–2008) married James Thomas Hall Lourie (1909–91), born at Marton, Manawatu-Wanganui, in 1935. They had three daughters. Both of them died at Tauranga Bay, Bay of Plenty.
- Possibly Jean Elizabeth Forsyth (1918–2012). No trace of her birth or her parents could be found. Jean married Harold Jesse Smith (born 1917), a motor mechanic, in 1939. They lived at 187 Thornton Quay, Wellington. By 1949 he was a driver for New Zealand Railway and they were living at 18 Melrose Street, Upper Hutt.
- Robert James Forsyth (1918 or 1920–1968) married Melva Joyce Edge (1925–2006), born at Waimangaroa, West Coast. He was a battery assembler in 1949 and they were living at 132 Ghuznee Street, Wellington. By 1954 he was a labourer and they were living at 64 Romilly Street, Westport, Buller District, West Coast and were still there in 1964. They had two children.
- Valerie June Forsyth (1928–29).

• Ellen Margaret Daisy Brown Forsyth (1898–1971) married Lyall Rayner Thomas (23rd August 1896–5th December 1957), born at King St, Newtown, Wellington, in 1927. Lyell enlisted in 1st Wellington (33478) as Rayner Lyall Thomas on 18th September 1916 and was posted to B Company, 21st Reinforcements the same day. He was a metal worker for Kirori Galvanising Co, Wellington and was living with his father (next of kin), Frederick William Thomas, at 152 Adelaide Road, Wellington. He was described as 5′ 8″ tall, weighing 140 lbs, with fresh complexion, brown eyes, brown hair and his religious denomination was Church of England. He was admonished and forfeited two days pay for overstaying his leave from 8.15 p.m. on 10th December 1916 until 1 p.m. on 12th December. On 19th January 1917 he embarked on HMNZT No.74 *Ulimaroa* at Wellington from 17th Ruahine Company, 3rd Reserve Battalion, Wellington Regiment, disembarking at Devonport on 27th March. He joined 2nd Wellington Company, 3rd Reserve Battalion at Sling Camp, Bulford, Wiltshire next day. On 24th April he joined 17th Company, 3rd Wellington Battalion, 4th Brigade at Codford, Wiltshire and departed for France on 27th May. He was appointed cook on 17th November. On 8th February 1918 he was attached to XXII Corps Reinforcement Camp and relinquished his appointment as cook. He was appointed cook again with No.1 New Zealand Entrenching Battalion 26th March–31st August, was granted leave in Britain 17th August–6th September and rejoined the Battalion as a cook until 15th October. The following day he joined 17th Company, 2nd Wellington and was promoted lance corporal on 10th December. He returned to Britain on 9th February 1919 and was posted to Sling Camp, Bulford on 13th February. He applied for discharge overseas on 5th March but did not follow it through. He was probably at Sling Camp when rioting broke out on 14th March as a result of the slow pace of repatriation. On 10th May he embarked in London on SS *Waimana* and disembarked at Auckland on 23rd June. His address was 11 Gerton Terrace, Wellington South when he was discharged in Wellington on 21st July 1919. Ellen and Lyell lived at 56 Cooper Street, Wellington and had at least one son, Frank Thomas, who lived at Makara Beach, New Zealand.

Nothing is known about Samuel's paternal grandparents. His maternal grandparents were Robert Dalgleish (1832–8th June 1889), born at Kells, Kirkcudbrightshire, Scotland, and Mary Scott née Hope (c.1830–17th May 1920), also born in Scotland. Mary emigrated to New Zealand with her daughter Grace and died at Waipawa, Hawke's Bay. In addition to Grace, Mary and Robert had another thirteen children:

- Robert Dalgleish (20th September 1856–28th September 1909), born at Kells, Kirkcudbrightshire, emigrated to Utah, USA and was naturalized on 3rd July 1890 at Salt Lake City. He worked as a miner and married Catherine Gray (12th May 1870–8th June 1913), born at Old Monkland, Lanarkshire, Scotland, on 14th September 1887 at Blackfoot, Bingham, Idaho. Robert died of miner's consumption at Park City, Utah. She also died there of general debility and cirrhosis of the liver. They had six children – Robert Dalgleish 1888, John G Dalgleish 1889, David Dalgleish 1891), James Dalgleish 1892, Rolland Chester Dalgleish 1894 and Margaret M Dalgleish 1901.
- Elizabeth Dalgleish (3rd July 1858–12th August 1930) never married and died at Wellington, New Zealand.
- Thomas Dalgleish (1st–11th June 1860).
- Mary Jane Dalgleish (28th April 1861–2nd January 1940) married William Muir (c.1863–16th June 1912) in 1898 in New Zealand. They had two daughters – Mary Muir 1900 and Agnes Muir 1901.
- John Dalgleish (15th–27th April 1863).

- David Dalgleish (1st August 1864–3rd April 1934) emigrated to the USA in 1888. He married Elizabeth Frances Williams (born June 1875), born in Pennsylvania, USA, on 5th October 1892 at Park City, Summit, Utah. Her father was Welsh and her mother was born in North Carolina, USA. David was a copper miner in 1900 and they were living at 263 Beginbere Street, Bisdee, Arizona. He subsequently died at Bisdee. They had eight children – an unnamed male 1892, David Reese Dalgleish 1893, Raymond Dalgleish 1897, Theodore Dalgleish 1899, Gilbert Burns Dalgleish 1901, Mary Elizabeth Dalgleish 1903, an unnamed male 1908 and Dorothy Ruth Dalglish 1919.
- Agnes Dalgleish (18th April 1866–31st July 1946) never married and died at Hawke's Bay, New Zealand.
- James Dalgleish (27th March–8th April 1868).
- James Dalgleish (12th July 1869–17th December 1915) emigrated to the USA in 1890 and was a copper miner in 1900 living at 1291 Beginbere Street, Bisdee, Arizona. He married Nellie L Hughes (March 1880–1975), born in California, USA, on 17th February 1902 at Tombstone, Arizona. Her parents were of Welsh origin. James was a silver miner in 1910 and they were living at 2nd Street, Tombstone. He was a mine foreman with Bunker Hill Company at the time of

Thorndon School was established on 5th April 1852 as St Paul's School in Sydney Street. In 1873 it was taken over by the education board of Wellington Province and the name changed to Thorndon School. It moved to a new site in 1880 and in the early 1900s was the largest school in the city. It also housed the Teachers' Training College for a while. It currently has about 300 pupils. The School is reputed to be the setting for Katherine Mansfield's 1921 short story, *Her First Ball*.

Clifton Terrace School had 750 former pupils and staff serving during the Great War. Almost one in six pupils (118) did not return, two of them were the sons of prime ministers and another was one of the school's four Rhodes Scholars. Governor General John Jellicoe dedicated a cenotaph to their memory in 1924, and the ceremony is seen in this picture. In November 1971 work on a new motorway near the school caused the memorial to collapse twenty metres down a slope. A new memorial, consisting of a three metre high triangular concrete column with a separate plaque naming those killed, was dedicated on 19th November 2018.

his death at Park City, Utah. They had four children – Camilla Hope Dalgleish 1903, Grace Dalgleish 1905, Robert Hughes Dalgleish 1906 and Joseph Whitman Dalgleish 1909.
- Thomas Dalgleish (4th–18th December 1871).
- William Dalgleish (25th March–18th April 1873).
- John Dalgleish (born and died 19th August 1874).
- Margaret Dalgleish (21st–23rd August 1875).

Samuel was educated at three schools in Wellington. First, Thorndon School 1900, then Terrace School, Clifton Terrace 1902–04 and probably Wadestown School, as his name appears on the school's roll of honour.

Samuel worked as a cabinet-maker before becoming a battery hand and an amalgamator with Monowai Gold Mining Co, Thames, Wellington. He served in the reserve forces, joining the Field Engineers in 1910. He was also a member of the Kent Terrace Bible Class and worked enthusiastically for the Sailors' Friend Society in Wellington.

Samuel enlisted in the New Zealand Engineers, New Zealand Expeditionary Force on 13th August 1914, described as 5′ 11″ tall, weighing 147 lbs, with fresh complexion, hazel eyes, fair hair and his religious denomination was Presbyterian. He embarked on HMNZT No.3 *Maunganui* on 15th October and disembarked

SS *Maunganui* (7527 tons), a twin screw passenger steamship built by Fairfield Shipbuilding & Engineering Co, Govan, Glasgow for the Union Steamship Co of New Zealand, is seen here in Wellington harbour during the Great War. Her maiden voyage was on 15th February 1912 from Wellington, via New Zealand southern ports, to Melbourne, Australia. At the start of the Great War she was requisitioned as a troop transport and was in the first convoy on 1st November 1914 to assemble in King George's Sound, Albany, Western Australia. She was designated flagship of the ten New Zealand transports in the convoy. She made ten round trips from New Zealand to Egypt and Britain. *Maunganui* was converted from coal to oil in 1922. She serviced the Auckland–Sydney–Vancouver route and later San Francisco until 1936, when that service was discontinued. From 1937 she ran the Trans-Tasman route between New Zealand and Sydney until June 1940 when she was requisitioned as a hospital ship, serving in that role until the end of 1945, when she was laid up at Wellington. In 1947 she was sold to GM Lykiardopulo under the Panamanian flag and in 1948 was owned by Cia Naviera del Atlantico (Hellenic–Mediterranean Line). She was refitted at Piraeus, Greece, renamed *Cyrenia* and delivered migrants to Australia from Genoa in Italy, Valetta in Malta and Piraeus in Greece. She was sold to Italian shipbreakers and scrapped in February 1957.

Biographies 77

HMT *Kingstonian* (6,454 tons) was torpedoed off San Pietro Island, Italy by UB-68 on 11th April 1918. She was beached in Carloforte Bay, but was torpedoed by UB-48 on 29th April, resulting in her being a total loss.

No.2 Australian Stationary Hospital at Mudros.

Samuel Forsyth was evacuated to Britain aboard HMHS *Aquitania*. RMS *Aquitania* was built for Cunard on Clydeside by John Brown and her maiden voyage to New York commenced on 30th May 1914. She was in use for thirty-six years and served in both world wars. The author's grandfather, John Camplin, was evacuated from Gallipoli on *Aquitania* at the same time as Samuel Forsyth. John awoke in a delirious state to see angels floating above him and thought he was dead, until he realised he was looking at the painted dining room ceiling.

From 1909 the new buildings of the University of Birmingham were earmarked as a war hospital of 520 beds. The first casualties arrived on 1st September 1914. More University and other suitable buildings were taken over and at its peak 1st Southern General Hospital had space for 130 officers and 2,357 other ranks. In May 1917, the former Poor Law Infirmary on Dudley Road was separated and became 2/1st Southern General Hospital.

at Alexandria, Egypt on 3rd December. On 9th May 1915 he embarked at Alexandria on HMT *Kingstonian* for Gallipoli and served there until 4th July, when he was taken aboard SS *Alnwick Castle*. He was evacuated to Egypt, where he was admitted to the Egyptian Army Hospital, Pont-de-Koubbeh, Cairo on 7th July. He returned to Gallipoli and was slightly wounded on 28th August but remained at duty. On 6th November he was admitted to the New Zealand Field Ambulance and transferred to No.2 Australian Stationary Hospital at Mudros on Lemnos. On 25th November he embarked on HMHS *Aquitania* for transfer to 1st Southern General Hospital, Birmingham, where he was treated from 5th to 16th December.

Samuel was granted leave 17th December–5th January 1916 and moved to the New Zealand Base Depot at Hornchurch, Essex on 14th January. He was admitted to No.2 New Zealand General Hospital, Walton-on-Thames 18th

At the outbreak of war the Army took over Grey Towers at Hornchurch, a country mansion with eighty-five acres of ground, for a military depot. A hutted camp was ready by November 1914 and was first used by 23rd Royal Fusiliers (First Sportsman's Battalion) until June 1915. In January 1916 the site became the first Command Depot for the New Zealanders in England. When wounded began arriving from the Western Front in April, it was realised that the site was too small for a Command Depot and it became the New Zealand Convalescent Hospital, opening in July with 1,500 beds. The aim was to return soldiers to the front within six months. If this could not be achieved it was more economical to return them to New Zealand. Hospitals were established for New Zealanders at Brockenhurst in Hampshire, Codford in Wiltshire and at Mount Felix in Surrey, but more capacity was required and Hornchurch also became an auxiliary hospital. Its capacity expanded to 2,500 patients. By the end of 1918 about 20,000 patients had been treated at the Hospital. The New Zealanders departed in June 1919 and the huts were taken over by No.2 Transfer Centre, which organised the staffing of demobilisation centres. It disbanded in November 1919 and the military occupation of Hornchurch ended. Grey Towers was demolished in 1931 and much of the site is now covered by housing.

At the outbreak of war, Sir Thomas MacKenzie, the New Zealand High Commissioner in London, formed the New Zealand War Contingent Association (NZWCA) to provide comforts for the troops, visit them in hospital, find accommodation for convalescents and keep in touch with soldiers and their relatives. With the end of the Gallipoli campaign and the move of New Zealand troops to the Western Front, there was a need to establish a hospital for New Zealand casualties. When war broke out the War Office requisitioned the Mount Felix estate at Walton-on-Thames, Surrey, to house British troops. They moved out in June 1915 and the estate was offered to the NZWCA as a hospital. Lady Islington undertook its conversion into a 350 bed facility with a large operating theatre. The New Zealand War Contingent Hospital, usually known as the New Zealand Walton Hospital, opened in August 1915. Within two days the first patients arrived from Gallipoli. The Chief Medical Officer was a New Zealander and about three-quarters of the staff came from, or were associated, with New Zealand. On 3rd August 1915 the King, Queen and Prince of Wales visited. In January 1916 five large ward huts were added, increasing the bed capacity to 1,040. In August 1916, No.1 New Zealand General Hospital opened at Brockenhurst, Hampshire and the Hospital at Mount Felix was renamed No.2 New Zealand General Hospital. In general, New Zealand wounded arriving at Dover were taken to Mount Felix, while those arriving at Southampton went to Brockenhurst. More huts were built at Mount Felix in October 1916, adding 500 beds and Oatlands Park Hotel nearby was acquired to increase accommodation. In 1919 a fire destroyed five marquees and a considerable amount of equipment. The number of patients was gradually decreased and No.2 New Zealand Hospital closed in March 1920, having treated 27,000 patients. In 1965 the Mount Felix estate was sold for housing development. A fire in 1966 damaged the mansion house so badly that it had to be demolished. A commemorative plaque to the New Zealanders was rescued and placed in the new Walton Town Hall in New Zealand Avenue. When the Town Hall was demolished, the plaque was donated to Elmbridge Museum. The only surviving estate buildings are the clock tower, brewhouse and laundry, which later became a coach house, and the stables, which have been converted into six houses.

February–9th March with an in-growing right big toenail. He travelled to France on 14th April and joined the New Zealand Infantry and General Base Depot, Étaples on 29th April. On 29th July he was attached to 2nd Anzac Entrenching Battalion and rejoined 3rd Field Company, New Zealand Engineers at Armentières on 8th August. On 24th December he was appointed acting lance corporal (later substantive from the same date).

On 3rd January 1917 Samuel Forsyth married Mary Sked Gardner (1st July 1894–13th June 1970), born at Montgomery Street, Eaglesham, Renfrewshire, at the YWCA, 80 Bath Street, Glasgow, Scotland. Mary was a head waitress, living at 79 John Knox Street, Dennistoun, Glasgow, when they met, as he addressed a Christian Association meeting in Glasgow while on leave in 1916. There were no children.

Mary's father, John Brown Gardner (1856–6th March 1937), born at Rutherglen, Lanarkshire, was a stationer in 1871, living with his parents. He had a daughter, Joan Gardner (born c.1878), whose mother is unknown. By 1881 he was a paper ruler, living with his parents at 38 Gilmour Street, Glasgow. He married Annie née Bell (c.1855–1st August 1925) in 1886 at Calton, Glasgow. He was a foreman paper ruler and they were living at 70 Fisher Street, Dennistoun, Lanarkshire in 1891 and 1901. By 1915 they were living at 79 John Knox Street, Glasgow. In addition to Mary they had three other children:

Samuel's wife, Mary Gardner, was born on Montgomery Street, Eaglesham, Renfrewshire.

- Isabella McLaren Gardner (1887–1968), born at Dennistoun, Glasgow, married William Andrew Ramsay Marshall (1883–1919) in 1913 at Calton, Glasgow. They had a son, Andrew Gardner Marshall (1916–95). They were living at 80 Cardross Street, Glasgow in 1918.
- Andrew Brown Gardner (1890–1915) served as a sergeant in 1/7th Highland Light Infantry (604) and died of wounds at Gallipoli on 15th July 1915 (Helles Memorial, Turkey).
- Robert Bell Gardner (1892–1918) was educated at Eaglesham School and became a printer. He joined 7th Highland Light Infantry on 26th June 1910 (280037). He was appointed company sergeant major on 21st February 1916 and applied for a

Samuel's brother-in-law, Andrew Brown Gardner, is commemorated on the CWGC Helles Memorial, Sedd el Bahr, Turkey. It sits on a headland at the tip of the Gallipoli peninsula overlooking the Dardanelles. The Memorial commemorates 20,956 Commonwealth servicemen with no known grave who died in the Gallipoli campaign 1915–16, including those who died or were buried at sea in Gallipoli waters. There are other Commonwealth memorials to the missing at Lone Pine (Australians who died in the Anzac area and New Zealanders prior to August 1915), Chunuk Bair (New Zealanders who died in the Battle of Sari Bair and other operations in that area) and Twelve Tree Copse (New Zealanders who died outside the limits of Anzac). Naval casualties buried at sea are commemorated on the Portsmouth, Plymouth and Chatham Naval Memorials. Four VCs are commemorated on the Helles Memorial – Major Cuthbert Bromley, Captain Gerald Robert O'Sullivan, Sergeant Frank Edward Stubbs and Sub-Lieutenant Arthur Walderne St Clair Tisdall (Harvey Barrison).

Ramleh War Cemetery and Memorial is for personnel who died in both World Wars and during the Palestine Mandate period until May 1948. It is located in Ramla, Israel and is the largest CWGC cemetery in that country. The cemetery dates to when Ramleh was occupied by 1st Australian Light Horse Brigade on 1st November 1917. Field ambulances and later casualty clearing stations were located at Ramleh and Lydda from December 1917 and the cemetery was begun by medical units. Other graves were brought in later from the battlefields and other military and Indian cemeteries. During the Second World War the cemetery was used by RAF Ramla and various Commonwealth hospitals.

There are 3,300 burials from the First World War (964 unknown), 1,168 burials from the Second World War, in addition to 892 graves of other nationalities from both World Wars and 525 non-war burials, many from RAF and garrison stations at Ramleh in the inter-war years and until the end of the British Palestine Mandate in 1948. The Ramleh 1914–18 Memorial was built in 1961 to commemorate over 300 Commonwealth, German and Turkish servicemen who are buried in other cemeteries in Israel where their graves can no longer be maintained. Only seventy-four are named. The Ramleh 1939–45 Memorial commemorates twenty-eight Jewish and non-Arab servicemen of the Second World War and six non-war casualties of the Palestine Police Force, who are buried in cemeteries elsewhere in Israel where their graves cannot be maintained. The picture was taken when the Cemetery was dedicated on 6th May 1927.

commission on 27th July 1917 while serving in 1/7th Highland Light Infantry in Egypt. He was a second lieutenant with 1/5th Highland Light Infantry when he was killed in action near Jaffa on 7th January 1918. He was buried at El Jalil and his remains were later moved to Ramleh War Cemetery, Israel – R 25.

Samuel was appointed acting 2nd corporal on 22nd March 1917. On 29th June he was detached to the Reinforcement Camp en route to the Rest Camp as a sapper. He was appointed temporary 2nd corporal on 16th July (substantive 17th August) and was granted leave 12th–23rd September. On 12th October he was appointed temporary corporal and was promoted corporal on 12th November and sergeant on 12th May 1918.

On 18th August Samuel was attached to 2nd Auckland to gain infantry experience prior to being commissioned. **Awarded the VC for his actions at Grévillers on 24th August 1918, LG 22nd October 1918.** The VC was presented to his widow by the King at Buckingham Palace on 23rd November 1918. Samuel was killed by a sniper during the VC action. His body was exhumed by a grave registration unit on 11th June 1919 two miles west of Bapaume, northeast of Loupart. He is buried in Adanac Military Cemetery, near Miraumont, France (I 1 39). He is commemorated in a number of other places:

New Zealand
- Forsyth Barracks, Linton Military Camp, Linton, near Palmerston North.
- Forsyth Street, Taradale, Napier.
- Family headstone, Karori Cemetery, Wellington.
- Roll of Honour, Wadestown School, Rose Street, Wellington dedicated in July 1919.
- Memorial tablet Sailors' Friend Society Institute, Whitmore Street, Wellington, dedicated on 26th January 1919.
- Named on one of eleven plaques honouring 175 men from overseas awarded the VC for the Great War. The plaques were unveiled by the Senior Minister of State at the Foreign & Commonwealth Office and Minister for Faith and Communities, Baroness Warsi, at a reception at Lancaster House, London on 26th June 2014 attended by The Duke of Kent and relatives of the VC recipients. The New Zealand plaque was unveiled on 7th May 2015 at a ceremony attended by Defence Minister Gerry Brownlee and Defence Force Chief Lieutenant General Tim Keating. Corporal Willie Apiata VC read the names of the sixteen men on the plaque, which is displayed in the grounds of Parliament in Wellington.
- An obelisk surmounted with a sundial in the centre of the War Memorial Wall, Caroline Bay, Timaru bears the names of eleven New Zealand VCs, including Samuel Forsyth.
- Victoria Cross winners' memorial dedicated by the Reverend Keith Elliott VC outside the Headquarters of the Dunedin Branch of the Returned Services Association

Samuel Forsyth's grave in Adanac Military Cemetery. Also buried there is Piper James Clelland Richardson VC, whose story is related in the third volume in this series, *Victoria Crosses on the Western Front: The Somme 1916*. Other notable burials are Thomas Alexander Jackson, who made six appearances in the Scottish football team 1904–07, and three sixteen year olds – Russell Lewis Collingridge, Joseph Lorne Dewart and Thomas Ethelbert Tombs.

Forsyth Barracks, Linton.

Memorial sundial at Caroline Bay, Timaru.

Victoria Cross memorial near Dunedin Cenotaph.

Forsyth family headstone in Karori Cemetery, Wellington.

Samuel Forsyth 60c stamp issued by New Zealand Post on 14th April 2011.

and unveiled by Governor General Sir Charles Willoughby Moke Norrie GCMG GCVO CB DSO MC on 29th January 1956, the centenary of the institution of the VC by Queen Victoria. The memorial was transferred to Anzac Square in front of the railway station. It was moved again to near Dunedin Cenotaph in Queen's Gardens and rededicated on 11th November 2001.
* An issue of twenty-two 60c stamps by New Zealand Post entitled 'Victoria Cross – the New Zealand Story', honouring New Zealand's twenty-two Victoria Cross holders, was issued on 14th April 2011.

United Kingdom
* Communities and Local Government commemorative paving stones for the 145 VCs born in Australia, Belgium, Canada, China, Denmark, Egypt, France, Germany, India, Iraq, Japan, Nepal, Netherlands, Newfoundland, New Zealand, Pakistan, South Africa, Sri Lanka, Ukraine and United States of America were

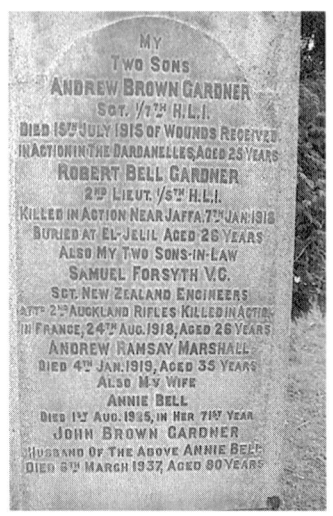

Samuel's commemorative paving stone at the National Memorial Arboretum.

Gardner family headstone in Linn Cemetery, Glasgow.

unveiled at the National Memorial Arboretum, Alrewas, Staffordshire by Prime Minister David Cameron MP and Sergeant Johnson Beharry VC on 5th March 2015.
* Gardner family headstone, Compartment 2A, Linn Cemetery, Glasgow, Scotland.
* Memorial headstone erected in Knockbreda Cemetery, Church Road, Belfast, Co Antrim, Northern Ireland by his widow.

Mary worked as a missionary, living at 12 Donegall Avenue, Belfast, Northern Ireland. She died at Belfast City Hospital and is buried in Cathcart Cemetery, 106 Brenfield Road, East Renfrewshire, Scotland.

In addition to the VC Samuel was awarded the 1914–15 Star, British War Medal 1914–20 and Victory Medal 1914–19. When Mary died the medals passed to a nephew in Scotland. They were sold at a Sotheby's auction in November 1981 to Ken Downie, a dealer from Melbourne, Australia, for £9,500. He resold them for $AI7,500 on 26th January 1982. The medals were purchased by Lord Ashcroft in a private sale in 1992. The VC is held by the Michael Ashcroft Trust and is displayed in the Imperial War Museum's Lord Ashcroft Gallery.

Mary's headstone in Knockbreda Cemetery, Church Road, Belfast.

23 LANCE CORPORAL BERNARD SIDNEY GORDON
41st Battalion AIF

Bernard 'Barney' Gordon was born on 16th August 1891 at Beaconsfield, Tasmania, Australia. His father, Charles Gordon (born c.1865) was a cabman and hotel proprietor. He married Mary Agnes née Roland (born c.1866), of 50 Frankland Street, Launceston, Tasmania on 26th January 1887 in Tasmania. She was living at 101 George Street, Launceston in August 1916. Barney had five siblings:

- Charles Roland Gordon (23rd December 1887–24th January 1909) died in an accident.
- Evelyn Mary Gordon (born 25th September 1889).
- James Edward Gordon (born 7th October 1893) was a jockey. He enlisted in 7th Reinforcements, 40th Battalion AIF at Claremont, Tasmania on 15th August 1916 (T3617 and later 3087), described as 5′ 4″ tall, weighing 138 lbs, with dark complexion, brown eyes, dark hair and his religious denomination was Roman Catholic. His next of kin was his mother. James embarked on HMAT A48 *Seeang Bee* at Adelaide on 10th February 1917 and disembarked at Devonport on 2nd May. He was posted to 10th Training Battalion, Durrington, Wiltshire and

The area around Beaconsfield was first explored by Europeans in 1804 and a settlement was established at York Town. Beaconsfield was known originally as Brandy Creek and was not established until the 1850s. Limestone mining led to the discovery of gold in 1847 but it was not until 1877 that a payable reef was discovered and mining commenced. The population boomed and the settlement was renamed Beaconsfield in 1879 after Benjamin Disraeli, Earl of Beaconsfield. At the peak of the gold rush, 700 men were involved in mining and twenty-six tons of gold were recovered. Beaconsfield became the richest gold town in Tasmania and by 1881 there were fifty-three companies working there. In 1903 an English company bought the Tasmanian Gold Mining & Quartz Crushing Co and formed the Tasmanian Gold Mining Co Ltd. The gold mine closed in 1914 due to flooding but re-opened in 1999. In April 2006 a small earthquake caused a fall in the mine. Fourteen miners escaped but one was killed. Two other men, trapped a kilometre underground, were found alive five days later and were eventually rescued after nearly two weeks. In September 2007, the Foo Fighters released a tribute, *Ballad of the Beaconsfield Miners*. Gold mining ended in June 2012.

left 12 Camp there on 30th August for Southampton and passage to France. He joined 3rd Australian Division Base Depot, Le Havre on 31st August. James was taken on strength of 40th Battalion on 13th September and was attached to 10th Light Trench Mortar Battery on 25th September. He was admitted to No.17 Casualty Clearing Station and the New Zealand Stationary Hospital with shell shock on 13th October and rejoined his unit on 4th November.

Barney's mother was living at 50 Frankland Street, Launceston when she married Charles Gordon.

On 1st December he was absent without leave 2 p.m.–9.30 p.m., for which he was awarded two days' Field Punishment No.2 and forfeited three days' pay. He was admitted to 9th Australian Field Ambulance with measles on 26th January 1918 and transferred to 7th General Hospital, St Omer on 28th January. On 2nd April he joined the Base Depot, Rouelles and rejoined 40th Battalion on 26th April. He was granted leave in England on 21st October but was absent without leave there from 7 a.m. on 25th October until 7 a.m. on 26th October, for which he was admonished. He was absent without leave again from midnight on 20th March 1919 until 4 p.m. on 21st March, for which he forfeited seven days' pay. James returned to England on 14th April and joined No.3 Group, Codford, Wiltshire next day. He returned to Australia on HT *Rio Padro*, embarking on 27th May and disembarking on 21st July. He was discharged from 6th Military District on 6th September 1919. He was living at 119 Queensberry Street, North Melbourne in 1935 and at Brewarrina, New South Wales in 1941.
- Ruby Ann Gordon (born 20th November 1895).
- Percy Gordon (born 5th August 1898) was living at 12 Doolan Street, Launceston, Tasmania in June 1942.

Barney was educated at Deloraine and Devonport in Tasmania. He was apprenticed to Mr J Robins as a cooper's machinist at Beaconsfield and later moved to Townsville, Queensland, where he was in charge of remounts en route to India. Barney was a keen amateur rider, a horse-breaker, sportsman and promoted racing, cycling, boxing and football. He won many amateur boxing tournaments and a canteen of cutlery for running. He also won the 100 and 200 yards championships in Launceston.

On 27th September 1915, Barney enlisted in the AIF at Townsville, described as 5' 7" tall, weighing 126 lbs, with fair complexion, hazel eyes, auburn hair and his religious denomination was Roman Catholic. He was posted to 7th Depot Battalion on 3rd October. On 29th December 1915, Barney married Evelyn Catherine Lonergan (10th September 1892–6th August 1938) under Catholic rites. They had six children:

Townsville, on the northeast coast of Queensland, had a population of 174,000 in 2016. James Cook visited the area on his first voyage in 1770 but the first Europeans to land were in 1819. The first party of settlers arrived in 1864. In 1866 Robert Towns visited for three days and agreed to provide financial assistance to the new settlement. Townsville was named after him. It developed rapidly as a major port and service centre. When Lord Hopetoun opened the town hall in 1901, it was the first vice-regal ceremony at which the Australian national flag was used. During the Second World War there were more than 50,000 US and Australian service personnel in the area and the, by then, city was a major staging point for the southwest Pacific. There were seven airfields in the area and raids against Japanese held territory were launched from there. In July 1942 the Japanese launched three small air raids against Townsville, with very limited effect. Today the Australian Army's 3rd Brigade is based in Townsville. The world number one ranked golfer in the 1980s and 1990s, Greg Norman AO (born 10th February 1955), was educated at Townsville Grammar School.

- Aquain Imelda Margaret Lonergan (born 27th June 1914), born at Launceston, Tasmania.
- Sylvia Clare Gordon (born 2nd October 1916) married Raymond Neville Smith (18th February 1913–14th December 1981) on 28th January 1942 in Queensland.
- Charles Bernard Bray Gordon (6th September 1920–25th July 1968), born at Brisbane, Queensland, married Daphne Ida Hawkins on 21st January 1941. He enlisted in the AIF on 11th January 1941 at Toombul, Brisbane (Q63453) and served as a dental mechanic with 17 Works Company until discharged on 10th October 1945.
- Joan Monica Gordon (12th November 1921–20th June 1986), born at Beaudesert, Queensland, married William Alex McCullagh (born 4th November 1913) on 12 December 1942.
- Damien John Vivian Gordon (born 27th January 1923) served during the Second World War and became a prisoner of war on Java.
- Eileen Patricia Gordon (born 28th August 1924) married Vincent Thomas Raleigh (born 30th August 1907) on 4th November 1944.

Evelyn's father, John Robert Lonergan, married Eveline Jane née Farrelly (born 12th May 1871) on 13th October 1891 at Tasmania

Barney transferred to 41st Battalion on 16th February 1916. He embarked with it aboard HMAT A64 *Demosthenes* at Sydney, New South Wales on 16th May and departed the following day. He was charged with being absent without leave whilst aboard 15th–17th June and was awarded twenty-one days detention and forfeited twenty-three days' pay. He disembarked at Plymouth, Devon on 20th July and moved to Salisbury Plain, Wiltshire. He was admitted to Fargo Military Hospital, Larkhill with tonsillitis on 2nd November and transferred to 1st Australian Dermatological Hospital, Bulford Camp on 6th November, having been diagnosed with venereal disease. On 20th November he transferred to Parkhouse Military Hospital near Tidworth and was discharged on 23rd December. Barney embarked at Folkestone, Kent on SS *Princess Victoria* on 31st December and joined 3rd Australian Division Base Depot at Étaples, France on 1st January 1917.

HMAT A64 *Demosthenes* (11,223 tons) leaving Port Melbourne carrying Australian troops on 16th July 1915. She was built for the Aberdeen Line by Harland & Wolff, Belfast in 1911 for the UK to Australia route. She made five trips as a troopship for the Commonwealth of Australia until being taken over by the Admiralty on 16th March 1917. In 1923 she was bought by G Thompson & Co of London and in 1928 was managed by Oceanic Line, carrying passengers between UK and Brisbane. She was scrapped in 1931.

Barney rejoined 41st Battalion on 5th January. He was charged with conduct to the prejudice of good order and military discipline by leaving the ranks without permission and urinating on a military parade ground on 9th August. He forfeited three days' pay. He was absent without leave from 9 p.m. on 24th August to 3 p.m. on 25th August and was awarded twenty-one days Field Punishment No.2 and forfeited twenty-six days' pay. He was

1st Australian Dermatological Hospital was established at Abbassia, Egypt in 1915. In September 1916 it relocated to Bulford Camp on Salisbury Plain and became a specialist hospital for venereal diseases. At its peak the hospital could accommodate over 1,500 patients, some under guard. However, security was not tight and eventually criminal patients were treated at Lewes Prison, Sussex.

again absent without leave from 9 p.m. on 24th September until 10 a.m. on 28th September, for which he was awarded twenty-eight days' Field Punishment No.2 and forfeited thirty days' pay. However, on 2nd February 1919 General Birdwood ordered that forty-nine of the total of fifty-six days' pay that he lost in these two cases be restored.

On 2nd October, Barney was wounded by shrapnel in the face and hand near Passchendaele, Belgium. He was admitted to No.10 Casualty Clearing Station and transferred to 14th General Hospital, Wimereux, France on 7th October. Next day he transferred to 1st Convalescent Depot, Boulogne and to 3rd Australian Division Base Depot, Rouelles on 12th November. He rejoined his unit on 23rd November. While on leave in England on 13th February 1918, he was found guilty of drunkenness but was admonished. He rejoined the Battalion on 28th February, was promoted lance corporal on 8th June and was granted leave in Paris 7th–21st July.

Awarded the MM for his actions east of Hamel on 8th August 1918, when he single-handedly attacked a machine gun crew that was holding up his section, killing the crew and capturing the gun. Later that day he stalked and killed an enemy sniper, LG 24th January 1919. Awarded the VC for his actions east of Bray, France on 26th August 1918, LG 26th December 1918. His left index finger was shattered by a bullet near Mont St Quentin on 1st September and he was admitted to 6th Australian Field Ambulance before being transferred later that day to No.37 Casualty Clearing Station. He transferred to 6th General Hospital, Rouen on 2nd September and was evacuated to England aboard SS *La Marguerite* on 4th September. He was admitted to the Military Hospital, Boscombe, Hampshire and later to Queen Alexandra Hospital, Cosham, where the finger was amputated. A medical report from 1st Australian General Hospital dated 12th March 1919 indicated that there was no other disability.

Barney was discharged on leave on 12th October and reported to No.4 Command Depot, Hurdcott, Wiltshire on 26th October. He joined No.2 Command Depot, Weymouth, Dorset on 3rd December and was discharged the following day. He embarked on HT *Margha* on 18th January 1919 and arrived at Melbourne, Victoria on 5th March, for onward travel by sea to Brisbane, Queensland. When he and fellow VC Henry Dalziel arrived, they were given a civic reception in Brisbane attended by the Governor, Sir Hamilton Goold-Adams, the acting Premier, Mayor and about 5,000 spectators. He was discharged on 19th April 1919 as medically unfit for service. The MM was presented by Sir Ronald Craufurd Munro-Ferguson GCMG, Governor General of Australia, in Brisbane on 26th July 1919. The VC was sent to the Commandant, 1st Military District, Queensland from Central Army Records Office, Melbourne on 9th September 1919. The VC was presented by Lieutenant General Sir Harry Chauvel GCMG KCB, Inspector General of the Australian Army, in Brisbane on 13th December 1919. It is not known why the VC was not presented before Bernard left Britain or why there were two separate investitures in Australia.

Barney worked as a grocer at Clayfield, Brisbane before becoming a dairy farmer, running a Jersey stud at Lincolnfield, Beaudesert, Queensland. He founded a junior farmers' club, the first of many similar clubs formed in Queensland. He had a milk round at one time and delivered mail on horseback to supplement his meagre dairying income. He sold it to buy a pie stall in Woolloongabba, Brisbane, which

General Sir Henry George Chauvel GCMG KCB (1865–1945), known as Sir Harry, served in the 1891 shearer's strike and was part of the Queensland contingent for the 1897 Diamond Jubilee of Queen Victoria in Britain. He served in the Second Boer War and afterwards was involved with training the Australian Light Horse. In the Great War he served at Gallipoli, in Sinai and Palestine. He was the first Australian officer to be promoted lieutenant general and general and also the first to command a corps (Desert Mounted Corps). In 1919, he was appointed Inspector General and was concurrently Chief of the General Staff from 1923 until retiring in 1930. During the Second World War he was recalled as Inspector in Chief of the Volunteer Defence Corps.

he ran for night workers. He also had a retail pie business and employed a cart driver to deliver the hot pies to factory workers in the Brisbane industrial areas. He moved to Hervey Bay through ill health in early 1962.

An Anzac Dinner on 23rd April 1927, hosted by Lieutenant General Sir John Monash GCMG KCB VD, was attended by twenty-three VCs including Bernard Gordon. For an unknown reason the Duke of York was not invited. Barney also attended the ANZAC Commemoration Service on 25th April 1927 at the Exhibition Building, Melbourne in the presence of the Duke of York (future King George VI), with twenty three other VCs. Bernard married Caroline Edith Manley née Victorsen (14th August 1902–15th June 1993), a widow, of Eaglesfield Street, Beaudesert,

Beaudesert is about ninety kilometres south of Brisbane and has a predominantly rural economy. It was first settled in 1847 with the intention of growing cotton and raising sheep. However, the area suffers from a shortage of water and cotton was not successful. Despite this there are also frequent floods. The railway opened in 1888 and at that time timber, cattle and dairying were the main industries (JW Stark).

The Logan and Albert Hotel, built in 1934, is now on Brisbane Street, but was originally on the corners of Logan and Albert Streets, from which it takes its name.

The congregation of the Ann Street Presbyterian Church originated in 1849 and a small wooden church was built in 1851 in Grey Street, South Brisbane. The congregation divided in 1857, with some moving to the north side of the river and became the Ann Street congregation. A church opened on the present site in 1858 and was rebuilt after a fire in 1871. It was reconstructed and enlarged in 1897 and extended in 1936. The church survived an attempt to redevelop the site in the 1960s and has been a listed building on the Queensland Heritage Register since October 1992.

Queensland, on 15th September 1938 at Ann Street Presbyterian Church, Brisbane. She was the cook at the Logan and Albert Hotel, Beaudesert. They later moved to Bayhome, 35 The Esplanade, Torquay, Queensland, and to Sandgate Road, Nundah, Queensland in 1940. They had three children:

- Bernard Edwin Gordon (born 15th June 1939).
- Caroline Louise Gordon (born 27th March 1941) married as Gee.
- David Leron Gordon (born 24th February 1943).

Barney attended the VC Centenary Celebrations at Hyde Park, London on 26th June 1956, travelling on SS *Orcades* along with other Australian VCs who were part of the 301 Victoria Cross recipients from across the Commonwealth to attend. Barney suffered from pulmonary tuberculosis for many years and died at his home at Torquay, Queensland on 19th October 1963. He was cremated at Mount Thompson Crematorium, Brisbane and his ashes are interred in Pinnaroo Lawn Cemetery, Graham Road, Bridgeman Downs, Albany Creek, Queensland. There is a commemorative plaque there on the Queensland Garden of Remembrance Memorial Wall 3, Row G. Bernard is commemorated in a number of other places:

- Australian Capital Territory
    - Australian Victoria Cross Recipients plaque on the Victoria Cross Memorial, Campbell, dedicated on 24th July 2000.

Barney's memorial plaque at Pinnaroo Lawn Cemetery.

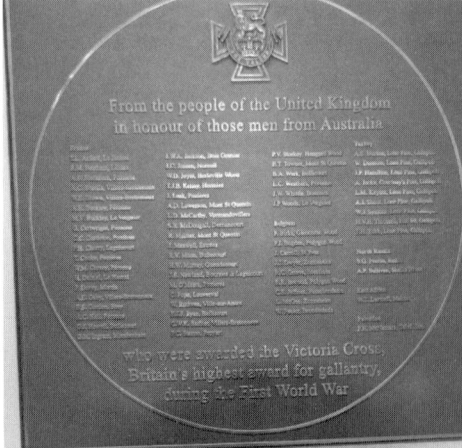

Australian VC plaque at the Australian War Memorial unveiled at Lancaster House, London on 26th June 2014.

- Named on one of eleven plaques honouring 175 men from overseas awarded the VC for the Great War. The plaques were unveiled by the Senior Minister of State at the Foreign & Commonwealth Office and Minister for Faith and Communities, Baroness Warsi, at a reception at Lancaster House, London on 26th June 2014 attended by The Duke of Kent and relatives of the VC recipients. The Australian plaque is at the Australian War Memorial.
- Display in the Hall of Valour, Australian War Memorial.
* New South Wales
    - Victoria Cross Memorial, Queen Victoria Building, George Street, Sydney dedicated on 23rd February 1992 to commemorate the visit of Queen Elizabeth II and Prince Phillip on the occasion of the Sesquicentenary of the City of Sydney. Sir Roden Cutler VC AK KCMG, Edward Kenna VC and Keith Payne VC were in attendance.
    - VC Memorial, 119 Borella Road, Peard's Complex, East Albury.
* Tasmania
    - Victoria Cross Memorial, Hobart Cenotaph, Tasmania dedicated on 11th May 2003.

Victoria Cross Memorial, either side of Hobart Cenotaph, Tasmania. The walls contain soil from the birthplace of all thirteen Tasmanian VCs and from the battlefields where their VCs were earned. Two of the thirteen were during the Boer War and eleven during the Great War. The Tasmanian awards include the first two VCs awarded to Australians serving in Australian forces.

- Memorial at Battery Point, Anglesea Barracks Memorial Garden, Hobart, Tasmania.
- Gordon Soldiers' Club opened at HQ 101st Wireless Regiment (now 7th Signal Regiment), Cabarlah, Queensland in January 1960.
- Communities and Local Government commemorative paving stones for the 145 VCs born in Australia, Belgium, Canada, China, Denmark, Egypt, France, Germany, India, Iraq, Japan, Nepal, Netherlands, Newfoundland, New Zealand, Pakistan, South Africa, Sri Lanka, Ukraine and United States of America were unveiled at the National Memorial Arboretum, Alrewas, Staffordshire by Prime Minister David Cameron MP and Sergeant Johnson Beharry VC on 5th March 2015.

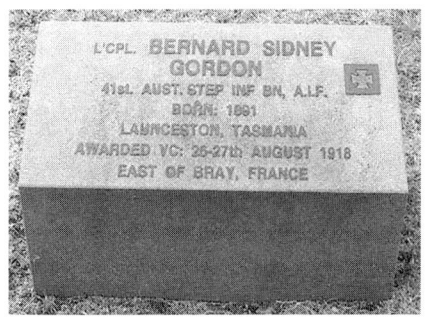

Memorial plaque at Battery Point, Anglesea Barracks Memorial Garden, Hobart.

In addition to the VC and MM he was awarded the British War Medal 1914–20, Victory Medal 1914–19 George VI Coronation Medal 1937 and Elizabeth II Coronation Medal 1953. The VC and two coronation medals were sold by his granddaughter, Margaret Schofield, to Kerry Stokes, chairman of Seven Network broadcasting corporation, at Bonhams & Goodman's Sydney office on 28th November 2006 for $AUS 486,000. Stokes then presented the VC to the Australian War Memorial, Treloar Crescent, Campbell, Australian Capital Territory, where it is held.

Kerry Matthew Stokes AC (born John Patrick Alford 1940), a businessman with interests in a wide range of industries, including electronic and print media, property, mining and construction equipment. He was born in Melbourne and adopted by Matthew and Irene Stokes. He dropped out of school aged fourteen and started off installing TV antennas in Perth, before getting into property and other interests. He has been married four times, including to actress Peta Toppano. Stokes is believed to be worth over A$3 billion. In 1995 he was appointed an Officer of the Order of Australia for service to business, commerce, the arts and the community. In 2008 Stokes became a Companion of the Order of Australia for service to business and commerce through strategic leadership and promotion of corporate social responsibility, to the arts through executive roles and philanthropy, and to the community, particularly through contributions to organisations supporting youth. He was chairman of the National Gallery of Australia for several years and has made multimillion-dollar donations to it. Stokes is a life member of the Returned and Services League of Australia. He has acquired three VCs (Alfred Shout, Bernard Gordon and Peter Badcoe) and a GC (George Gosse), which he donated to the Australian War Memorial.

LIEUTENANT WILLIAM DONOVAN JOYNT
8th Australian Infantry Battalion AIF

William Joynt, known as Don, was born on 19th March 1889 at Elsternwick, Melbourne, Victoria, Australia. His father, Edward Kelly Joynt (1846–8th March 1912), was born at Crossmollina, Co Mayo, Ireland. His ancestors were French Huguenots named de Joyance, who fled after the Edict of Nantes in 1598 and settled in England. Later two brothers, captains in Cromwell's army, were granted lands in Co Mayo. Edward failed the entrance examination for the Royal Irish Constabulary and emigrated to Australia. He married Alice née Woolcott (10th September

The first settlement at Ballina appears to date from 1375, when an Augustinian friary was founded there, but the town was established officially in 1723. In the early 19th century the area was heavily dependent on potatoes and, when the potato blight struck in 1846, there was widespread starvation. Many people requested admission to the overcrowded Ballina workhouse. By February 1847 the death rate had risen to almost ninety people per week. Mary Therese Winifred Robinson (née Bourke), seventh President of Ireland, was born in Ballina in May 1944. She was the first woman to hold the office. She was the UN High Commissioner for Human Rights 1997–2002.

Bendigo is just over ninety miles north of Melbourne. The discovery of gold in the 1850s turned it into a boomtown. The finds intensified the Victorian gold rush and brought in numerous migrants from around the world. When the alluvial gold had been worked out, companies were formed to exploit the underground gold and it became the most productive goldfield in Australia in the 19th century. Since 1851, about 780,000 kilograms of gold have been extracted from Bendigo's goldmines. As the gold industry declined, the town suffered a reversal of fortune in the early 20th century but this was reversed in the post-war years.

The Joynt family lived on Glen Huntly Road, Elsternwick.

1858–1913), also born at Crossmollina, Co Mayo, at All Saints' Church, St Kilda, Victoria on 1st June 1882. He joined William Dodgshun & Sons, soft goods merchants, an English company, and became their agent in Bendigo, Victoria. When the gold mining industry failed in Bendigo, they moved to Melbourne, living in Glen Huntly Road before moving to Lara, Shoobra Road, Elsternwick. He died at Elsternwick and she at Caulfield, Melbourne, Victoria. In addition to William they had two other sons:

- Gerald Victor Woolcott Joynt (13th September 1883–25th September 1917), born at Windsor, Melbourne, was educated at The Grange School, South Yarra and Caulfield Grammar School. He was a clerk living at Elmore, Glen Huntly Road, Elsternwick, Victoria in February 1913, when he married Phyllis Gwendoline Beryl Fenton (c.1890–3rd January 1973). They lived at Lara (also seen as Shoobra), Shoobra Road, Elsternwick, Victoria before moving to St Sidwell's, Kallista, Victoria. They had a daughter:
  - Gwendoline Alice Margaret Joynt (1914–2000) became an allergy physician. She married Russell Hughes Oxby-Donald (1902–81) in 1940 in Victoria. He was born at Lindfield, New South Wales and qualified as a doctor. He was commissioned as a flight lieutenant in the Medical Branch of the Royal Australian Air Force on 4th May 1942 (255253) and was serving at No.5 Medical Receiving Station, Morotai Island, Indonesia at the time of his discharge on 14th June 1945. Russell became an ear, nose and throat surgeon. They had two children.

Gerald served for fifteen years in various volunteer forces, including two years in the ranks of the Senior Cadets before being commissioned. He served for two years as a second lieutenant before joining 6th Australian Infantry Regiment (Militia) in January 1906. He was promoted first lieutenant in February 1908 and captain in January 1911. Gerald was a cashier with the Orient Steam Navigation Co in Melbourne when he enlisted in 8th Reinforcements, 57th Battalion AIF on 25th September 1916, described as 5′ 5″ tall and weighing 126 lbs. Phyllis' address was The Bungalow, Rosanna, Victoria in 1915 when she was nominated as Don's next of kin. By September 1916 she was living at Croydon, Victoria and by February 1918 had moved from 10 Florence Street, Surrey Hills, Victoria to Woodcote, Bay View Crescent, Black Rock. In October 1918 she moved to The Bungalow, Rosanna Road,

Rosanna and by September 1919 had moved to 10 Marine Parade, St Kilda, Victoria. Gerald embarked at Melbourne on HMAT A7 *Medic* on 16th December 1916 and disembarked at Plymouth, Devon on 18th February 1917. He joined 15th Training Battalion, Hurdcott, Wiltshire the same day. On 29th April he left Tidworth and crossed to France, joined 5th Australian Division Base Depot, Étaples on 3rd May and was taken on strength of 57th Battalion on 5th May. He was a lieutenant when he was killed in action on 25th September 1917 and is buried in The Huts Cemetery, Ypres, Belgium (VII D 18). In his will, dated 15th January 1917, he left everything to his wife. She was granted a war pension of £3/10/- per fortnight and her daughter was granted £1/-/- per fortnight from 6th December 1917, when they were living at 18 Long Street, Elsternwick. Phyllis married Arthur Leslie Hargrave (1879–1969) in January 1922 and they lived at Jaringa, Hopetown, Malvern, Victoria. She lost her war pension but it was still paid for her daughter. Phyllis died at Caulfield.

Gerald Victor Woolcott Joynt's grave (right) in The Huts Cemetery, Ypres, Belgium.

The CMS Roper River Mission, established in 1908 at Mirlinbarrwarr, included a school and dormitories for Aboriginal children aged five to eighteen. Some children were moved between Roper River and Groote Eylandt Missions in the years 1924–33. After severe floods in 1940 the Mission moved to Ngukurr. The Government took it over in 1968 and in 1988 the township became Ngukurr.

- Reginald Desmond Joynt (21st May 1885–3rd November 1946), born at Prahran, Melbourne, became a teacher and commenced missionary training in February 1906. He was one of three founders of the Church Missionary Society Roper River Mission, Arnhem Land in 1908. Living conditions were so harsh that he was the only one left in 1910. Circumstances improved when the Reverend Hubert Ernest Warren took charge in 1913. Reginald was made deacon by the Bishop of Bendigo on 15th September 1918 and was ordained priest in Christ Church Darwin, Northern Territory on 1st December 1921. He was registered as an officiating minister on 15th March 1922 with power to conduct marriage ceremonies. He was also appointed an acting Officer of Customs on 20th October 1927. Reginald left the Mission in 1928 and resigned from the CMS on 30th April 1930. He sailed for England and became an Anglican minister, living at South Croxted Road, Camberwell, London in 1935. He travelled to Japan and returned to England aboard SS *Rajputana* on 29th July 1938. He was living at The Colt, Vinery Lane, Plympton, Devon in 1939. He was living at Ecila, Elburton Road, Elburton, Plympton at the time of his death there.

Don's paternal grandfather, William Joynt (29th May 1812–21st August 1892), was born at Crossmollina, Co Mayo, Ireland. He married Margaret née Kelly (1822–28th May 1905). She was living at 7 Arthur Street, Ballina, Co Mayo in 1901. In addition to Edward they had ten other children:

- Henry Joynt (born c.1840) married Thomasina Briscoe and they had a son, Dudley Francis Briscoe Joynt, born on 30th November 1864 at Ballina.
- Charles Joynt (born c.1842).
- John Kelly Joynt (25th December 1847–1921) married Catherine Robinson (1847–1920) in 1872 in Victoria. They settled at South Yarra, Victoria and were living there at 470 Punt Hill in June 1915. They had six children – Margaret Mary Kelly Joynt (1874–94), Violet Maude Joynt (1875–1900), Amy May Joynt (born 1877), Edna Victoria Katherine Joynt (1879–1952), unnamed (born 1880) and Oswald Joynt (14th October 1885–6th May 1938). Oswald Joynt MB MS attested for the AIF in the Australian Army Medical Corps as a medical officer on 25th June 1915. He was described as 5′ 8½″ tall, weighing 140 lbs, with fair complexion, grey eyes, dark hair and his religious denomination was Church of England. His appointment as a captain dated from 27th May 1916 as MO aboard No.1 Hospital Ship *Karoola*, departing Australia on 18th (sic) May 1916. He was recommended for termination of appointment on completion of duty on 13th February 1918 but it was not terminated until 13th December 1918.
- William Joynt (born c.1848).
- Esther Joynt (born c.1850) was a spinster living with her mother in 1901. She died between 1910 and 1916.
- Eleanor Johnson Joynt (24th March 1856–30th June 1932) married William Leitch (3rd April 1846–10th April 1927) on 20th April 1881. He was born at Glenwherry, Ballymena, Co Antrim, Ireland. They both died at Ballina. They had eleven children – Irene Margaret Leitch (1882), William Lawrence Leitch (1883–1917), John Wilson Leitch (1884–1954), Henry Brennan Leitch (1886–1952), Mary Jane Leitch (1887–1971), Josephine Martha Leitch (1889–1969), Archibald Robinson Leitch (1890–1936), Oswald Johnson Leitch (1892), Anna Sara Leitch (1894–1924), Eleanor Leitch (1896–1998) and Charles Alexander Leitch (1898). William Lawrence Leitch was serving as a lance corporal (1909) in 2nd Irish Guards when he was killed in action in France on 27th November 1917 (Cambrai Memorial, Louverval, France – Panels 2 & 3).
- George Lawrence Joynt (born 1863) was a civil engineer, town surveyor of Ballina 1900–37 and Assistant County Surveyor for Co Mayo. He married Annie Baillie

McKee (born 1856), born in England, in 1886. They had three children, including – George Edgeworth Joynt (1890–1971) and Annestalia May Baillie Joynt (1895). George junior lived at 9 West Walnut Street, Pasadena, California, USA, having migrated there in 1937.
* Margaret Joynt (9th July 1864–1885).
* Isaac Joynt (born 1866).
* James Joynt (born 1868).

His maternal grandfather, William Spark Woolcott (c.1827–16th January 1883), was born at Exeter, Devon. He was descended from an old Devonshire family dating back to the time of William the Conqueror. He was a solicitor's clerk living at 5 Pedley Street, Bethnal Green, London when he married Mary Crump (c.1823–7th August 1893) at St Matthew's Church, Bethnal Green on 16th November 1845. They emigrated to Victoria, Australia and William became one of Melbourne's first solicitors. They first lived in a tent in Canvas Town, South Melbourne. He died at East St Kilda and she at Elsternwick, Victoria. In addition to Alice they had seven other children:

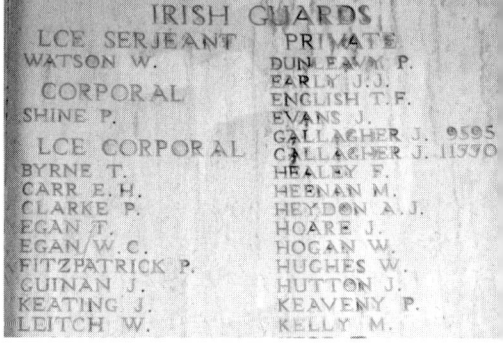

William Lawrence Leitch is commemorated on the Cambrai Memorial. His name is bottom left.

* William John Crump Woolcott (11th December 1848–23rd June 1916), born at 75 Great George Street, Bermondsey, London, married Emily Annie Corlett (28th November 1852–15th January 1925) on 26th April 1876 at All Saints Anglican Church, St Kilda. She was born at 18 Hemus Terrace, St Luke, London. William died at Hexham, 83 Alma Road, St Kilda and Emily at Hawthorn, Victoria. They had six children – Ernest Woolcott (1876–99), Theodora Elsa Woolcott (1878–1965), William Spark Woolcott (1880–1959), Arthur Francis Woolcott (1881), unnamed stillborn in 1883 and Beatrice Victoria 'Queenie' Woolcott (1886–1979).
* Mary Elizabeth Woolcott (1851–11th May 1929), born in Victoria, married Leopold Quintin de Soyres (c.1841–19th September 1884), born at Clifton, Gloucestershire, England, on 15th September 1875 at Balaclava, Victoria. They had five children – Lionel Francis de Soyres (1876–89), Fernie de Soyres (1877–1931), Isabella Mary de Soyres (1879–1972), Louis John de Soyres (1881–1945) and Leopold Woolcott de Soyres (1884–1944). Leopold died at Dookie, Victoria. Mary was living at St Quintin's, Grosvenor Street, Balaclava, Victoria in 1889. She married Mark John Brady (1866–1922), a wool classer, on 23rd June 1891 at Holy Trinity Church, Balaclava, Victoria. He was born at Waterview, Breakfast

Creek, Brisbane, Queensland. They both died at La Serra, 13 Iona Street, Black Rock, Victoria.
* Amelia Emily Woolcott (1852–10th May 1853).
* Emily Harriett Woolcott (17th February 1854–15th July 1935), born at Richmond, Victoria, married William Francis Nash (22nd October 1849–1914), a barrister-at-law born at Clapham, London, England, on 24th October 1877 at All Saints Anglican Church, St Kilda. He died at Dookie, Victoria and she at Malvern. They had four children – Frances May Nash (1878–1960), Florence Emily Nash (1880–95), Clifford Woolcott Nash (1882–1949) and Llewellyn Nash (1884–1959).
* Louisa Woolcott (1856–28th October 1918), born at Darebin Creek, married Joseph Walter Lush (6th March 1856–1940), born at Elmore, Victoria, there on 10th September 1879. They were living at Bondi, 36 Elm Grove, East St Kilda, Victoria in 1914. She died at Haig Street, Caulfield and he at Prahran. They had seven children:
  - Studley Woolcott Lush (1880–1949) was educated at St Kilda Scotch College, Moore Park Grammar School and privately. He became a schoolmaster with the Department of Public Instruction, Sydney, New South Wales in 1897 but resigned in August 1898 and joined Goldsbrough, Mort & Co, Melbourne. During the South African War he rose to staff sergeant, serving with the Marquess of Tullabadine in the Scottish Horse. He joined Vacuum Oil Co in 1903, transferred to South Australia as chief accountant in 1919 and resigned in 1921 to join Neptune Oil Co, Kent Street, Sydney as assistant manager. He became manager in 1927. Studley married Caroline Hogan (1888–1975) in 1909 and they had three sons and two daughters. They lived at Bywong, Prince Street, Mosman, Sydney. Studley was appointed a magistate for New South Wales in 1920.
  - Alfred Joseph Lush (born and died 1882).
  - Ruby Louise Lush (1883–1940).
  - Walter Gordon Lush (1884–1951) enlisted at Melbourne in 1st Division Signal Company AIF (107) on 19th August 1914. He declared twelve years previous service in Victorian forces. He was described as a clerk, 5′ 6½″ tall, weighing 146 lbs, with dark complexion, brown eyes, black hair and his religious denomination was Church of England. Walter departed Melbourne on HMAT A10 *Karroo* on 20th October and was promoted corporal on 30th November. He transferred to the Divisional Artillery HQ on 1st June 1915, to 3rd Australian Signal Company at Gallipoli on 20th June and to 2nd Division Signal Company on 26th July. He was detached to Egypt the same day and disembarked from SS *Minneapolis* at Alexandria on 29th July. He was commissioned on 27th August, backdated to 27th July 1915, and embarked on SS *Menominia* at Alexandria from Base Details on 5th October for Gallipoli. Promoted lieutenant 22nd October. Disembarked at Alexandria from SS *Simla* on 4th January 1916.

He travelled from Egypt to Marseille, France aboard SS *Themistocles* 16th–21st March. Walter was Mentioned in Sir Douglas Haig's Despatch of 9th April 1917, LG 1st June 1917. Promoted captain 15th April and was granted leave in Britain 28th November–12th December. He was awarded the MC for continuously showing courage and devotion to duty in maintaining intercommunications in the Division's artillery. During operations against the Hindenburg Line he maintained effective communications for nine brigades of artillery under the most difficult circumstances, showing fearlessness and initiative of the highest value, LG 28th December 1917. He was granted leave to Paris 10th–20th February 1918. Walter was detached to the Australian Corps Signal Company as OC Heavy Artillery Section 8th–13th March 1918 and transferred to it on 2nd June. He was granted leave in Britain 22nd July–4th August and 8th–24th October. On 14th October he was appointed OC Australian Corps Signal Company. He was granted seventy-five days long service leave in Britain 9th November 1918–25th January 1919, then reported to AIF HQ in London for early repatriation on 29th January. Walter married Ethel Mary MacPhail (1894–1982) at St Giles, Edinburgh, Scotland in 1919. She was living at 5 Archibald Place, Lauriston, Edinburgh. They returned to Australia aboard SS *Wahehe*, departing from Tilbury on 16th May and arriving at Melbourne on 28th June. His appointment was terminated in 3rd Military District on 23rd October 1919. Walter worked for the State Electricity Commission of Victoria. They were living at 66a Grosvenor Mansions, William Street, Balaclava, Victoria in the 1920s.
  - Mervyn Drummond Lush (born 1886).
  - Mary Woolcott (1888–90).
  - Charles Williatt Lush (1892–1950) was a clerk when he enlisted as a sapper in 1st–5th Division Signal Companies Reinforcements on 13th August 1917 (21118). He departed Melbourne aboard HMAT A71 *Nestor* on 28th February 1918 and returned to Australia on 6th September 1919. Charles married Blanche Muir McComb (1891–1972) in 1922 at Brighton, Victoria. He re-enlisted in the Australian Army on 5th December 1940 at Kew, Victoria (V91153) and was promoted through the ranks to sergeant. He was discharged from 9th Garrison Battalion on 23rd October 1945.
- Florence Woolcott (22nd January 1861–16th December 1934), born at Balaclava Road, St Kilda, married Alfred Brett on 26th March 1890 at Holy Trinity Church, Balaclava, Victoria. They were living at 4 Kinross Avenue, Caulfield, Victoria in May 1916, at 11 Dover Parade, Caulfield in July 1918 and at Victoria Coffee Palace, Pitt Street, Sydney in October 1918. She died at Corinan Private Hospital, Murrumbeena. They had five children:
  - Jack Goodall Brett (1891–99).

- Roy George Woolcott Brett (1893–1971), born at Armadale, New South Wales, was a bank clerk when he enlisted in 12th Reinforcements, 5th Battalion AIF on 3rd August 1915 at Ouyen, Victoria (3270). He was described as 5′ 5½″ tall, weighing 129 lbs, with fair complexion, blue eyes, brown hair and his religious denomination was Church of England. He embarked at Melbourne aboard HMAT A40 *Ceramic* on 23rd November 1915 and was allocated to the HQ staff of Major General Sir Herbert Vaughan Cox at Zeitoun, Egypt on 8th March 1916 from No.2 Training Battalion. Roy was attached to AIF HQ on 5th May 1916. He embarked at Alexandria on 2nd June and disembarked at Marseille, France on 8th June 1916. He was taken on strength of the Australian HQ Egypt on 1st August and was promoted corporal and temporary sergeant on 19th August. Roy was admitted to No.3 Australian General Hospital with debility on 20th September and transferred to No.14 Australian General Hospital, Cairo with neurasthenia. He transferred to the British Red Cross Convalescent Hospital, Montazah, Alexandria on 26th September and returned to duty on 15th October. He was promoted sergeant on 1st August and staff sergeant on 1st November 1917. He was mentioned in General Sir Edmund Allenby's despatch dated 23rd October 1918, LG 21st January 1919. A medical board at No.14 Australian General Hospital, Port Said found he was suffering from neurasthenia, debility and cardiac (sic) and was graded B2 on 13th January 1918. Medical boards on 3rd August 1918 and 7th September 1919 graded him B and B2 respectively. Promoted extra regimental warrant officer class one on 1st November 1918 and was attached to HQ Desert Mounted Corps until 5th December. He was attached to HQ Desert Mounted Corps again on 9th January 1919 and was stationed at Aleppo, Syria from 17th March and Cairo from 22nd March. Roy was awarded the French Médaille d'Honneur avec Glaives en Bronze (LG 15th December 1919). He embarked at Port Said for Britain aboard HT *Ellenga* on leave on 10th June until 11th August. He returned to Alexandria on 6th September and to Australia aboard HT *Berrima*, arriving on 25th October 1919. Roy married Lily Carroll (1893–1970) in 1919 in Victoria.
- Percy Laurence Brett (1894–1947) enlisted in Melbourne on 6th May 1916 (2381), described as a clerk, 5′ 6½″ tall, weighing 120 lbs, with medium complexion, grey eyes, black hair and his religious denomination was Church of England. He joined 5/59th Battalion, 3rd Training Brigade at Castlemaine on 22nd May. He was found to be physically weak, unable to withstand full training and did clerical work instead. He never went to France. Appointed voyage only corporal and acting CQMS on 25th September, embarking at Melbourne on HMAT A9 *Shropshire* the same day and disembarking at Plymouth, Devon on 11th November. He reverted to private on 21st November on joining 15th Training Battalion. Appointed acting lance corporal on 15th February 1917 and transferred to HQ No.5 Group on 29th

May on the permanent cadre as an extra regimental corporal. Appointed extra regimental sergeant on the permanent cadre of HQ 3rd Training Brigade at Codford, Wiltshire on 7th November and reverted to private on 3rd December on ceasing duty there. Appointed temporary corporal on 1st January 1918 on transferring to the permanent cadre of No.2 Command Depot, Weymouth. On 8th March he was declared fit for Home Service but permanently unfit for General Service. Appointed temporary RQMS on 28th October and extra regimental RQMS on 1st May 1919. Percy was granted leave on 30th November. Appointed extra regimental WO1 on 19th January 1920. He embarked on SS *Wahehe* in London on 31st August as SQMS aboard and disembarked on 21st October at Melbourne. Discharged from 3rd Military District on 7th February 1921. Percy married Vera May Hunt (1898–1992) on 24th November 1928 at Northcote, Victoria. He was an accountant at the time of his death in South Melbourne.
- Edward/Edwin Vernon Brett (1899–1975) enlisted on 26th October 1918 (N96011) at the Central Depot, New South Wales. His father had to verify his date of birth and give his consent. He was described as a traveller, 5′ 5½″ tall, weighing 120 lbs, with fair complexion, blue eyes, fair hair and his religious denomination was Church of England. He was discharged on 31st December 1918. Edwin married Margaret Gladys Broderick (1900–88) in 1924 in Victoria and they had a son. Edwin enlisted in the Royal Australian Air Force on 19th August 1941 at Carnegie, Victoria (42346). He was discharged as a flight sergeant on 18th December 1945 from 1 Aircraft Depot, Laverton, Victoria. He died at Carnegie, Victoria.
- Geoffrey William Alfred Brett (1902–24) enlisted at Melbourne (V78512) on 15th July 1918 as Edwin Vernon Brett. He was described as a National Bank clerk, 5′ 5″ tall, weighing 113 lbs, with fresh complexion, blue eyes, fair hair and his religious denomination was Church of England. He declared service in the Senior Cadets and 2/7th Infantry in Caulfield for four years, including camp at Bendigo in November 1917. Due to his physique he was retained for three months to build up. He joined the Recruit Depot Battalion, Broadmeadows Camp on 1st August. He was admitted to No.5 Australian General Hospital with influenza 17th–28th August, transferred to No.16 Australian General Hospital until 7th September and then to light duties. On 10th September he transferred from 47th Infantry to 66th Infantry for training. On 16th September he made a statement that he had enlisted as his brother, Edward/Edwin. He gave his age as eighteen years and seven months (born on 31st (sic) November 1899), although he was actually only fifteen years and eleven months. He was discharged on 21st October 1918 for being under military age and was reprimanded for making a false statement.
• Amelia Woolcott (24th June 1864–7th January 1865) was born at Carlisle Street, St Kilda.

Don was educated at Orrong Road Kindergarten, Elsternwick, Melbourne, at Grange Preparatory School, Toorak, South Yarra, Melbourne and at Melbourne Grammar School. He studied accountancy until 1909 with a firm of chartered accountants, Densham & Sherlock. He was not happy and headed north for Rockhampton, Queensland in search of adventure, with the intention of learning about the cotton industry. He travelled overland to Mackay with a fellow traveller named Lancaster. When they ran out of food they shot wild game. They found nothing in Mackay, moved on to Cairns aboard a small coastal ship and worked in a number of jobs. Don became disillusioned with cotton and returned to Melbourne, working his passage aboard SS *Grantala*, on 15th November 1910. He then tried sheep and wheat farming in the Mallee in Northern Victoria, gaining experience with Mr Sands. However, a disagreement with Sands ended his employment and he found work on Tyrell Downs sheep station, where he worked in a range of appointments for nine months. Next he moved to Perth, Western Australia, where he purchased land to grow peas and potatoes, while also working for the Jarrah Timber & Trading Co. He lost his potato crop to Codlin moth and his peas withered under bush fires. His own condition deteriorated and leeches infected his leg. He contracted blood poisoning and would have died if his friend, Tom Harris, had not called in to see how he was getting along. Don was unable to move and was rushed to hospital. If they had waited another day, he would not have survived. Whilst recovering he learned that his mother was seriously ill, so left his property to a couple who promised to pay him when they made good. He never heard from them again. Don then purchased a property on Flinders Island in the Bass Strait to grow potatoes but sold it in 1915 to enlist. He was fiercely pro-British and a royalist.

Don served in the Victorian Rifles, a Militia unit, on and off from 1909, when he passed the 1st class certificate of special training at Port Melbourne. While serving

Melbourne Grammar School soon after it opened. The foundation stone was laid on 30th July 1856. It was officially Melbourne Church of England Grammar School but was known as the Grammar. It was based on the principles of the English public schools and opened on 7th April 1858 with seventy-seven pupils. Enrolments grew to 272 in 1889 but had fallen to 117 by 1894 and a group of former pupils decided to save it by forming the Old Melburnians Society in 1895. The buildings were expanded and second stories were added to existing ones. The early 20th century saw enrolments increase steadily. Over 200 former pupils were killed in the Great War and about 3,500 served in the Second World War, during which part of the School was used by Australian and US forces. Another building programme commenced in the 1950s. The School currently has 1,800 pupils, including 120 boarders. It has produced numerous prominent alumni, including Richard Casey, the sixteenth Governor General, three Prime Ministers (Alfred Deakin (2nd), Stanley Bruce (8th) and Malcolm Fraser (22nd)) and six state premiers. In addition to Don Joynt, the School produced another VC – William Ellis Newton (1919–43).

SS *Wiltshire* (10,390 tons) was built in 1912 by John Brown on Clydebank for the Federal Steam Navigation Co, London for the UK–Australia–New Zealand route. She was leased by the Commonwealth as HMAT A18 *Wiltshire* until 27th December 1917, when she was taken over by the British Admiralty. Wiltshire completed nine voyages from Australia, including the first convoy from Albany in October 1914. She was wrecked on 31st May 1922 in Rosalie Bay, Great Barrier Island, New Zealand. All 103 men aboard were saved.

with the Victorian Rifles he met Lord Kitchener during his visit to Australia in January 1910. Kitchener asked him to relay a message to his CO during an exercise. Don served for twenty months as a corporal according to his service record. He enlisted in the AIF at Sturt Street, Melbourne on 21st May 1915, described as 5′ 5″ tall, weighing 152 lbs, with dark complexion, blue/grey eyes, black hair and his religious denomination was Church of England. He gave his address as that of his brother, Gerald. Don applied for a commission and trained at No.4 Officers Training School from 7th July and at No.7 Officers Training School from 10th October. He trained at 23rd Depot Battalion, Royal Park, Melbourne 21st September–4th December with 23rd Depot Battalion and was posted to Broadmeadows, Victoria on 5th December. He was commissioned on 24th December and embarked at Melbourne aboard HMAT A18 *Wiltshire* bound for the Middle East with the 15th Reinforcement Group, 8th Battalion on 7th March 1916, arriving at Suez, Egypt on 10th April. He joined 2nd Training Battalion.

On 9th May he embarked at Alexandria, Egypt aboard HT *Caledonia*, arriving at Marseille, France on 17th May. He joined the Base Depot, Étaples on 19th May and was posted to A Company, 8th Battalion on 25th July. **Commended by Major General Harold Bridgwood Walker, GOC 1st Australian Division, for his actions on 30th September, when he led a successful raid near Pozières during which he was wounded by shrapnel in the right shoulder (1st Australian Division Routine Orders 6th October 1916).** During the raid he became caught up in the enemy wire and was rescued by the CO of 6th Battalion, Lieutenant Colonel Henry Gordon Bennett (later Lieutenant General CB CMG DSO VD). This commendation has been cited as a mention in despatches but no evidence of such an award has been found. Don was admitted to 1st Australian Field Ambulance and transferred to No.10 Casualty Clearing Station and 7th Stationary

HMHS *St Andrew* (2,495 tons), built in 1908 by John Brown, operated by Great Western Railways between Fishguard in Wales and Rosslare in Ireland. It was one of the first ships to be taken over in 1914 and was fitted out as a hospital ship. She was in use until 29th May 1919, when she returned to her normal service and was renamed *Fishguard* in 1932. A year later she was sold for scrap.

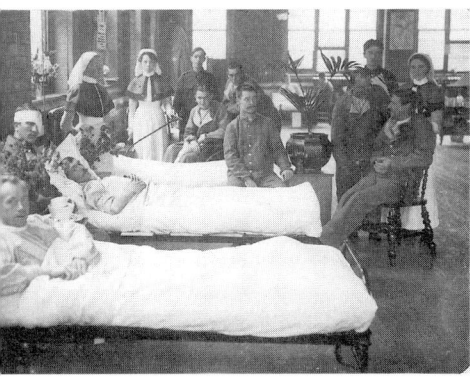

Manchester was a major centre for wounded servicemen during the Great War, with the main military hospital being 2nd Western General Hospital. It was mobilised in August 1914, with most of the staff coming from Manchester Royal Infirmary and Manchester University. It originally had 520 beds but the capacity was extended greatly. The Hospital was based in Central Higher Grade School on Whitworth Street and the Day Training College on Princess Street. Later there was a branch at the School of Domestic Economy on High Street (Hathersage Road). By November 1918 there were 5,239 beds and 220,548 patients had been treated. The Hospital was decommissioned in 1919 (Sue Light & Nick Metcalf).

Hospital, Boulogne on 1st October. On 9th October he was evacuated to England on HMHS St Andrew from Boulogne and was admitted to 2nd Western General Hospital, Manchester. A medical board there on 22nd November found him unfit for General Service for four weeks. A medical board at the Australian Military Offices, London on 14th December found him fit for General Service. He was discharged to Perham Down Depot, Wiltshire on 16th December and was promoted lieutenant on 31st December.

Don returned to France on 5th January 1917 and joined 1st Australian Division Base Depot, Étaples next day. He rejoined 8th Battalion on 15th January, taking part subsequently in operations at Bullecourt and Ypres. He was posted to the Second Army School 10th November–18th December and was granted leave 11th–27th January 1918. He was posted to 1st Australian Division Reinforcement Camp for duty on 28th April.

Awarded the VC for his actions at Herleville Wood, near Chuignes, Péronne, France on 23rd August, 1918, LG 27th November 1918. The original recommendation by Lieutenant Colonel John Wesley Mitchell DSO, CO 8th Battalion, on 31st August 1918 was for the DSO, but this was raised to a VC by General Sir Henry Rawlinson, commanding Fourth Army, on 18th October. Don received a gunshot wound to the left thigh/buttock on 26th August near Péronne and was evacuated to No.41 Casualty Clearing Station. He was admitted to 2nd General Hospital, Le Havre on 27th August and later that day was evacuated to England aboard HMHS Guildford Castle for admission to 3rd London General Hospital on 29th August. Promoted captain on 29th October. He was convalescing 2nd–16th December, then a medical board found him fit for overseas service. He was posted to the Overseas Training Brigade on 31st December 1918 and was attached to HQ AIF, London on 1st March 1919. The VC was presented by the King in the quadrangle at Buckingham Palace on 10th July.

Don was granted leave with pay (26/- per day, plus subsistence allowance of 6/-) for non-military employment, i.e. agricultural and sheep breeding with Mr E Smith at Bransford, Worcester from 31st July to 31st October 1919. He was admitted to 1st Australian General Hospital, Sutton Veny, Wiltshire 14th–28th August and during that period his subsistence reduced to 3/6 per day. He was granted leave with allowances 3rd–7th November and reported to Sutton Veny on 3rd December. Before leaving Britain, Don organised several parties of AIF soldiers to tour farming areas in England in order to gain experience as part of a repatriation education programme. Major Henry Murray VC DSO DCM was also involved in this work. Don embarked on HMT Themistocles on 22nd December 1919 and arrived in Melbourne on 11th February 1920. He was admitted to the Repatriation Hospital, Caulfield, Victoria for a full medical check up. His wounds had healed but there was some neurasthenia. His next of kin in February 1920 was his aunt, Mrs Florence Brett. On 11th June 1920 Don's appointment was terminated

The AIF Headquarters in London on Horseferry Road, Westminster (Australian War Memorial).

SS *Guildford Castle* (8,036 tons) built in 1911 by Barclay Curle & Co in Glasgow for the Union Castle Mail Steamship Co. When the Great War broke out she participated in the first troop convoy to Europe and on 22nd September 1914 was commissioned as a hospital ship with 427 beds. During the German West and East African campaigns in 1915 she remained in Southern African waters. Most patients were suffering from diseases rather than wounds. On 10th March 1918, inbound to Avonmouth, she was hit by a torpedo that failed to explode. On 9th November 1918 she returned to civilian service with Union Castle on the London to South Africa service and later on the round Africa service. On 31st May 1933 she was in collision with SS *Stentor* near Oste Riff, Elbe and two lives were lost. Next day she was beached and was declared a total loss.

and he transferred to the Reserve with the rank of captain. His second cousin, 38713 Private Charles Henry Joynt, Taranaki Company, 2nd Wellington NZEF was killed in action on 31st July 1917 (Messines Ridge (New Zealand) Memorial, Belgium).

3rd London General Hospital in Wandsworth. Before the war it was the Royal Victoria Patriotic School for orphans. By May 1917, the Hospital had almost 2,000 beds, many in hutted wards behind the main building. It closed in August 1920 having treated 62,708 patients and became an orphanage again until the Second World War. The children were evacuated and MI6 used it as a clearing, detention and interrogation centre. Post-war it became a teacher training college and later a school. By the 1970s the building was badly run-down. In 1980, the Greater London Council sold it for £1 on condition that it was properly restored and it has since been divided into apartments. Arthur Blackburn VC (see the third book in this series, *Victoria Crosses on the Western Front – Somme 1916*) was also treated there September–October 1916.

The entrance to 1st Australian General Hospital, which opened at Sutton Veny on 15th January 1919 after moving from Rouen, France, was on the main road from Warminster to Sutton Veny (Australian War Memorial).

Henry Murray VC DSO DCM. His exploits are covered in the fourth book in this series, *Victoria Crosses on the Western Front – 1917 to Third Ypres – 27th January 1917–27th July 1917*.

Don farmed one hundred acres at Berwick, Victoria under the Soldier Closer Settlement Scheme. A series of droughts forced him to quit the land, which was seized by the Closer Settlement Board after he fell behind with his rent. He was living at Kainga, Seymour Grove, Brighton Beach, Victoria at some time in the early 1920s. He returned to Melbourne and founded the WD Joynt & Co and Dominion Press printers, North Blackburn. Don was a foundation member of the Legacy Club, Melbourne and was President of the Old Melbournians. He was also a

Charles Henry Joynt is commemorated on the Wellington Regiment panel on the Messines Ridge (New Zealand) Memorial.

TSS *Themistocles* (11,231 tons), built by Harland & Wolff in Belfast and launched on 22nd September 1910, was owned by the Aberdeen Line and worked the London–Cape Town–Australia route, carrying one hundred first and 250 third class passengers. During the Great War she was leased by the Commonwealth until 20th October 1917. In 1932 she was sold to the Shaw, Savill & Albion Line. During the Second World War she survived a number of convoys. *Themistocles* was scrapped at Dalmuir in August 1947.

member of several Freemason lodges in Melbourne – Old Melbournians Lodge (No.317), Berwick Lodge (No.359) and Bolton Memorial Lodge (No.758).

He attended a function in the Public Library, Melbourne on 28th May 1920 in honour of the visit of the Prince of Wales. During the 1920s he petitioned with his friend, Sir Alfred Kemsley, for the raising of funds to build the Shrine of Remembrance in Melbourne. This brought them into conflict with the Returned Services League, which had other plans for the site.

An Anzac Dinner on 23rd April 1927, hosted by Lieutenant General Sir John Monash GCMG KCB VD, was attended by twenty-three VCs including Don Joynt. For an unknown reason the Duke of York was not invited. He attended the ANZAC Commemoration Service on 25th April 1927 at the Exhibition Building, Melbourne in the presence of the Duke of York (future King George VI), with twenty three other VCs. Don attended a garden party at Parliament House, Melbourne, hosted by the Duke of Gloucester KG PC KT KP GCVO on 9th November 1934. He was also present at the official opening by the Governor General, Lord De L'Isle VC, of VC Corner at the Australian War Memorial in 1964, with seventeen other Australian VCs.

On 19th March 1932, Don married Edith Amy Garrett (1896–30th May 1978), born at Box Hill, Victoria, at Hawthorn, Victoria. She was a nurse at Melbourne Hospital in 1923 when they met. They were living at 23 Isabella Grove, Hawthorn, Victoria in 1936 and at 424 Elgar Road, Box Hill, Melbourne in September 1939. By December 1942 they were living at 447 Law Courts Place, Melbourne, where he also worked at some time. Edith died at Kallista, Victoria. There were no children.

Sir Alfred Newcombe 'Kem' Kemsley (1896–1987), the son of English born parents, was educated at Nailsworth Public School in Adelaide, at Howard's Commercial and Correspondence College and at the Adelaide Shorthand and Business Training Academy. From 1911 he was a clerk in the State Lands Department until enlisting in the AIF on 5th March 1915. He was employed on supply duties in Egypt and on the Western Front. He was awarded the MSM and was demobilised as an honorary captain in December 1919. In 1920 he moved to Melbourne to join Broken Hill Proprietary Ltd. Next year he married Glydus Annie May Logg (died 1922) and in 1925, Janet Oldfield in Bendigo. When she died he married Annie Elizabeth Copsey in 1972. With Don Joynt he advocated the creation of a Shrine of Remembrance as a memorial to Victoria's efforts during the Great War and played an active role in defeating a counter-proposal. In 1938 he was appointed to the trust established to administer the Shrine and was its deputy chairman in 1952 and chairman 1978–84. Kem had extensive involvement in a wide variety of other appointments:

1921–28	Militia and the League of National Security.
1923	Secretary Special Constabulary Force during the police strike.
1923	Foundation member Melbourne Legacy Club and President 1932–33.
1923–29	Secretary Melbourne Metropolitan Town Planning Commission.
1930–34	Secretary Liquor Trade Defence Union.
1934	General manager of radio-station 3UZ.
1935–36	Vice-president Australian Federation of Broadcasting Stations.
1941	Full-time service in Militia and AIF as director of organisation and recruiting at Army HQ as a colonel.
1943–46	Business adviser to Department of the Army and Army representative on the Board of Business Administration.
1946	Established United Service Publicity Pty Ltd – director 1946 and chairman 1960–64.
1946–68	Victorian Town and Country Planning Board.
1947–76	Melbourne Chamber of Commerce.
1948–68	Trustee Henry George Foundation.
1948–83	Council (War) Nurses Memorial Centre.
1954	Blamey Memorial Committee, chairman 1978.
1956–68	Represented Associated Chambers of Commerce of Australia on the Australian National Travel Association.
1958–74	Member of National Trust of Australia (Victoria).
1964–69	Director of Ponsford Newman & Benson Ltd.
1969–74	Discharged Servicemen's Employment Board.

He also supported many charities and other causes and was a member of Melbourne's Naval and Military Club from 1936. Kem was appointed CBE 1960, CMG 1973 and was knighted in 1979.

Edith's father, Thomas Henry Garrett (4th May 1862 or 1863–5th January 1951), was born in Birmingham, Warwickshire and emigrated to New Zealand with his parents on 14th March 1865. He married Elizabeth née Robertson (9th September 1855–9th December 1938), born at Box Hill, Victoria, on 24th November 1884 in Auckland, New Zealand. They were living at Avonlea, Carrington Road, Box Hill, Melbourne, Australia in October 1916. They both died at Box Hill. In addition to Edith they had four other children:

23 Isabella Grove, Hawthorn, Victoria.

- Walter Henry Alexander Garrett (1885–1962), born at Auckland, married Marjorie Halhed Belcher (1884–1956), born at Ledbury, Herefordshire, in 1913 at Sydney, New South Wales. Marjorie was a governess in 1909, living on Balaclava Road, St Kilda, Victoria. In 1931 he was a clerk and they were living at 31 Munster Avenue, Glenhuntly, Victoria. They both died in Melbourne. They had two children – Thomas Halhed Garrett (1914–86) and Elizabeth Joan Garrett (1919–2000).
- Alfred Garrett, born and died 1889 at Box Hill.
- Mabel Isabella Garrett (1891–1961) married John Stewart Spence (1894–1949), born at Birkenhead, Cheshire, in 1923. They had three daughters including, Marjorie Isobel Spence (1925–2008). John died at Coburg, Victoria and Mabel at Hawthorn, Victoria.
- Stanley George Garrett (1894–1958), born at Bendigo, Victoria, served for two and a half years in 48th Kooyong Infantry as a second lieutenant from 16th May 1914 and a lieutenant from 1st July 1915. He applied for a commission in the AIF field engineers on 18th March 1916 and attended an aviation course at the Central Flying School from 1st August. On 1st October he joined No.2 Australian Flying Squadron as a second lieutenant, described as a junior architect, 5' 10½" tall, weighing 158 lbs and his religious denomination was Presbyterian. He embarked at Melbourne on HMAT A38 *Ulysees* on 25th October and disembarked at Devonport on 28th December. Stanley joined No.49 Reserve Squadron RFC, Spittlegate, Lincolnshire for elementary instruction on 8th January and No.44 Reserve Squadron RFC, Harlaxton, Lincolnshire on 24th February. He joined No.3 Squadron AFC (also known as No.69 Squadron RFC to avoid confusion with No.3 Squadron RFC/RAF), South Carlton, Lincoln on 23rd March and attended a course at the School of Aerial Gunnery, Turnberry, Ayrshire 7th May– 11th July. He was attached to No.16 Squadron RFC in France for instruction

on 25th July. Promoted lieutenant 3rd August and was detached to First Army Artillery School 6th–8th August. He returned to England to No.69 Squadron on 12th August and was posted to France on 21st August. He was detached to 51 Heavy Artillery Group 25th–29th November and was granted leave in UK 14th–31st January 1918. Stanley joined No.3 Squadron AFC on 1st April. On 21st April 1918 he was flying with observer, Lieutenant Alfred Victor Barrow, and another aircraft of No.3 Squadron AFC, when they were attacked near Le Hamel at 7,000′ by four enemy aircraft. Two enemy aircraft dived on them and the observer fired 120 rounds. One enemy aircraft went down, although it is not thought that it was hit by Barrow. The downed aircraft was almost certainly hit by ground fire and was flown by Baron Manfred von Richthofen, the Red Baron. Stanley joined the Home Establishment in Britain on 12th May, HQ 1st Wing AFC on 20th May, No.7 Training Squadron AFC Leighterton, Gloucestershire on 1st June and No.7 Group RAF Instructors School for a course at Weyhill, Andover, Hampshire 12th–23rd June. He rejoined No.3 Squadron AFC in France on 24th July and was attached to HQ Australian Corps 2nd–24th October. On 27th December he rejoined the Squadron from leave in Italy. On 4th March 1919 he disembarked at Weymouth, Dorset and joined 3rd Training Brigade, Hurdcott, Wiltshire. He was granted leave 10th March–10th September, extended to 30th June 1920, with pay and subsistence, for a course at the Architectural Association School, Bedford Square, London. Stanley reported to HQ AIF, London on 1st July. He embarked for Australia on SS *Wiltshire* on 14th July, arriving on 9th August. His appointment terminated in 3rd Military District on 13th November 1920. He transferred to the Reserve of Officers on 16th February 1921 and was placed on the Retired List on 27th November 1943. Stanley married Eva Lilias Bertha McMillan (1901–91), born at Childers, Queensland, on 1942 at Box Hill. He died at Mont Albert, Victoria and she in Melbourne.

Don joined the 24th Battalion on 22nd June 1926 and transferred to 6th Battalion, Royal Melbourne Regiment on 16th February 1927. He was promoted major and appointed second-in-command on 11th February 1930. He transferred to the Unattached List on 1st July 1932

Manfred Albrecht Freiherr von Richthofen (2nd May 1892–21st April 1918), the 'Red Baron', a German fighter ace with eighty officially credited victories. He commanded Jasta 11, then the larger fighter wing Jagdgeschwader 1, known as 'The Flying Circus' because of the bright colours of its aircraft and because it was transferred from area to area, like a travelling circus. Richthofen became a national hero in Germany. He was shot down and killed near Vaux-sur-Somme. This was credited to Canadian Captain Arthur 'Roy' Brown but more recent research indicates that the fatal shot almost certainly came from ground fire and to the Reserve of Officers on 9th August 1935. Don was commissioned in the Australian Citizen Military Forces on 23rd March 1939 (V80044) and was mobilised on 26th September 1939 with the rank of major. A medical the following day graded him Class II with pulmonary fibrosis. He was promoted lieutenant colonel, with seniority from 23rd September, to raise and command 3rd Garrison Battalion. The Returned Services League carried out preliminary interviews and selection before Don selected his officers, giving preference to members of the old 8th Battalion. They were sworn in at Victoria Barracks, Melbourne and the Battalion entrained for Queenscliff, Victoria on 19th October. Don was granted recreation leave 21st–22nd August and 7th–20th December 1940.

Don ensured that there was a 'wet canteen' at Queenscliff, in contravention of regulations that forbade the sale of intoxicating liquor in camps of continuous training. Don was aware of this and also that the regulations did not apply to war service and continued to run the canteen. The beer was much cheaper than in town and this kept the men in barracks instead of making a nuisance elsewhere. Don refused to occupy a series of trenches dug by the Royal Australian Engineers along the extremities of the barracks, because he considered them unsafe and exposed. An engineer lieutenant was sent by Commander Coast Defence to report on the defence system. He confronted Don, asking if he had ever occupied a fire trench. At this Don lost his temper and pulled the young officer's head into the medal ribbons on his tunic. Shortly afterwards a letter was sent to the Ministry of Defence complaining about the standard of discipline at Queenscliff. Don replied but received no acknowledgement and was appointed Camp Commandant at Puckapunyal, Victoria on 28th March 1941.

After taking over his new appointment, he was informed that a Court of Enquiry was to be held over the loss of £300 from the 'wet canteen' at Queenscliff. Don was summoned to appear at Southern Command Headquarters, where he was informed that he would not be charged with any offence but would be required to refund the full amount. Don asked the authorities if they had examined the canteen account ledger and informed them that he wanted to see the book immediately. He opened it at a certain page and read out an entry commencing with, ... *as I have found we are making too much profit which we have to return to Southern Command, take notice that from today all prices of goods sold must be reduced by 2½%*. When the takings were calculated from that day forward and the profit was reduced by 2½%, the amount came to £300 exactly. Don heard nothing more about the matter and did not receive an apology.

Don was granted annual recreation leave 21st April–5th May 1941. He used Italian prisoners of war to straighten out and revet a creek that wound across Puckapunyal Camp. His superiors claimed it was against regulations, even though the Italians were happy to do it. Don was transferred to a similar appointment as Camp Staff Officer at Seymour, Victoria from 22nd June 1942 and as Quartermaster from 1st October. He was granted leave 2nd–9th November. On 15th December he

Don's grave marker in Brighton Lawn Cemetery, Melbourne.

Don's funeral was held at St Mary's Church, Caulfield. The church began in 1858 when the first service was held in a cottage on Park Street. The following year a wooden church was built, known as All Saints. In 1863 Caulfield Parish was created and the church became St Mary's the following year. A new stone church was opened by Bishop Perry on 26th May 1871. It was enlarged in 1885, increasing the number of seats to 555. In 2014 St Mary's Anglican Church merged with St Clement's to form Oaktree Anglican.

was classified A2 medically and considered young enough for service in the Second AIF. He was detached to Camp Pell, Royal Park, Melbourne for fire protection training instruction 4th–13th January 1943. He was appointed Quartermaster Seymour Camp on 9th December on the Permanent Short List Australian Infantry. He relinquished the appointment on 3rd August 1944, marched out to the Rehabilitation Section, General Details Depot Royal Park, Melbourne to be placed on the Retired List on 26th September and was discharged on 10th October 1944 as an honorary lieutenant colonel. He received a personal letter of commendation from General Blamey for his services in all three appointments.

Don attended the VC Centenary Celebrations in Hyde Park, London on 26th June 1956, travelling on SS *Orcades* with other Australian VCs who were part of the 301 VC recipients from across the Commonwealth to attend. Don broadcast to Australia from the dinner given by the Lord Mayor of London during the celebrations. He attended the third and fifth VC & GC Association Reunions at the Café Royal, London on 18th July 1962 and 14th July 1966. He was also a committee member of the VC & GC Association.

In later life, Don wrote three books. The first, *To Russia and Back Through Communist Countries*, was published in 1971 about travels through the Soviet Union. *Saving the Channel Ports* 1918 followed in 1975 and was a history of the 8th Battalion. It was somewhat controversial in its claims that the Australians had saved the Channel ports during the German Spring Offensives. His autobiography, *Breaking the Road for the Rest*, was published in 1979.

Don died peacefully in his sleep at the Freemason's Centennial House, Windsor, Melbourne on 5th May 1986, having spent the last six years of his life there. He was the last surviving Australian VC from the Great War. His funeral, with full military honours, was held at St Mary's Anglican Church. He is buried in Brighton Lawn Cemetery, Melbourne, Victoria. Don is commemorated in a number of other places:

- Victoria
    - Joynt Street, Wodonga on White Box Rise estate, built on land formerly part of Bandiana Army Camp.
    - Victoria Cross Memorial, Springvale Botanical Cemetery, Melbourne, Victoria unveiled on 10th November 2013.
    - Donovan Joynt VC Memorial Sportsmen's Club, Puckapunyal. He attended the opening ceremony and assisted with funding the construction, which was carried out by 21st Construction Squadron and 19th Chief Engineer Works, based at Puckapunyal. The Club was opened by the Chief of the General Staff, Lieutenant General Sir Phillip Harvey Bennett KBE AO DSO, on 23rd March 1983.
    - Joynt Street, Macleod.
- Australian Capital Territory
    - Australian Victoria Cross Recipients plaque on the Victoria Cross Memorial, Campbell, dedicated on 24th July 2000.
    - Named on one of eleven plaques honouring 175 men from overseas awarded the VC for the Great War. The plaques were unveiled by the Senior Minister of State at the Foreign & Commonwealth Office and Minister for Faith and Communities, Baroness Warsi, at a reception at Lancaster House, London on 26th June 2014 attended by The Duke of Kent and relatives of the VC recipients. The Australian plaque is at the Australian War Memorial.
    - Display in the Hall of Valour, Australian War Memorial.
- New South Wales
    - Victoria Cross Memorial, Queen Victoria Building, George Street, Sydney dedicated on 23rd February 1992 to commemorate the visit of Queen Elizabeth II and Prince Phillip on the occasion of

The Australia Service Medal 1939–1945 was awarded to members of the Australian armed forces, Mercantile Marine and Volunteer Defence Corps. The qualifying period was eighteen months full-time service at home or overseas or three years part time service between 3rd September 1939 and 2nd September 1945. There was no minimum qualifying period for those killed, wounded or disabled due to service. In August 1996 the qualifying period was reduced to thirty days for full-time service and ninety days for part-time service.

the Sesquicentenary of the City of Sydney. Sir Roden Cutler VC AK KCMG, Edward Kenna VC and Keith Payne VC were in attendance.
    - Victoria Cross Recipients Wall, North Bondi War Memorial, donated to the community of Waverley on 27th November 2011 by The Returned & Services League of Australia.
    - VC Memorial, 119 Borella Road, Peard's Complex, East Albury.
 - Communities and Local Government commemorative paving stones for the 145 VCs born in Australia, Belgium, Canada, China, Denmark, Egypt, France, Germany, India, Iraq, Japan, Nepal, Netherlands, Newfoundland, New Zealand, Pakistan, South Africa, Sri Lanka, Ukraine and United States of America were unveiled at the National Memorial Arboretum, Alrewas, Staffordshire by Prime Minister David Cameron MP and Sergeant Johnson Beharry VC on 5th March 2015.

In addition to the VC he was awarded the British War Medal 1914–20, Victory Medal 1914–19, War Medal 1939–45, Australia Service Medal 1939–45, George VI Coronation Medal 1937, Elizabeth II Coronation Medal 1953 and Elizabeth II Silver Jubilee Medal 1977. The current location of the VC is not known.

LIEUTENANT LAWRENCE DOMINIC McCARTHY
16th Battalion AIF

Lawrence McCarthy was born on 21st January 1892 at York, Western Australia. He was named Florence (sic) Joseph McCarthy but later changed this to Lawrence Dominic McCarthy. To his family and friends he was 'Sykes' and in the Army he was 'Fats', because of his bulk, or 'Mac'. His father, also Florence McCarthy (c.1853–22nd July 1918), was born in Cork, Ireland. He emigrated to Australia, where he became a station hand. Florence married Ann 'Annie' née Sherry (1867–17th January 1896) at York, where she was born, in 1887. Anne contracted pertussis (whooping cough) about September 1895 and subsequently died from the illness. Florence died at the Hospital for the Insane, Claremont, Western Australia.

Lawrence had three brothers. He, James and Patrick were admitted to Subiaco Boys' Orphanage, run by the Sisters of Mercy, on 21st January 1896. They were transferred to the Christian Brothers at St Joseph's Orphanage, Subiaco in 1899, and in 1901 to their new

York in Western Australia, where Lawrence was born in January 1892 (Johnstone, O'Shannessy & Co).

A site at Claremont was chosen for a new Hospital for the Insane, accessible from Perth and Fremantle, administered under the Lunacy Act 1903 and managed by the state government Lunacy Department. Temporary buildings were set up and in August 1903 twenty patients were moved there from Whitby Falls Hospital to help clear the scrub and prepare the site. By 1904 all male wards were under construction, but the female wards were not completed until 1934. Transfer of patients from Fremantle began in 1904. The hospital was renamed Claremont Mental Hospital in 1933. A physical treatment block, built in 1939, was taken over by the military at the beginning of the Second World War. From 1945 it accommodated former servicemen with psychiatric disorders. In April 1959 Australia's first psychiatric day hospital was established there. In 1954 a tuberculosis block was added and in 1961 an

Industrial Rehabilitation Unit was constructed. By 1966 Claremont had almost 1,700 long-term patients but numbers began to reduce with improved medication. In September 1972, Claremont closed and was divided into two establishments – Swanbourne Hospital for psychogeriatric patients and adults with developmental disabilities and Graylands Hospital for acute psychiatric patients. The number of patients continued to fall and in 1979 it was decided to close Swanbourne. Part of the site was redeveloped for John XXIII College and the remainder for residential purposes. The last elderly patients left in April 1985 and much of the site has been demolished (Jessica Barratt).

In 1897 the Christian Brothers assumed control of the Sisters of Mercy orphanage in Subiaco. Shortly afterwards land on the banks of the Canning River near Manning was obtained and a new St Joseph's Boys' Orphanage was completed in September 1901, later renamed St Peter's Intermediate Orphanage. By 1919 it was Clontarf Boy's Orphanage. By the 1930s Clontarf was almost self-sufficient with an orchard, vegetable garden, dairy, poultry, piggery and other livestock. It housed up to 150 boys aged six to fourteen. They received primary education, religious teaching and training in basic manual skills and farm practices. An apprenticeship scheme was introduced

to provide boys with trade skills and they provided the labour for the construction of many new buildings. In 1941 it was renamed Clontarf Boys' Town and began to accept orphans from Britain. During the Second World War the RAAF used the site as a training school, while the orphanage moved to new farm schools at Bindoon and Tardun. After the war a junior secondary school was introduced and some boys moved to nearby Aquinas College to complete their education. In 1961 it opened to day pupils and boarders and in 1964 was renamed Clontarf School, with a peak enrolment of 303 boys. In the early 1970s the Christian Brothers started to use the facilities as a treatment centre for adolescents with behavioural problems and dayboys ceased by 1977. The orphanage closed in April 1984 but reopened as Clontarf Aboriginal College in May 1986. In the late 1980s allegations of abuse were made against the Christian Brothers by former students and residents of their institutions, including Clontarf. The Christian Brothers accepted that many allegations were true and made a public apology. A legal action brought by over 200 former students was settled out of court in 1996.

orphanage at Clontarf on the Canning River. The brothers were:

- James Cyril McCarthy (1888–1967), of Lion Hill, WA, married Ida Grace Madden (1894–1964). She was born at Perth, WA.
- Patrick John McCarthy (1890–February 1959) married Amy Susannah Linto (1890–6th September 1939) in 1912 at Northam, WA. Patrick enlisted at 62nd Depot on 10th April 1916 (6301), described as a labourer, 5′ 5½″ tall, weighing 130 lbs, with fresh complexion, blue eyes, black hair and his religious denomination was Roman Catholic. He was posted to 21st Reinforcements, 11th Battalion on 1st May and to 20th Reinforcements, 11th Battalion on 22nd July. He allotted 4/- per day from his Army pay to his wife from 2nd August. Patrick was discharged on 6th September at his own request on payment. They had a son, Thomas William McCarthy (1916–92). He married Irene Beatrice Harrison (1920–97) and they had five daughters.
- John Edward 'Ted' McCarthy (1894–1967) was raised by his aunt and uncle, Jack and Mildred Sherry. He married Ruby Ruth Rebena Crawford (1897–1970) and they had four sons and a daughter, including Reginald McCarthy, who served in the Royal Australian Air Force during the Second World War.

Clontarf Boy's Orphage, now Clontarf Aboriginal College (Moondyne).

Lawrence's paternal grandfather, Patrick McCarthy, a farm labourer, married Mary née Moloney. His maternal grandfather, Peter Sherry (1829–4th July 1905), was born in Co Monaghan, Ireland and emigrated to York, WA. He married Mary née Morgan (1833–7th April 1888), also born in Co Monaghan, on 1st January 1861. Both died at York. In addition to Ann they had two sons:

- John 'Jack' Sherry (6th December 1862–8th October 1945) married Mildred Sturtridge (2nd January 1866–31st July 1947) at York in 1890. She was born at Bodmin, Cornwall, England. They had two children – Patrick Sherry (1891–1968) and Ada Mary Sherry (1898–1985).
- Patrick Sherry (died 1906).

Lawrence left the orphanage on 30th November 1905, having been educated at various Catholic schools in Perth, WA. Life at Clontarf was not always pleasant. During a visit there later in life with his brother Ted, he was asked by one of the Christian Brothers if he was pleased to see the buildings again. He replied, *Yes I am, but I must say that if, when I die, there is a Hell for me, then there will be a Hell*

Mount Helena, a suburb of Perth, originally White's Mill built by Abraham White and others in 1882 for the construction of the Eastern Railway. From 1898 it was known as Lion Mill. Robert Bunning purchased the site in 1905 and next year other mills to the north and northwest. Bunning built a new mill at Lion Mill to the north of the old mill. Until it closed in 1923, the Bunnings operated Lion Mill as their main mill in Western Australia. In 1924 the site was renamed Mount Helena. The picture shows workers at Lion Mill in its early days. Robert Bunning (1859–1936), born in Hackney, London, arrived in Fremantle with his brother Arthur in 1886 and they

set up as building contractors. By January 1887 they had been awarded contracts for additions to Fremantle Lunatic Asylum and Roebourne Hospital. During the 1896–97 boom in the export of jarrah, the Bunning's turned their attention to timber. Robert bought his first sawmill at North Dandalup in 1897 and in the early 1900s concentrated on expanding sawmills and timber yards. He established sawmills throughout the southwest, imported the first band saw in Western Australia to Lion Mill and installed the first timber-drying kiln. In 1907 the company was incorporated and timber yards were established in Murray Street, Perth. He imported a locomotive (Dirty Mary) and was one of the first to use tractors for hauling logs in the bush. Robert collapsed and died in 1936, while replying to a toast during a dinner to celebrate fifty years in business. Bunnings made bricks during the Second World War and teamed up with rival Perth group Millars at the request of the Ministry of Munitions to build small boats used by Z Force to land on Japanese territory in Asia. In the post-war housing boom, Bunnings became the largest logging operators in Australia. In 1952 the company went public as Bunning Timber Holdings. In the mid-1950s it diversified into hardware and opened its first retail store in West Perth in 1961. In 1968, the timber yards were relocated to Welshpool and by 1970 had become one of the biggest producers of building materials in the State. In 1983 the company bought out Millars and in 1990 Alco Handyman hardware operations. Bunnings was bought out by Wesfarmers in 1994 but the name lives on in more than 250 hardware stores across Australia. In 2016 Bunnings expanded into Britain.

for some of the Brothers who were here too. His brother Patrick said that Clontarf was the cruellest place on Earth. Lawrence was apprenticed for four years as a farmer to John White of Jennacubbine, near Northam, WA. He subsequently worked as a contractor for Bunning Brothers at a sawmill, cutting sleepers for Western Australia Railways. At that time he was living at Lion Mill (later Mount Helena), Perth, WA with his brother Patrick and his wife Amy. Lawrence lost three fingers on his left hand in a mill accident.

Lawrence is believed to have had an affair with Mabel Grace Thackrah (9th August 1896–15th June 1971) and she became pregnant in May 1914. Lawrence sought permission from Mabel's father, Albert Louis Thackrah, to marry her. This was refused because Lawrence was a Catholic and Albert was not going to allow his Protestant daughter to marry one. Lawrence was devastated. Their daughter, Marjorie Ida Thackrah (born 11th February 1915) was brought up as Albert's eleventh child. Marjorie was not aware of the true situation until her late teens. It is understood that Lawrence sent money for Marjorie's education but they never

SS *Indarra* (9,735 tons), built by William Denny & Bros at Dumbarton for the Australian United Steam Navigation Co, was launched in 1912. She arrived at Fremantle on 1st January 1913 and continued around the coast to Brisbane, calling at various ports for public inspection. She was the most palatial liner ever to serve the Australian coast. There were berths for 150 first, 200 second and 120 third class passengers. Serious problems became apparent early in her career. An eight degree list to port had to be solved by loading eighty tons of stone ballast. She was longer than previous ships, which led to difficulties manoeuvring in the docks in Melbourne and Sydney. At Albany she could not be berthed at all if there was a wind. Coaling had to be done from each side and this necessitated the ship being turned in dock. At sea *Indarra* rolled heavily and there were rumours that she was top heavy. She was requisitioned in October 1917 and converted into a troopship at Sydney. After the Armistice she repatriated British soldiers from India and other areas and also carried Australian troops home. The liner returned to civilian ownership and was chartered to the Orient Line but proved to be too slow and unreliable. In 1920 she was purchased by Compagnie Maritime Belge and renamed *Pays de Wael*. In October 1923 she was sold to Osaka Shasan Kaisha of Japan, renamed *Horai Maru* and was extensively refitted. This included removing the upper part of the superstructure to reduce the draft and made her more stable. She operated between Kobe and Keelung until war broke out in late 1941 and she was converted into a troop transport. On 1st March 1942 *Horai Maru* was attacked by Allied aircraft and warships in the Sunda Strait during the Battle of Java. She was accidently torpedoed and sunk by the Japanese ship *Ijn Mogami* when she fired six torpedoes against USS *Houston* and USS *Perth* and missed them. In 1947 the wreck was raised by Japanese salvage companies for scrap.

met. Mabel married William Charles Walker (1892–26th May 1975) at Northam, WA in 1919. He was a cleaner and they were living at 61 Central Avenue, Perth, WA in 1954 and at Princess Road, Mount Helena from 1958. Marjorie married Kevin Anthony Mannion Cruse and they had two children – David Cruse (1940) and Judith Cruse.

Lawrence served in 18th Australian Light Horse for two and a half years before war broke out. He attempted to enlist in the regular forces but was rejected due to the missing fingers on his left hand. Having informed the authorities that he had won shooting competitions at Northam Rifle Club, he was recruited on 23rd September 1914 at Blackboy Hill Camp, Helena Vale, WA. He was attested and posted to C Company, 16th Battalion on 16th October 1914 (422). Lawrence was described as a contactor, 5′ 7″ tall, weighing 182 lbs, with fair complexion, grey eyes, brown hair and his religious denomination was Roman Catholic. His next of

HMAT A40 *Ceramic* loading at Port Melbourne c.1915. SS *Ceramic* was built in Belfast for the White Star Line 1912–13 and worked the Liverpool–Australia route. In 1914 she was requisitioned and survived a number of U-boat attacks. She returned to the White Star Line to resume civilian service in November 1920. When White Star merged with Cunard in 1934, *Ceramic* was sold to Shaw, Savill & Albion, but worked the same route. In February 1940, she was requisitioned as a troopship. In the South Atlantic on 11th August she collided at speed with the cargo ship *Testbank*. Both ships were damaged, but remained afloat. *Testbank* made Cape Town under her own power. *Ceramic*'s passengers were transferred to RMS *Viceroy of India* and she was assisted to Walvis Bay in South West Africa by a tug. After emergency repairs she went to Cape Town for renovation before resuming service. On 3rd November 1942, *Ceramic* left Liverpool for Australia carrying 641 passengers and crew and 12,362 tons of cargo in Convoy ON 149. When it dispersed, she continued unescorted and at midnight on 6th/7th December was hit by a torpedo from U-*515* in mid-Atlantic. A few minutes later, two more torpedoes hit the engine room. However, she remained afloat and was abandoned in good order. Three hours later, U-*515* fired two more torpedoes, which sank her immediately. It was a stormy night and the heavy sea capsized some lifeboats. U-*515* returned to look for *Ceramic*'s Master, Herbert Elford, to ascertain the ship's destination. One lifeboat was sighted around noon, but with the storm raging, the U-boat crew seized the first available survivor, Sapper Eric Munday RE. Despite searches by neutral craft, no other survivors were picked up. Munday spent the rest of the war at Stalag VIII-B in Silesia (Australian War Memorial).

HMHS *Formosa* in the Grand Harbour, Valetta, Malta. SS *Formosa* (4,508 tons) was built by London & Glasgow Engineering & Iron Shipbuilding Co Ltd, Govan for Société Générale des Transports Maritimes à Vapeur, Marseille in 1906. She carried fifty-seven first, seventy second and forty-four third class passengers for the South America service. On 23rd June 1915 she was commissioned as a hospital ship with accommodation for 417 patients and sixty-three medical staff, including some Australians. By August she was operating between Mudros and Egypt. She resumed her civilian service in July 1919. On 25th October 1927 *Formosa* went to the assistance of the Italian liner *Principessa Mafalda*, which sank with the loss of 314 lives off Brazil.

kin was his brother, Patrick, at Lion Mill; but in some documents his brother James was nominated. He sailed from Fremantle to Melbourne aboard SS *Indarra* on 21st November and was based at Broadmeadows Camp for training. The Battalion sailed

Luna Park in Heliopolis, Cairo, Egypt opened in 1911 as the first Western-style amusement park in Africa and the Middle East. In January 1915 the buildings and grounds were converted for No.1 Australian General Hospital. Demand for bedspaces increased and the facilities were expanded to include No.1 Auxiliary Hospital in the ice-rink, with 500 beds. Further accommodation was provided in the haunted house, roundabout, scenic railroad and pavilion. The ticket office became an operating theatre. By mid May 1915 the hospital had over 1,200 beds and was treating casualties from Gallipoli. The General Hospital moved to France in July 1916. No.1 Auxiliary Hospital then closed. It was a separate organization to No.1 Australian Auxiliary Hospital, which opened at Harefield, England in March 1915. Luna Park is now covered by Roxy Square and, although a few original buildings remain, there is no trace of the former amusement park (Ellen Thompson).

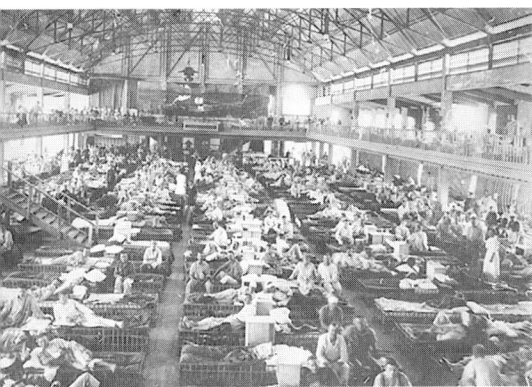

The interior of No.1 Auxiliary Hospital inside the Luna Park ice-rink. The beds, made of local palm wood, were known as angeribs (Australian War Memorial).

from Melbourne for Egypt aboard HMAT A40 *Ceramic* on 22nd December, arriving at Alexandria on 3rd February 1915.

On 12th April 1915 the Battalion embarked aboard HMT *Hyda Pasha* at Alexandria for Lemnos and took part in operations at Gallipoli from 25th April. Lawrence was promoted lance corporal on 13th May, corporal on 19th July and sergeant on 1st September. He was taken ill with diarrhoea and was admitted to 4th Australian Field Ambulance on 10th September before being transferred to No.25 Casualty Clearing Station, Imbros on 12th September. He was evacuated to Port Said aboard HMHS *Formosa*, arriving on 21st September and was treated at No.1 Auxiliary Hospital, Luna Park, Cairo until being discharged

SS *Ascanius* (10,048 tons) was built in 1910 by Workman, Clark in Belfast for the Ocean Steamship Co, Liverpool. She was leased to the Australian Commonwealth as HMAT A11 *Ascanius* until 30th July 1917 and was part of the first convoy transporting 3rd Australian Infantry Brigade to Egypt in November 1914. She completed nine trips from Australia and was later re-employed as HMT *Ascanius*. After the war she resumed a refrigerated meat service between Liverpool and Australia. *Ascanius* was also a troopship in the Second World War and, although torpedoed, made it to port for repairs. She resumed civilian service in 1946. In 1949 she was sold and renamed *San Giovannino*. She was scrapped in Italy in 1952.

to the Convalescent Camp at Helouan on 5th October. He embarked at Alexandria on 4th November and rejoined the Battalion at Gallipoli on 13th November. Lawrence was among the last in the Battalion to leave Gallipoli for Lemnos on 20th December. It moved to Alexandria, Egypt aboard HMT *Ascanius* and arrived at Tel el Kebir on 30th December.

Lawrence embarked with the Battalion at Alexandria on 1st June 1916 and disembarked at Marseille, France on 9th June. He took part in heavy fighting on the Somme around Pozières and Mouquet Farm in August. **Awarded the French Croix de Guerre with Palm for his actions at Beaumetz, France on 13th February 1917, LG 1st May 1917.** He was appointed CSM on 8th March 1917. On 2nd April he was wounded by a gunshot to the left arm near Bullecourt and was treated at 4th Australian Field Ambulance that day and at 1/1st South Midland Casualty Clearing

Codford Camp, Wiltshire was used by ANZAC forces as a training and transit depot. The AIF badge was carved into the chalk on the hillside above the camp (53 × 45m) in 1916. The soldiers of 13th Training Battalion, who had to maintain the badge, named it 'Misery Hill'. The nearby CWGC cemetery contains the graves of sixty-six New Zealanders and thirty-one Australians. The local community still feels a strong bond with the ANZAC troops and hold a remembrance ceremony on Anzac Day every year. A similar bond exists at nearby Sutton Veny (Australian War Memorial).

Station and 8th Stationary Hospital, Wimereux on 3rd April. He was evacuated to England aboard HS *Princess Elizabeth* from Boulogne and admitted to Norfolk War Hospital, Norwich on 5th April. While there he was commissioned on 10th April. On 18th May he transferred to No.1 Convalescent Depot, Perham Down, Wiltshire. He proceeded overseas from AIF Depot, Tidworth on 4th July, joined 4th Australian Division Base Depot, Le Havre on 6th July and rejoined 16th Battalion in France on 9th July.

On 1st November, Lawrence was promoted lieutenant and on 31st January 1918 he was posted to 13th Training Battalion, Codford, Wiltshire. He attended the Lewis gun course at the Australian School of Musketry, Tidworth from 21st February and qualified 1st class on 7th March. He rejoined 13th Training Battalion on 9th March and transferred to 12th Training Battalion on 11th April. He embarked at Southampton, Hampshire on 1st August and joined the Australian Infantry Base Depot, Le Havre next day. He rejoined 16th Battalion on 8th August. **Awarded the VC for his actions near Madame Wood, east of Vermandovillers, France on 23rd August 1918, LG 14th December 1918.**

On 19th November Lawrence transferred to the Divisional Liaison Party. He was taken ill with influenza and was admitted to 4th Australian Field Ambulance and No.50 Casualty Clearing Station on 23rd November. He was transferred by 28 Ambulance Train on 29th November to 8th General Hospital, Rouen on 30th November and to 39th General Hospital, Le Havre the following day. He

SS *Runic* (12,490 tons), constructed by Harland & Wolff for the White Star Line in Belfast, was launched on 25th October 1900. Her maiden voyage to Cape Town commenced on 3rd January 1901. She had an eventful life. On 25th November 1901 she towed the crippled Union Castle liner *Dunottar Castle* into Dakar. She was leased as a troopship (HMAT A54 *Runic*) during the Great War until 27th November 1917, when she operated under the Liner Requisition Scheme for the rest of the conflict. On 3rd November 1920 she collided with HMS *London* at Gourock on the Clyde. She was sold to Christian Salveson Whaling Co in 1930 and was converted to a whaling factory ship, renamed *New Sevilla*. She was torpedoed and sunk on 20th September 1940 off Islay, Scotland by *U-138*, with the loss of two crewmen.

Collins Street in Melbourne.

was discharged to the Base Depot on 31st December, joined the Australian Infantry Base Depot on 1st January 1919 and rejoined the Battalion on 7th January 1919. Lawrence was granted seventy-five days leave in Britain from 12th January 1919, during which he married. He was appointed North Dublin Union Area Officer for Australian soldiers based in Ireland on 14th April. The VC was presented by the King at Buckingham Palace on 12th July, the last Australian to receive the VC from King George V personally.

Lawrence was granted leave in London 28th November–19th December and embarked for Australia on 20th December aboard SS *Runic* as Ship's Adjutant, arriving on 29th January 1920. He was admitted to the Base Hospital, Fremantle, WA and was discharged from the Army on 6th August 1920. He transferred to the Reserve of Officers in Victoria and was attached to 59th Battalion (Militia) in Victoria from 29th October 1927.

Lawrence McCarthy married Florence 'Flossie'/'Polly' Minnie Norville (1892–15th April 1995), born at Axbridge, Somerset, on 25th January 1919 at Weston-super-Mare, Somerset. She was a wool shop assistant, living with her parents in 1911, and a housemaid in a hotel when they met while he was on an earlier leave. Polly followed Lawrence, arriving in Western Australia on 28th February 1920. They lived initially at 42 Union Street, Subiaco, WA. They were living at 73 Alma Road, St Kilda, Melbourne c.1932. They later arrived at 401 Collins Street, Melbourne, at 205 Dandenong Road, Windsor, Victoria by April 1957 and at Flat 1,

In the wake of the gold rush, land and funds were granted by the Victoria government to four religious groups, including in 1854 to the Wesleyan Methodist Church, for the establishment of colleges in Melbourne. The foundation stone was laid at the St Kilda Road campus on 4th January 1865 and the school opened on 11th January 1866. By 1896 pupils had dropped to just ninety boys and closure was threatened. The appointment of Lawrence Adamson as headmaster in 1902 saw a reversal in the school's fortunes. The St Kilda Road campus was expanded 1933–39 with a bequest from philanthropists Alfred and George Nicholas. In 1942 the campus was

requisitioned for the Australian Army and the school moved to Scotch College. The school purchased land at Syndal in 1955, which became the Junior School in 1966. Girls were admitted in 1978 and boarding ended in 1980. Wesley amalgamated with Cato College in 1986. In 1989 a fire damaged the St Kilda Road campus and the library was lost. A fire in 2016 at the Glen Waverley campus destroyed ten classrooms. Amongst its numerous famous alumni are:

- Robert Cuthbert Grieve VC.
- Australian Prime Ministers Harold Edward Holt (1908–67) and Sir Robert Gordon Menzies (1894–1978).
- Ian Johnson (1917–98) Australian Test Cricket Captain.
- Katie Mactier (born 1975) Olympic, Commonwealth and World cycling medallist.
- Mark Philippoussis (born 1976), US Open and Wimbledon tennis finalist.

14 Rosslyn Street, Hawthorn East, Victoria by June 1969, before moving to Lorne Parade, Mont Albert, Victoria in 1975. When Polly died she was cremated and her ashes interred with those of her husband at Springvale Cemetery, Melbourne.

Lawrence and Polly had a son, Lawrence Norville McCarthy (9th April 1921–20th May 1945), born in Perth, WA and educated at Wesley College, Melbourne. He enlisted in 24/39th Battalion AIF (V40561 later VX104484) on 3rd August 1941 at Seymour, described as a warehouseman, with fair hair and blue eyes. He was called up for full time duty on 31st October and was granted leave without pay 3rd–9th November. On 15th December he was promoted corporal. He made a will on 13th

Lawrence Norville McCarthy is buried in Port Moresby (Bomana) War Cemetery, Papua New Guinea in the closest block on the left of picture (Papua New Guinea Tourism).

Collins Street Independent Church in Melbourne. The first church on the site was built in 1839 and demolished in 1866 to make way for the current larger church. It was designed by Joseph Reed, who also designed Melbourne Town Hall and the Royal Exhibition Building. It was known as the Independent Church and the Congregational Church before its present name of St Michael's Uniting Church.

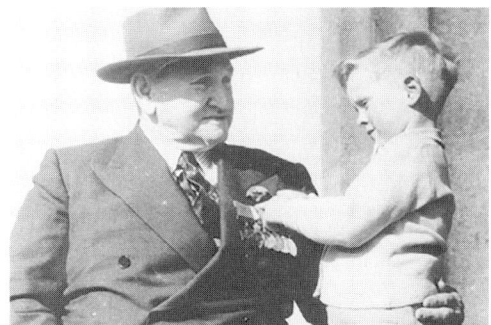

Lawrence McCarthy with Ross Bastiaan in 1956.

March 1942, leaving all his property to his father, Lawrence Joseph (sic) McCarthy. He moved to Bonegilla, Victoria by train on 25th May and transferred to the AIF, receiving a new Army number on 24th July. Lawrence joined No.3 Course at Small Arms School, Bonegilla on 28th August and returned to 24th Battalion on 11th November. He embarked on MV *Duntroon* at Brisbane on 23rd February 1943 and disembarked at Port Moresby on 1st March. On 19th April he was evacuated to 2/9th Australian General Hospital with a sprained ankle and was discharged to No.1 Australian Corps Recovery Camp on 25th April before rejoining 24th Battalion on 30th April. He attended Weapon Training Course No.2 at New Guinea Force Training School on 1st January 1944 but was evacuated to 47th Australian Camp Hospital, Goondiwindi with otitis externa of the left ear on 7th January. He transferred to 113th Australian Convalescent Depot with malaria on 19th January, was discharged to New Guinea Deployment Depot on 7th February and rejoined 24th Battalion on 10th February. Lawrence attended Weapon Training Course No.5 at the Medium Machine Gun Wing, New Guinea Force Training School 20th April–21st May and rejoined 24th Battalion on 26th June. He embarked

The Norville family home was at 37 Meadow Street, Weston-super-Mare in 1911.

on SS *Van Heutz* on 3rd August and disembarked at Townsville on 10th August. On 23rd December he was promoted lance sergeant. He embarked on SS *Van Heutz* on 29th December and disembarked as Torokina on 2nd January 1945. He joined 3rd Australian Division Training School for Booby Traps, Mines and Demolitions Course No.2, 29th January–9th February. Lawrence was killed in action on 20th May 1945 on Bougainville Island. He was buried in the field on 22nd May and was reburied on 15th July in Torokina War Cemetery. His remains were subsequently moved again and are buried in Port Moresby (Bomana) War Cemetery, Papua New Guinea (CIA18). Lawrence senior's Catholic religion lapsed after the death of his son and thereafter attended the Independent Church, Collins Street, Melbourne.

Lawrence junior was engaged to Nancy (died 1997 aged seventy-three), who married Jan Bastiaan (died 2007 aged eighty-six) and they had a son, Ross J Bastiaan (born January 1951). Ross studied dentistry in London and qualified as a periodontist in 1977, eventually running three practices in Melbourne. Lawrence McCarthy became a defacto grandfather to Ross and was known by him as Uncle

The Sunshine Harvester Works at Braybrook (Sunshine from 1907), Melbourne, was founded by industrialist Hugh Victor McKay (1865–1926) in 1906 and was named after his Sunshine Harvester, the first commercially successful combine harvester. The factory became the largest in the Southern Hemisphere and by 1911 the workforce had expanded to 1,500. At its peak it employed nearly 3,000 workers and Sunshine was known as the 'Birmingham of Australia'. In 1907 a dispute between McKay and the unions went to court, which ruled McKay was to pay his employees a wage that guaranteed a standard of living that was reasonable for 'a human being in a civilised community'. McKay appealed successfully but the judgment became a benchmark industrial decision, leading to the creation of a minimum wage for workers and dominated Australian industrial relations for the next eighty years. The Works developed the world's first self-propelled harvester in 1924. In 1930 Canadian farm machinery manufacturer Massey Harris bought a controlling interest in HV McKay Propriety Ltd and the Australian operations merged under the title HV McKay Massey Harris Pty Ltd. During the Second World War the company exported 20,000 Sunshine drills, disc harrows and binders to Britain to help increase food production. In the 1950s the McKays sold out to Massey Ferguson, a combination of the Canadian and American interests of Massey Harris and the British tractor firm of Harry Ferguson. However, in the 1970s the business contracted and most of the factory was demolished in 1992. The former bulk store, factory gates, clock tower, pedestrian footbridge, factory gardens and head office are listed on the Victorian Heritage Register.

Dom. He helped to finance Ross's education at Wesley College, following in the footsteps of his natural son. Ross was appointed Deputy Chairman of the Australian War Memorial in 2003 and was made a Member of the Order of Australia in 2006. He has erected over 200 bronze commemorative plaques around the world where Australian troops fought, including a special one at Vermandovillers close to where Lawrence McCarthy won his VC. He is also a colonel in the Australian Army Reserve.

Polly's father, Arthur Ernest Norville (1861–1926), married Rosina Harriett née House (1862–1938), a tailoress, in 1881 at Axbridge, Somerset, England. Rosina had a son prior to her marriage, Gilbert Norville House (1881–1968). Gilbert was an upholstery journeyman in 1901 and married Pamela Lizzie Lock (1883–1966), born at Upton, Worcestershire, in 1908. He changed his name to Norville and served in the Wiltshire Regiment during the Great War (26472). They had two daughters and were living at 32 Glendor Gardens, Hendon, Middlesex in 1939. She died at Battle, Sussex and he at Hastings, Sussex. Arthur and Rosina were living at 56 Alfred Street, Weston-super-Mare in 1891 and at 37 Orchard Street, Weston-super-Mare in 1901 and 1911. By 1911 Arthur was a master tailor. In addition to Polly they had five children, including:

- Ada Geraldine J Norville (1884–1960) was a milliner in 1901. She married Evan Hughes (born c.1877), born at Llantwit Fardre, Glamorgan, in 1908 at Bridgend, Glamorgan. Evan enlisted in the Royal Artillery at Tonyrefail on 11th December 1915 (189269), described as 5′ 4″ tall, weighing 129 lbs, with light brown hair and brown eyes. He transferred to the Army Reserve the following day. On 28th September 1916 he was examined by a medical board and was mobilised on 1st December. Next day he was posted to No.2 Depot RFA, Preston, Lancashire as a driver and the following day to No.8 Reserve Battery RFA. He transferred to the ASC Remounts on 13th March 1917 (310862) and was posted to Ormskirk, Lancashire on 11th May. On 16th July he was posted to Shirehampton Remount

The Trustees, Executors & Agency Co Ltd building on Collins Street, Melbourne.

Depot, Bristol. He was graded Medical Category C1 (garrison duty at home) and was upgraded to Category B1 (lines of communication in France) on 9th October. He was admitted to Shirehampton Hospital on 5th June 1918 and transferred to the Class Z Reserve at Woolwich Dockyard on 5th April 1919. Ada was boarding at 2 Coombe Road, Weston-super-Mare in 1939, recorded as married but her husband was not with her. They had two sons – Evan Haydn Hughes (1909–73) and Edgar Norville Hughes (born and died 1911).

* George Louis Norville (1887–1925) married Edith Mary Morris (17th March 1890–25th May 1977), born at Pancras, London, in 1915. She was living at 37 Woodman Road, Coulsdon, Surrey in 1939. She died at the Royal West Sussex Hospital, Chichester, Sussex.
* Nelly/Nellie Rose Norville (13th March 1890–1977) married Arthur Harold Penberthy (2nd December 1889–5th May 1970) in 1915. Arthur was an electrical engineer and they were living at Newton Hayes, Norris Green, Callington, Cornwall at the time of his death there. She died at Weston-super-Mare.
* Gladys Beatrice Norville (16th January 1898–5th July 1976) never married. She was living at 19 Upper Bristol Road, Weston-super-Mare at the time of her death.

Lawrence was endorsed as the Labor Party candidate for the Legislative Assembly seat of Swan for the election on 12th March 1921. However, he was again admitted to the Base Hospital in Fremantle and had to resign. In January 1924 he was appointed manager of the RSL League Employment Office and was elected honorary secretary of the North Perth-Mount Lawley sub-branch. As a result of an illegal Digger's Tipping Competition being run on RSL premises, Lawrence resigned his position on 24th November 1926. The extent of his involvement was never clearly ascertained. There were moves to have him expelled from the RSL completely but there were insufficient votes in the Executive to achieve this. However, with a cloud hanging over him, Lawrence decided to move to Melbourne for a fresh start and the family departed on 21st May 1927. Lawrence joined the staff of HV McKay Sunshine Harvester Works, working mostly as a commercial traveller in the Mallee region of Victoria. In 1934 the Depression forced staff reductions and Lawrence was employed until his retirement in 1969 as superintendent (caretaker) of the Trustees, Executors & Agency Co Ltd building, 401 Collins Street, Melbourne. He and Polly made morning tea for the staff and clients and lived in a flat on the roof of the building. Lawrence attended a number of significant events/celebrations connected with the VC:

* Banquet at Government House, Western Australia, in honour of the Prince of Wales on 3rd July 1920.
* Anzac Dinner on 23rd April 1927, hosted by Lieutenant General Sir John Monash GCMG KCB VD, attended by twenty-three VCs. The others were – TL Axford, A Borella, WE Brown, G Cartwright, WM Currey, H Dalziel, JJ Dwyer, JP Hamilton,

GJ Howell, GM Ingram, WD Joynt, TJB Kenny, AD Lowerson, SR McDougall, RV Moon, W Peeler, W Ruthven, PC Statton, AP Sullivan, ET Towner, JW Whittle and J Woods. For an unknown reason the Duke of York was not invited.
* ANZAC Commemoration Service on 25th April 1927 at the Exhibition Building, Melbourne in the presence of the Duke of York (future King George VI) and the march past. The other VCs who attended were – TL Axford, A Borella, J Carroll, G Cartwright, WM Currey, H Dalziel, JJ Dwyer, BS Gordon, RC Grieve, GJ Howell, GM Ingram, W Jackson, WD Joynt, TJB Kenny, AD Lowerson, SR McDougall, RV Moon, W Peeler, I Smith, PC Statton, AP Sullivan, ET Towner and J Woods.
* VC Centenary Celebrations at Hyde Park, London on 26th June 1956. He travelled on SS *Orcades* with other Australian VCs.
* Official opening by the Governor General, Lord De L'Isle VC, of the VC Corner at the Australian War Memorial in 1964, with seventeen other Australian VC's.

Lawrence returned to Gallipoli in 1965 to mark the 50th anniversary of the landings. Following retirement in 1969, he and Polly moved to a small house in Mont Albert, Melbourne. He was admitted to the Repatriation General Hospital, Heidelberg, Melbourne, where he died three weeks later on 25th May 1975. His funeral, with full military honours, was held at the Wycliffe Anglican Church, Surrey Hills, Melbourne and he was cremated at Springvale Crematorium on 28th May. His ashes were interred at Springvale Cemetery, Melbourne (Section C, Plot 015). He is commemorated in a number of other places:

* Australian Capital Territory
    ○ Australian Victoria Cross Recipients plaque on the Victoria Cross Memorial, Campbell, dedicated on 24th July 2000.
    ○ Named on one of eleven plaques honouring 175 men from overseas awarded the VC for the Great War. The plaques were unveiled by the Senior Minister

Lawrence McCarthy died at Heidelberg Repatriation Hospital, Melbourne.

of State at the Foreign & Commonwealth Office and Minister for Faith and Communities, Baroness Warsi, at a reception at Lancaster House, London on 26th June 2014 attended by the Duke of Kent and relatives of the VC recipients. The Australian plaque is at the Australian War Memorial.
- Display in the Hall of Valour, Australian War Memorial.
- McCarthy Place, Canberra.
- Western Australia
  - RSL Branch, 164 Avon Terrace, York – McCarthy VC Memorial Garden, the latter was dedicated by Reg McCarthy on 25th April 2007.
  - McCarthy, Place, York.
  - York District Honour Board at York Town Hall.
  - LT LD McCarthy VC Handicap Pace-York Harness Racing Club pacing race (2,150m) run each November at Northam Harness Racing Club's track at Burwood Park, Northam.
  - Plaque at the State War Memorial, King's Park, Perth dedicated on 26th January 1996.
  - The wards at Hollywood Private Hospital, Perth are named after VCs and GCs, including Lawrence McCarthy.
- Victoria
  - McCarthy Street, Wodonga on White Box Rise estate, built on land formerly part of Bandiana Army Camp.
  - Victoria Cross Memorial, Springvale Botanical Cemetery, Melbourne, Victoria unveiled on 10th November 2013.
  - Victoria Cross Monument, Esplanade & Albert Street, Alfred Square, St Kilda dedicated on 21st April 1985.
- New South Wales
  - Victoria Cross Memorial, Queen Victoria Building, George Street, Sydney dedicated on 23rd February 1992 to commemorate the visit of Queen Elizabeth II and Prince Phillip on the occasion of the Sesquicentenary of the City of Sydney. Sir Roden Cutler VC AK KCMG, Edward Kenna VC and Keith Payne VC were in attendance.
  - Victoria Cross Recipients Wall, North Bondi War Memorial donated to the community of Waverley on 27th November 2011 by The Returned & Services League of Australia.
- Communities and Local Government commemorative paving stones for the 145 VCs born in Australia, Belgium, Canada, China, Denmark, Egypt, France, Germany, India, Iraq, Japan, Nepal, Netherlands, Newfoundland, New Zealand, Pakistan, South Africa, Sri Lanka, Ukraine and United States of America were unveiled at the National Memorial Arboretum, Alrewas, Staffordshire by Prime Minister David Cameron MP and Sergeant Johnson Beharry VC on 5th March 2015.
- Plaque by Ross Bastiaan on the outside wall of the village school, Vermandovillers, France, dedicated on 23rd August 1993, the 75th anniversary of the VC action.

In addition to the VC he was awarded the 1914–15 Star, British War Medal 1914–20, Victory Medal 1914–19, George VI Coronation Medal 1937, Elizabeth II Coronation Medal 1953 and the French Croix de Guerre with Bronze Palme. There is a palm device from a Belgian Croix de Guerre on the ribbon of the Victory Medal. The medals were presented to the Australian War Memorial by his widow and are held in the Hall of Valour, Australian War Memorial, Treloar Crescent, Campbell, Australian Capital Territory.

12311 PRIVATE HUGH McIVER
2nd Battalion, The Royal Scots (Lothian Regiment)

Hugh McIver was born on 21st July 1890 at 30 Napier Street, Linwood, Kilbarchan, Paisley, Renfrewshire, Scotland. His father, Hugh McIver (c.1855–31st March 1919), born at Linwood, was an iron miner boarding with Mary Kennedy and her family at 2 Redan, Kilbarchan, Renfrewshire in 1881. He married Mary née Flynn (c.1860–4th September 1929), also born at Linwood, on 2nd October 1884 at St Margaret's Roman Catholic Church, Johnstone, Renfrewshire. She was a mill worker living with her parents in 1881 and was a thread mill hand at the time  of her marriage. Hugh was a shale miner and they were both living at Napier Street, Linwood at that time. The family moved to Newton Hallside, Glasgow, Lanarkshire in 1894 and was living at 34 Dunlop Street, Newton Hallside, Glasgow in 1899.

Hugh senior died from a fractured skull and abdominal injuries following a fall of stones from a roof at No.1 Pit, Newton Colliery, Cambuslang, Lanarkshire. Mary died at 19 Clyde Street, Cambuslang. In addition to Hugh they had seven other children:

- Margaret 'Maggie' McIver (28th February 1886–1967), born at 12 Napier Street, Linwood, married William McLaren (23rd December 1883–27th November 1920), a coal miner, on 26th October 1906 at St Charles Roman Catholic Chapel, Newton, Cambuslang. He was born at Johnstone, Renfrewshire and died at 32 Dunlop Street, Newton. Maggie married

Hugh's parents married at St Margaret's Roman Catholic Church in October 1884. It was built in 1852 but was greatly altered and reconstructed to designs by Messrs Pugin & Pugin in the late 1870s.

Thomas Loughrie (born c.1886) in 1926 at St Charles Roman Catholic Chapel. She died at Cambuslang. Maggie had seven children from her two marriages including:
- Mary McLaren (1907–88) married James Bloomer (1903–88), a steel worker born at 98 Hallside, Cambuslang, in 1927 at St Charles Roman Catholic Chapel, Newton. He was living at 36 Hallside and she at 27 Clyde Street at the time. They adopted a daughter.
- Margaret 'Peggy' McLaren (1909–2004) married Andrew Feeney (born c.1900), born at Renfrew, in 1931 at St Charles Roman Catholic Chapel, Newton. Peggy died at Cambuslang.
- James McLaren (1914–96), born at Newton and died at Rutherglen, Glasgow, Lanarkshire.
- Catherine 'Cassie' McLaren (1917–94) married Alexander McNeil (c.1908–c.1990) in 1937 at St Charles Roman Catholic Chapel, Newton. He was born and died at Cambuslang. They had five children.
- Williamina Loughrie (1927–2009) never married.
• John McIver (15th October 1888–21st January 1892) was born at Linwood, Renfrewshire.
• Patrick McIver (21st June 1892–17th March 1956), born at 30 Napier Street, Linwood, married Mary Kelly (1896–1943) on 4th March 1919. They had six children including:
  - Possibly Margaret McIver (born 1920), born at Cambuslang.
  - Hugh McIver (1922–71), born at Ashington, Northumberland, married Eva Alice Gertrude Maund (1922–2009), born at Kingston-upon-Hull, Yorkshire, in 1946 at St Joseph, Leyton Marshes, Essex. Hugh died at Cambuslang and Eva at Corsham, Wiltshire. They had six children.
  - Patricia McIver (1928–47), born at Cambuslang.
  - George McIver (born 1931).
  - Josephine McIver (1933–2001), born in Glasgow, married Patrick Kearney (17th March 1931–1998) in 1955 at St Charles Roman Catholic Chapel, Newton, Cambuslang, Lanarkshire. They emigrated to Australia, arriving in Sydney, New South Wales in October 1967. They both died at Albion Park Rail, Wollongong, New South Wales. They had three children.
• Mary McIver (15th June 1894–1974), born at 15 Dunlop Street, Newton, Cambuslang, never married.
• Catherine 'Kate' McIver (2nd July 1896–21st December 1948), a pithead worker, married James Farrell (c.1894–3rd September 1933), a coal hewer, on 9th April 1920 at Cambuslang. They had seven children including:
  - Bridget Farrell (born and died 1922).
  - Hugh Farrell (1923–98).
  - John Farrell (1925–2002).

- ○ Margaret Farrell (1928–2006) married James Donnelly Williamson (1926–92), born at Lesmahagow, at Cambuslang in 1949. He died at Martha Street, Glasgow and she at Cambuslang.
- Bridget McIver (born 2nd July 1897), born at 15 Dunlop Street, Newton, Cambuslang, married James McAuley (born c.1898), a steel worker, on 1st September 1922 at St Charles Roman Catholic Chapel, Newton. They had a daughter, Mary Flynn McAuley, in 1922.
- Jane McIver (27th October 1899–1998), born at 34 Dunlop Street, Newton, married James McGuinness (28th March 1896–c.1964), a coal miner born at Inkerman, Renfrewshire, on 27th October 1922 at St Charles Roman Catholic Chapel, Newton. He was a paper maker when he enlisted in the Royal Navy as an ordinary seaman (J80524) on 31st October 1917, described as 5′ 2½″ tall, with fair hair, blue eyes and fresh complexion. He served on HMS *Vivid I* and HMS *Resolution* 27th February 1918–12th January 1919. He deserted on 27th January and spent fourteen days in the cells. James was demobilised on 7th April 1919. They both died at Westburn, Cambuslang. They had four children including – Francis McGuinness (1923–96) and Joseph McGuinness (1933–2001).

Hugh's paternal grandfather, also Hugh McIver (born c.1816) was born in Ireland. He married Margaret née Morrison (c.1819–25th April 1877), also born in Ireland. She died at Kilbarchan, Renfrewshire. In addition to Hugh they had two other children, both born in Ireland – Catherine McIver c.1843 and Mary McIver c.1845.

His maternal grandfather, Patrick Flynn (also been seen as Flinn) (c.1820–20th January 1894), an agricultural labourer, was born in Ireland. He married Mary

Hugh's maternal grandparents married at the Abbey Church, Paisley, Renfrewshire in June 1848. A community was founded on the site in the 7th century, probably by Saint Mirin/Mirren. A charter for a priory was issued in 1163 and thirteen monks came from Much Wenlock, Shropshire to found the community. Paisley grew rapidly and the priory was raised to the status of an abbey in 1245. In 1307, Edward I of England burned it down but it was rebuilt later in the century. William Wallace, who was born nearby in Elderslie, is believed to have been educated in the abbey. In 1316, Marjorie Bruce, daughter of Robert I and wife of Walter Stewart, High Steward of Scotland, fell from her horse and was taken to Paisley Abbey as she was heavily pregnant. In the Abbey she gave birth to the future King Robert II by caesarean section. She was later buried there. There were a number of fires and collapses in the 15th and 16th centuries, which left the building partly ruined. It was reconstructed between 1858 and 1928. Paisley Abbey is the burial place of all six High Stewards of Scotland. King Robert III (c.1337/40 – 4th April 1406), who ruled from 1390, is also buried in the Abbey.

née Rafferty (c.1824–2nd March 1889), also born in Ireland, on 4th June 1848 at the Abbey Church, Paisley, Renfrewshire, Scotland. They were living at Napier's House, Kilbarchan, Renfrewshire in 1861, at Napier's Land, Linwood in 1871 and at 12 Napier Street, Kilbarchan in 1881. She died at 13 Napier Street, Linwood and he at 2 Bridge Street, Linwood. In addition to Mary they had four other children:

- Catherine Flynn (born c.1849).
- Bridget Flynn (born c.1855), a mill worker in 1881, married James McGinnis (born c.1848), an iron miner, on 1st January 1884 at St Margaret's Roman Catholic Church, Johnstone, Renfrewshire.
- James Flynn (22nd April 1857–1927) was a pithead man in 1881.
- Jane Flynn (1867–1949), birth registered as Flinn, was a mill worker in 1881. She married Barnard Lafferty in 1901 at Linwood.

Hugh was educated at St Charles' Roman Catholic School, Newton, Glasgow, Lanarkshire. From 1904 he worked as a miner at Newton No.1 Pit, Cambuslang, Lanarkshire, owned by Messrs James Dunlop & Co. He enlisted in the Highland Light Infantry Special Reserve on 26th March 1914 but was discharged after just fifty-five days on 19th May. His character was assessed as 'Bad' and he was considered unlikely to make a special reservist. On 18th August 1914 he enlisted in 12th Royal Scots at Glencorse, Midlothian, described as 5' 4½" tall, weighing 135 lbs, with fresh complexion, blue eyes, fair hair and his religious denomination was Roman Catholic. He declared his previous service and being discharged due to conviction, but gave no details.

Glencorse Barracks, just outside Penicuik, Midlothian, is one of three barracks making up the Edinburgh Garrison. The current buildings, constructed in 1803, were first used to house French prisoners of war. It was known as Greenlaw Military Prison and the only building from that time is the former guardroom, which is now the clocktower. The site was acquired by the War Office in 1812 and additional buildings were erected to house 6,000 prisoners and their guards. The facilities were little used until 1875, when they were converted into an infantry barracks. It became the depot for the 1st Regiment of Foot (Royal Scots), following the Cardwell Reforms. From 1960 the barracks were the Lowland Brigade Depot infantry training centre. In 1970 the Scottish Division was formed and junior soldiers moved to Aberdeen, while adult recruits moved to the new Scottish Division Depot at Glencorse Barracks. The barracks underwent a £60M reconstruction and since 2006 has been the base for The Royal Highland Fusiliers, 2nd Battalion, The Royal Regiment of Scotland. In November 2016 the MOD announced that the site would close in 2032.

At Aldershot, Hampshire on 20th October he made an improper remark to a non commissioned officer while in a drunken state and was confined to barracks for seven days. At Alton, Hampshire he was fined two days pay for being absent from tattoo until 10.20 p.m. on 28th December. He sailed for France on 11th May 1915 and became runner to Captain Alick 'Tam' Gordon MC & Bar DCM MM. He was admitted to 29th Field Ambulance with rheumatism on 17th March 1916, transferred to 27th Field Ambulance on the same day with myalgia and returned to duty on 23rd March. He was admitted to 27th Field Ambulance on 25th March with pyrexia of unknown origin (trench fever), transferred to 1st Field Ambulance on 1st April and was passed fit for duty on 8th April. He returned to the Battalion on 11th April.

Awarded the MM for his actions on 14th July 1916 during an attack on Longueval. The Battalion attacked with 11th Battalion, was caught by shell fire passing the western side of Montauban and suffered heavy casualties, LG 21st September 1916. He received a shrapnel wound to the right buttock on 12th October 1917 and was admitted to 28th Field Ambulance and No.64 Casualty Clearing Station. He was evacuated to England on 19th October and was on the strength of the Depot from 20th October while in hospital at Fort Pitt, Chatham, Kent. He transferred to hospital at Shoeburyness, Essex 4th–12th November and to the Scottish Command Depot on 24th November. Hugh joined 3rd Battalion at Mullingar, Ireland on 16th January 1918. He was passed fit for duty on 4th February at the Military Hospital, Mullingar and returned to France on 12th February 1918. He joined the Base Depot on 16th February and joined the 2nd Battalion on 23rd February.

Awarded a Bar to the MM for his actions on 15th July 1918 at Locon during a daylight patrol. He was in a party with Lieutenant Somerville, Sergeant Fraser and Lance Corporal McDonald, when they crawled through a belt

3rd (Reserve) Battalion, Royal Scots was based at Mullingar in Co Westmeath, Ireland from late 1917 until the end of the war.

VC memorial at Hawkhead Cemetery, Paisley.

Hugh McIver's grave in Vraucourt Copse Cemetery. Also buried there is Richmond Gordon Howell-Price MC. He was one of four brothers who served in the war, three of whom died. Between them they were awarded the DSC, four DSOs, three MCs and five MIDs.

of corn and captured four Germans, LG 21st October 1918. Awarded the VC for his actions at Courcelles-le-Comte, France, on 23rd August 1918, LG 15th November 1918. On 2nd September 1918 near Courcelles he was moving up a hill close to Captain Gordon to attack some machine guns when he was shot and killed. Gordon removed the MM ribbon and rosette from Hugh's chest and sent it to his mother with a letter of condolence. Hugh is buried in Vraucourt Copse Cemetery, Pas de Calais, France – I A 19.

The VC and MM & Bar were presented to his parents by the King at Buckingham Palace on 13th February 1919. Hugh is commemorated in a number of other places:

- Renfrewshire
    - Memorial at Hawkhead Cemetery, Paisley, Renfrewshire to the men of Paisley awarded the VC, dedicated on 26th June 2007.
    - Hugh McIver Avenue, Hawkhead Village, Paisley.
- Lanarkshire
    - Memorial to Glasgow VCs outside Glasgow Cathedral.
    - Family headstone in Westburn Cemetery, Old Mill Road, Cambuslang.
    - Cambuslang War Memorial.
    - Memorial arch in Hamilton to the sixteen Lanarkshire VCs. The others commemorated are – Frederick Aikman, William Angus, Thomas Caldwell, Donald Cameron, John Carmichael, William Clamp, William Gardner, John Hamilton, David Lauder, Graham Lyall, David MacKay, William Milne, John O'Neill, William Reid and James Richardson.

Biographies 137

Glasgow VC memorial outside the Cathedral.

McIver family grave in Westburn Cemetery, Cambuslang.

Memorial arch in Hamilton, Lanarkshire to the sixteen Lanarkshire VCs (Memorials to Valour).

Hugh McIver's memorial (bottom left) in front of the Mairie in Courcelles-le-Comte.

- Display at the Regimental Museum, Edinburgh Castle, Midlothian.
- Department for Communities and Local Government commemorative paving stones were dedicated at Linwood Community Centre and Library, Bridge Street, Linwood, Renfrewshire and Cambuslang Remembrance Garden, Hamilton Road, Toll Pitch, Glasgow on 23rd August 2018.
- Memorial unveiled by his fifteen years old great, great nephew, James Kellock, at the war memorial in Courcelles-le-Comte, France on 23rd August 2008. The ceremony was attended by a detachment from 1st Battalion, Royal Regiment of Scotland. The following day a service was held at his graveside.
- Ring of Remembrance (L'Anneau de la Mémoire), Ablain-Saint-Nazaire, Pas-de-Calais, France.

Cover of the 18th November 1972 Victor (Victor Comic).

The Royal Scots Museum within Edinburgh Castle.

- His VC action featured in Issue 613 of the Victor Comic entitled 'A VC for the Royal Scots' dated 18th November 1972.

In addition to the VC and MM & Bar he was awarded the 1914–15 Star, British War Medal 1914–20 and Victory Medal 1914–19. The VC was listed for sale in a coin and medal magazine for £2,065 by AD Hamilton in Glasgow, Lanarkshire on 1st January 1974. This was spotted by Major George Breach RA, HQ Lowland Area who notified the Royal Scots and the Regiment purchased it. The other medals were secured later. The VC is held by The Royal Scots Museum, Edinburgh Castle, Midlothian.

63514 LANCE CORPORAL GEORGE ONIONS
1st Battalion, The Devonshire Regiment

George Onions was born on 2nd March 1883 at Wellington Street, Bilston, Staffordshire. His father, Zachariah 'Zacary' Webb Onions (14th October 1857–27th August 1921), born at West Bromwich, Staffordshire, married Amy Susan née Skemp (14th March 1856–16th September 1884) on 23rd July 1880 at Wood Street Chapel, Bilston, where she was born. Amy was a descendant of Jan Ridd, who appears in the historical romantic novel *Lorna Doone*. Zachariah was the manager of an ironworks in 1881 Census and they were living at 27 High Street,

George Onions' parents and paternal grandparents were living on High Street, Bilston in 1881. His maternal grandparents were living there in 1871.

Bilston. He married Jane M Farquhar (20th April 1861–1927), born in Edinburgh, Midlothian, Scotland, on 15th October 1887 at Tynemouth, Northumberland. By 1891 they were living at 37 Bayley Street, Stalybridge, Cheshire, where he was an iron works manager. The family moved to Pontypool, Monmouthshire between 1894 and 1897. In 1901 they were living at Wainfelin, Abersychan, Monmouthshire, where he was a sheet iron works manager. In 1911 the family was living at 58 Liverpool Road, Chester, Cheshire but Jane was not present at the time of the Census. He later moved to White Lodge, 7 Church Road, Edgbaston, Birmingham, where he died. George had eight siblings from his father's two marriages:

- Eliza Onions (1881–1901) was born at Moxley, Staffordshire and died at Pontypool, Monmouthshire.
- Archibald 'Archie' Robert Farquhar Onions (8th September 1888–1962), born at Wallsend on Tyne, Northumberland, was an engineer mechanic in 1911. He served as a trooper (D9387) in 7th (Princess Royal's) Dragoon Guards, enlisting in August 1914. He was awarded the DCM as a stretcher-bearer for rescuing several wounded under intense shelling and on one occasion for carrying a man on his back, LG 26th June 1918. Archie married Elsie May Bernard Horrey (30th May 1892–24th November 1976), born at Grimsby, Lincolnshire, on 3rd June 1920

at Leeds, Yorkshire. She died in Manchester, Lancashire. They had a daughter, Christine Onions, in 1921 at Wolverhampton, Staffordshire. Archie and Elsie were living at 4 Manly Road, Manchester, Lancashire in 1939. She was recorded as 'incapacitated' and he was an engineer in a telephone company. During the Second World War he served as an Air Raid Precautions warden and signalling communicator. It is assumed that the marriage ended in divorce. Archie married Gladys Bentley in 1943 at Barton upon Irwell, Lancashire. He died at Andover, Hampshire. Archie and Elsie had three children:
- Christine Onions (1921–97) married Frank Bradshaw (1920–99) in 1945 at Manchester. They had two children.
- William J Onions (born 1922).
- Austen Robert Onions (1924–2000) was commissioned in the Royal Army Ordnance Corps on 15th July 1945 (354411) and was promoted war substantive lieutenant on 15th April 1946. He last appears in the Army List April-June 1947.

- Amy Barbara Onions (13th June 1890–1970) was born at Stalybridge, Cheshire. She emigrated to Canada where she married John Irvin Thomas Scallon (1st June 1895–16th July 1972), born at Wincanton, Somerset, in Alberta. He was living with his mother and siblings at 38 Norham Road, Oxford in 1901. John enlisted on 25th August 1916 as a 2nd air mechanic RFC (47357), described as a Sun Insurance clerk and motor cyclist. He joined at South Farnborough on 28th August and applied for a commission in the RFC but was rejected due to defective eyesight. He was ordered to join No.10 Officer Cadet Battalion, Gailes, Irvine, Ayrshire on 30th July 1917 but was unable to do so due to medical issues. However, he was commissioned in the Hampshire Regiment on 28th November. A medical board on 19th February 1918 found him fit for General Service. He embarked at Taranto, Italy on 20th May and disembarked at Salonica on 23rd May. He was posted to No.1 Base Depot on 26th May and to 10th Hampshire next day, joining on 31st May. He attended a course at 27th Division Grenade School on 7th June. On 21st June he was admitted to 63rd General Hospital with impetigo and transferred to 20th Stationary Hospital with scabies later the same day. He was discharged to the Infantry Base Depot on 5th July and rejoined the Battalion on 18th July. He was attached to HQ XII Corps Ammunition Column RFA on 10th October and was admitted to 28th General Hospital not yet diagnosed on 6th November. Approval for the Y Scheme (removal of those with malaria to a healthier environment) was granted on 7th December. He embarked at Salonica on HMHS *Gloucester Castle* on 30th December, arriving at Southampton on 10th January 1919. A medical board on 15th January at 5th Southern General Hospital, Portsmouth found him unfit for General Service for three months and for Home Service for one and a half months. Leave was granted to 27th February. Medical boards on 31st March and 17th April found him unfit for General Service for three months but fit for Home Service and on the latter occasion also for Garrison

Service abroad. A medical board on 22nd July found him fit for General Service and he embarked at Liverpool on 7th September, disembarking at Bombay on 1st October. He embarked at Bombay on SS *Vita* on 4th October and disembarked at Basrah, Mesopotamia on 10th October. He served with the Local Audit Office, Military Accounts Department, Basrah as a temporary captain from 23rd October. John was demobilised and relinquished his commission in Mesopotamia on 18th April 1920 to take up civil employment there. He retained the rank of lieutenant. He worked for the Director of Civil Stores, Civil Commissioner, Baghdad as a local audit officer. By August 1923 his address was c/o Reverend Harold Edward Scallon, St Paul's Mission House, Gough Lake Mission, Hartshorn, Alberta, Canada. There was protracted correspondence between him and the War Office over the alleged overpayment of £60/19/9, resulting from him overdrawing his pay after a pay increase and the addition of staff pay while serving in Mesopotamia. This went on into late 1925 when it was realised that he was not going to make the refund and, as he lived in Canada, nothing further could be achieved. He disputed the overpayment throughout. Amy and John were living at 121st Street, Jasper, Edmonton, Alberta in October 1928. They returned to Britain aboard RMS *Ascania*, arriving on 8th December 1931. John was an accountant and became Secretary of Vosper Ltd, Portsmouth, Hampshire. They were living at 79 High Street, Portsmouth, Hampshire in 1939, when they were both Air Raid Precaution wardens. He was awarded the MBE, LG 12th June 1958. Amy died at Herriard, Basingstoke, Hampshire and John at Alton, Hampshire. They had a son:
    ○ David Patrick Lindsay Scallon (1921–92), born in Canada, was a journalistic pupil in 1939, boarding with Arnold L Hodges, a journalist, at 20 Causeway, Horsham, Sussex. David was living at Brick Kiln Cottage, The Avenue, Herriard, near Basingstoke at the time of his death there.
- Margaret Jean Farquhar Onions (23rd April 1892–20th May 1968), born at Stalybridge, married Alan Symes (9th July 1889–28th December 1962), born at Chelsea, London, on 27th June 1918 at Edgbaston Parish Church, Warwickshire. He was commissioned in 3rd Dorsetshire on 22nd May 1915 and was promoted lieutenant on 1st July 1917. He was stationed as Westham Camp, Weymouth, Dorset at the time of his marriage. They emigrated to Canada in 1935 and were living at 199 Chapel Street, Ottawa, Ontario in 1940, at March Road RR1, Britannia Bay, Ottawa, Ontario in October 1941, at Saskatoon, Saskatchewan in 1942, c/o The Rectory, Onoway, Alberta in June 1943 and at 580 Mariposa Road, Rockcliffe, Ottawa, Ontario in November 1943. They returned to England. He was a civil servant in 1955 and they were living at Whitehill, near Borden, Hampshire. They both died on the Isle of Wight, Hampshire. They had a son:
    ○ Alan John Farquhar Symes (1921–43), born in Birmingham, Warwickshire, was educated at Westward Ho School, Somerset 1928–35, Garneau High School, Edmonton, Alberta 1935–39 and Lisgar Collegiate, Ottawa 1940.

He served as a trooper in 19th Alberta Dragoons (553) 16th November–7th December 1939. He was living at 199 Chapel Street, Ottawa, Ontario, while his permanent address was 12217–108th Avenue, Edmonton, Alberta, when he attested for the Royal Canadian Air Force at the RCAF Recruiting Centre, 90 O'Connor Street, Ottawa, Ontario on 20th August 1940. He took the oath on 18th November (R82041) and was described as 6' tall, weighing 158 lbs, with fair complexion, hazel eyes, fair hair and his religious denomination was Anglican. He was taken on strength of No.1 Manning Depot, Toronto on 19th November as an aircraftman class 2. He joined No.1 Auxiliary Manning Depot, Picton on 10th December, RCAF Station Rockcliffe on 3rd January 1941 and 12 Training School, Toronto on 7th April. He was promoted leading aircraftman on 15th May and next day commenced pupil pilot flying and ground training on Course No.28 at No.11 Elementary Flying Training School (FTS), Cap-de-la-Madeline, Québec until 3rd July, flying a Fleet Finch 2. As a result he was considered suitable for commissioned rank and for training as a pilot and secondarily as an air observer. Alan attended Course No.32 at No.8 Service FTS, RCAF Moncton, New Brunswick 3rd July–13th September, flying an Anson. He qualified as a pilot, was promoted temporary sergeant (paid) and was commissioned as a pilot officer, all on 13th September 1941 (J/7617). He was posted to Central Flying School, Trenton, Southern Ontario on 15th September and attended the Flying Instructors (Advanced) Course there 2nd October–12th December 1941. On 14th October he applied for an appointment in the Special Reserve. On 31st December he was posted to No.8 Service FTS, RCAF Moncton, New Brunswick as a flying instructor. He was granted annual leave 19th–30th March 1942. On 15th May he took off in a Harvard accompanied by a student pilot. During the latter stages of the flight he struck a tree in a low flying area, contrary to Command Instructions by failing to pull out at a minimum height of 250' above all obstacles. As a result he was placed in open arrest and remanded by his CO next day for taking of a summary of evidence. He was charged with negligently flying one of His Majesty's aircraft in an act likely to cause loss of life or bodily injury and causing considerable damage to the aircraft. He was reproved on 2nd June for carelessness, which caused a forced landing and was severely reprimanded on 26th June by Air Commodore A de Niverville, AOC No.3 Training Command. He lost six months seniority resulting in his promotion to pilot officer being amended to 13th March 1942. Alan attended a refresher drill course on 16th June. He was posted to No.11 Elementary FTS and was appointed acting flying officer on 28th August. Alan married Margaret Soame (born c.1923) on 5th September 1942 at St Bartholomew's Anglican Church, Ottawa. She lived at 32 Lindenlea Road, Ottawa, Ontario. Granted annual leave 14th–27th September. Alan was promoted temporary flying officer on 1st October and acting flight lieutenant on 13th February 1943. Granted semi-annual leave 7th–13th December 1942 and 23rd–29th March 1943. He was posted to No.1 General Reconnaissance School, Summerside, St Eleanors, Prince Edward Island on 2nd April and was granted embarkation leave 5th–19th June. He embarked at Halifax, Nova Scotia on 23rd June and disembarked in Britain on 1st July. He was posted to 3 Personnel Reception Centre on 2nd July and was attached to 412 Squadron RCAF. Alan was granted privilege leave 15th–21st July and was attached to the Medical Training Depot, Sidmouth 5th–8th August. He attended course No.29 at No.19 (Pilots) Advanced Flying Unit 10th August–22nd September and was posted to 8 (Coastal) Operational Training Unit, Dyce, 16 Group, Coastal Command on 12th October. Promoted temporary flight lieutenant on 13th September. Granted privilege leave 20th September–11th October. On 11th November he took off at 9.10 a.m. from RAF Dyce, Aberdeen on a high level (25,000') cross country training flight in Mosquito Mk IV DZ459 with Sergeant Edward Lyon (1433734) as navigator. The route was to be Barnes Ness, Kendal, Doncaster, St Abb's Head and back to Dyce. All went well until he attempted to land on No.3 Runway at RAF Thornaby, Yorkshire with the starboard engine feathered. He was too high (c.300–400') so retracted the undercarriage and turned the aircraft to port. However, with full flaps on and not having flown straight for long enough to gain height, he lost control. The Mosquito crashed vertically at Stanton Cross Road, near Goldie's Farm, High Leven, Yarm-on-Tees at 11.15 a.m. killing both crewmen. A Court of Enquiry on 15th November ruled that the accident was attributable to pilot error in not following correct procedures. The reason for attempting to land on one engine was never ascertained. Alan is buried at Thornaby-on-Tees Cemetery, Yorkshire (O N 20) and Lyon is buried at Burscough Bridge (St John the Baptist) Churchyard, Ormskirk, Lancashire. Alan's uncle, Major John Irvin Thomas Scallon, attended his funeral. Margaret received a war service gratuity of $367.49.

- Edith Mary Onions (22nd August 1894–7th May 1975) was a nurse in 1928 when she travelled to Canada aboard SS *Ascania*, with her sister Barbara, to visit their sister Amy Scallon. They departed Southampton, Hampshire on 13th October and arrived at Québec on 2nd October. She visited the USA and Canada in 1947, when her permanent address was 4 Sydney House, Elizabeth Street, London. Edith married Richard Perry Calvert Harvey (3rd April 1885–21st November 1971), born at Florence, Italy, in 1958 at Saffron Walden, Essex. He was educated at Heversham Grammar School, Cumberland and was the manager of an iron works. He enlisted as a cadet in the Inns of Court Officer Training Corps, Berkhamstead (5381) on 5th August 1915, giving his address as 52 York Road, Ilford. He was described as 5' 7½" tall and weighed 133 lbs. He was promoted lance corporal on 9th October. His next of kin was his mother at 409 Old Chester

Road, Rock Ferry, Cheshire. Richard applied for a commission on 11th October and was commissioned in the Devonshire Regiment on 29th October 1915. He was appointed acting captain whilst commanding a company in 3rd Devonshire at North Raglan Barracks, Devonport 26th September 1916–23rd April 1917. Richard was awarded the MC for leading a bombing party against an enemy strongpoint and later leading a party of forty men in capturing an enemy trench and taking twenty prisoners (LG 24th November 1916). He embarked in France on 28th April 1917 suffering with neurasthenia caused by the shock and strain of active service on Vimy Ridge when his company was badly cut up. He was granted leave until 25th June. A medical board at Millbank, London on 4th June found him unfit for service for three months, but fit for light duty after three weeks leave. He reported for duty at Plymouth on 25th June and was promoted lieutenant on 1st July. A medical board at the Military Hospital, Devonport on 8th September found him unfit for General Service for one month, but fit for Home Service. A medical board at Bedford on 11th October found him fit for General Service and he was ordered to report to No.2 School of Instruction, Elstow, Bedfordshire. He embarked at Southampton on 7th November 1918 and disembarked in France next day. He joined 6th Infantry Base Depot, Rouen on 12th November, 25th Division on 16th November and 9th Battalion on 18th November. Richard was appointed acting captain whilst commanding a company in 9th Devonshire, 17th November 1918–5th April 1919. He was granted leave to Britain 10th–26th March. He embarked at Boulogne on 4th April and was demobilised from No.2 Dispersal Unit, Crystal Palace on 5th April 1919. Richard relinquished his commission on 1st April 1920 and retained the rank of lieutenant. His address at that time was Shorendon, Wanstead, Essex. They were living at 6 Clatterford Shute, Carisbrooke, Isle of Wight, Hampshire at the time of their deaths there. Richard had married Gladys Eleanor Bressey (1887–18th June 1958) in 1913 at West Ham, London, where she was born. She died at 2 Calverley Park Gardens, Tunbridge Wells, Kent. Richard and Gladys had two children:

- Heath Laurence Harvey (1915–59) married Patricia Mary Temple Wilson (1916–86) in 1940 in Manchester, Lancashire. They emigrated to Johannesburg, South Africa, where he was a director and general manager. They were living at Ashley Cottage, Linden Road, Sandown, Johannesburg, South Africa at the time of his death there. She reportedly died in Jersey, Channel Islands. They had a son.
- Monica 'Nicki' Calvert (1917–2004) married Anthony 'Tony' William Wheldon Atkinson (1924–2017), born at Bilbao, Spain, in 1947 at Westminster, London. He enlisted in the RAF (1836694), reaching the rank of aircraftman 2nd class. He was commissioned as a pilot officer on 1st July 1946, with seniority backdated to 9th June 1945 (193431). He was promoted war substantive flying officer on 9th December 1945 and was involved in the Berlin Airlift 24th June 1948–12th May 1949. He was promoted flight lieutenant 9th December 1948 and was awarded the AFC

(LG 30th December 1952). Tony was promoted squadron leader on 1st July 1958, wing commander on 1st July 1966 and group captain on 1st January 1974. He was awarded the OBE (LG 1st January 1971). On 30th March 1973 he was appointed Group Captain Operations & Training, HQ No.18 Group, Northwood. Tony retired on 31st March 1978. Monica died at Henley-on-Thames, Oxfordshire. They had a son and two daughters. Tony married Eveline Loufte (c.1930–2017) in 2012 at Henley-on-Thames. She was born in France and they met through his work with NATO.

- Barbara Hislop Onions (30th July 1897–8th March 1982), born at Pontypool, never married. She was at boarding school at Hale, Cheshire in 1911 and was a secretary in October 1928, when she went to Canada, with her sister Mary, to visit their sister, Amy Scallon. She returned to Britain aboard RMS *Empress of Britain*, arriving at Southampton on 19th July 1934. Barbara became a church missionary and visited Amy again, travelling on RMS *Empress of Britain*, departing Southampton on 20th October 1934 and returning to Britain aboard SS *Montrose*, arriving at Southampton on 10th October 1937. Her address at the time was Old Farm Cottage, 70 High Street, Old Portsmouth, Hampshire. She travelled to Québec aboard RMS *Empress of Britain*, departing Southampton on 2nd July 1938 and to New York aboard RMS *Mauretania* from Liverpool on 25th October 1944. She was living at The Retreat, 100 Castle Street, Portchester, Hampshire in 1948. On 6th October 1948 she again travelled to Canada aboard RMS *Empress of Canada*, departing Liverpool for Québec and Montréal. She travelled to Canada aboard RMS *Scythia*, departing Southampton on 26th July 1951 for Québec. She returned to Britain aboard RMS *Samaria*, arriving at Southampton in July 1952. Her address was Blackmore Links House, Whitehall, Hampshire. Barbara died at Winchester, Hampshire.
- Hannah Onions (6th March 1900–March 1985) was at boarding school at Hale, Cheshire in 1911. On 2nd August 1930 she sailed from Southampton to Canada aboard SS *Aurania*, arriving at Québec on 10th August. Her occupation was recorded as a club leader. She became a church missionary and travelled to Natal, South Africa aboard SS *Winchester Castle*, departing Southampton on 6th December 1937. She travelled to Durban, South Africa aboard SS *Warwick Castle* from Southampton in 1939. Hannah never married and died at Winchester.
- Joseph Zac Onions (27th September 1902–6th May 1954) married Nellie Winfield (20th September 1906–12th February 1996) in 1927 at Basford, Nottinghamshire. They had three children:
    - Barbara J Onions (born 1928).
    - Peter Joseph Onions (1929–54) was living at 28 Tettenhall Road, Wolverhampton at the time of his death at Shrewsbury Road, near Bromfield, Shropshire.
    - Archibald Zac Onions (born 1932) was a company director with Realism Ltd, 14 Broad Street, Ludlow 1989–2010. He was involved in construction projects at El Sotillo, San Jose, Spain in the early 2000s and was living at Orelton, Shropshire in 2003.

George's paternal grandfather, also George Onions (23rd August 1827–16th May 1915), was born at Wednesbury, Staffordshire. He married Elizabeth née Webb (3rd November 1830–30th August 1906), born at Coseley, Staffordshire, on 13th July 1850 at St Mary's Church, Handsworth, Staffordshire. He was an iron puddler in 1851 and they were living at Hawkes Lane, West Bromwich, Staffordshire. By 1861 he was a mill and forge manager, boarding at 4 St James Terrace, Doncaster, Yorkshire, while the rest of the family was living at 2 Dudley Street, West Bromwich, Staffordshire. In 1871 he was a forge manager and they were living at 96 Green Lane, Walsall, Staffordshire. He was an ironmaster employing one hundred men and they were living at 25 High Street, Bilston, Staffordshire in 1881 and at 56 Wellington Street, Bilston in 1891. She was living at 8 Hope Street, West Bromwich at the time of her death there. He died at Handsworth. In addition to Zachariah they had six other children, all born at West Bromwich:

George's paternal grandfather was born in Wednesbury in 1827.

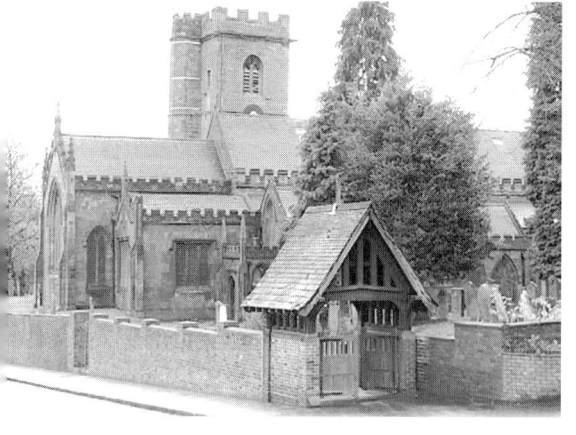

George Onions and Elizabeth Webb married at St Mary's Church, Handsworth in July 1850. It is particularly well known for its association with famous early industrialists and is sometimes referred to as 'the cathedral of the Industrial Revolution'. The first stone church was built c.1160 but little remains. A number of successors followed and there were major reconstructions in 1820 and 1870. The church has memorials to three pioneers of the industrial age. James Watt invented the separate condenser, possibly the most important major improvement to steam engine technology. This was applied by engineer Matthew Boulton in 1774 and the two formed one of the most famous partnerships in industrial history. William Murdoch perfected gas lighting and developed the high-pressure steam engine. He went into partnership with Boulton and Watt. James Watt was buried in the churchyard but an expansion of the church brought his tomb inside. Also buried there are:

- Harry Freeman (1858–1922), a famous music hall performer.
- George Ramsay (1855–1935), who managed Aston Villa, winning six League Championships and six Football Association Cup Finals between 1887 and 1920, a record not beaten until Arsene Wenger won the FA Cup seven times with Arsenal between 1998 and 2017.
- William McGregor (1846–1911), founding member of the Football league in 1888 and Director of Aston Villa FC.

- Hannah Onions (7th February 1851–3rd June 1899) married Samuel Onions (sic) (8th July 1850–22nd October 1877), born at Wednesbury, Staffordshire, on 25th November 1874 at Gartcosh, Lanarkshire. He died at Newcastle-upon-Tyne, Northumberland. She was a widow living with her parents in 1881 and 1891. Hannah married the Reverend John Williams (6th February 1840–7th November 1902), a Baptist Minister born in Pembrokeshire, on 8th April 1892 at Wood Street Chapel, Bilston. John had married Elizabeth Morgan Price (3rd April 1850–27th December 1887) in 1872 at Pembroke and they were living at Lower Park Terrace, Pontypool in 1881. John and Elizabeth had four children – Grace Williams 1875, Gwendoline Mary Williams 1878, William Percy Williams 1880 and Reginald John Price Williams 1885. Elizabeth died at Pontier, near Caerleon, Monmouthshire. John was living with two of his children at Lower Park Terrace, Pontypool, Monmouthshire in 1901. He died at Solva House, Caerleon. John and Hannah had a son, George Maurice Williams (1893–1959).
- Mary Onions (10th December 1853–8th May 1948) married the Reverend George Samuel (c.1854–4th August 1893), a Baptist minister born at Bothwell, Lanarkshire, on 15th August 1878 at Wood Street Chapel, Bilston, Staffordshire. They were living at 11 Howard Road, Penge, Surrey in 1881 and at Wilton Road, Aston, Warwickshire in 1891. He died at 205 Church Hill Road, Handsworth, Staffordshire. Mary was still living there in 1901. She was living at 52 Selly Park Road, Birmingham in 1919. She died at Sutton Coldfield, Warwickshire. They had five children:
    - Elizabeth Webb Samuel (1879–1967).
    - George Christopher Samuel (1881–1918), a consulting engineer, married Alma Gordon Willes (née Richards) (born c.1887), born at Rondebosch, Cape Colony, South Africa, at the Strand, London in 1912 and they had a son, Adrian Christopher Ian Samuel, born in Colchester in 1915. Alma had married Hubert William Heaton Willes (1885–1969) at Islington, London in 1907. They had a daughter, Phyllis Dorothy Willes, in 1908. They divorced in 1911. Hubert served as an officer in the Oxfordshire & Buckinghamshire Light Infantry during the Great War and later emigrated to Kamloops, British Columbia, Canada. George was embodied as a lieutenant in the Territorial Force on 5th August 1914. He was promoted captain in 3rd Midland Brigade RFA in September and was later a major seconded to the Artillery Training School. His addresses were 53 International Exchange, Birmingham and The Chalet, Durrington, Wiltshire. He was serving as a captain in C/82nd Brigade RFA when he died of wounds at No.1 (Presbyterian USA) General Hospital, Étretat, France on 16th August 1918 (Étretat Churchyard Extension – II F 3). George left a life interest in his estate to his widow and the remainder to his son. Alma moved to 102A Warwick Gardens, Kensington, London. She married John Clisdal at Kensington in 1919 and they lived at 92 Warwick Gardens, Kensington.

- Alexander Onions Samuel (1883–1942) was a Lloyds Bank clerk 1898–1902, followed by a few months working for a temperance organisation in Birmingham. He later worked for local newspapers in the city. He changed his middle name to Wenyon. Alexander married Eva Louise Huggins in 1906 at St George, Hanover Square, London and they had three children. Alexander moved to America in 1913, returning to England in 1915 to serve during the Great War. He was invalided in 1917 and was living at Dover House, Sizewell, Suffolk. He married Julia Lyle of New Jersey and changed his name by deed poll to Alexander Lyle-Samuel. He served as Liberal MP for Eye, East Suffolk 1918–23, when he lost his seat, then returned to America. He died in New York in November 1942.
  - Margaret Hannah Samuel (1885–1934).
  - Mary Gladys Samuel (1887–1970).
- William James Onions (5th January 1856–13th November 1936) was a stock taker in 1871 living with his parents. He married Catherine Simpson (1852–31st May 1922), born at Evesham, Worcestershire, on 19th June 1877 at Gartcosh, Lanarkshire, Scotland. He was an iron works manager in 1881 and they were living at Cadder, Lanarkshire. By 1891 they were living at 31 South Road, Harborne, Staffordshire. He was an iron merchant in 1901 and they were living at 95 Beeches Road, West Bromwich. They were living at Miramar, Forest Road, Branksome Park, Dorset at the time of her death. William married Maud Maria Houston on 12th September 1923 at the Baptist Church House, Kingsgate House, Camden, London. He was living at Flat 2, Branksome Court, Bournemouth, Dorset at the time of his death there. A Maud Maria Onions died on 10th May 1943 in Montréal, Canada but it is not clear if this was William's wife. William had two children from his first marriage, one of whom died in infancy, and:
  - George Gordon Onions (1884–1934) was educated at King Edwards High School, Birmingham and married Lucy Catherine Tickle (1881–1930) at the Cathedral Church of St Philip's, Birmingham on 22nd September 1910. He attested at Suffolk Street, Birmingham on 9th December 1915 and transferred to the Army Reserve next day. He was described as a metal broker/merchant (driver), 5' 10½" tall, weighing 152 lbs, with pale complexion, blue eyes and brown hair. He was mobilised on 10th July 1916 and was posted to the ASC Cadet Unit, MT Reserve Depot, Grove Park, Lee, London next day (M2/193514). His address was 24 Selbourne Road, Handsworth, Birmingham but his wife, his next of kin, was living at Philip Victor Road, Handsworth. Later his address was 3 New Street, Birmingham. He was posted to 201st Company ASC MT, Eltham. He left the ASC Cadet School on 29th August and applied for a commission in the RFC on 9th September. He was commissioned on probation on the General List on 30th September 1916 and was posted to the School of Military Aeronautics RFC, Reading

as an assistant equipment officer. George suffered from impetigo and was sent on sick leave 1st–25th November. This was extended by the Military Hospital, Birmingham and his address was the Royal Automobile Club, Pall Mall, London. A Medical Board at Adastral House, Victoria Embankment, London found him fit for General Service on 5th January 1917 and he was appointed equipment officer 3rd class on 14th February. He was confirmed in rank on 22nd February and was appointed equipment officer 2nd class on 1st March. He last appears in the Army List in August 1920. George and Lucy divorced and he married Irene Constance May Lawley (née Anstey) (1889–1960) in 1921 at Paddington, London. Irene had married Thomas Henry Lawley (born c.1885) in 1909 at Harborne, Staffordshire. He was a china merchant in 1911 and they were living at Oak Lodge, King's Norton. Irene died at Conway, Caernarvonshire.

- Elizabeth Onions (born 10th November 1859).
- John Thomas Onions (12th September 1861–18th January 1928) was an iron merchant employing three men in 1881. He married Elisabeth Anne Proffitt (4th March 1867–28th September 1937) on 12th June 1886 at Aldridge, Staffordshire. They travelled frequently to America, where their children, Florence and Forrest, were born. By 1901 he was a tea manufacturer and they were living at Bleak House, Mount Pleasant, Bilston. Elisabeth was living with her children at 88 Wellington Road, Westbourne, Bilston in 1911. The family travelled to New York aboard SS *Laurentic*, arriving on 17th January 1912. They moved to Philadelphia, Pennsylvania, became American citizens and John changed the family surname to Wenyon on 10th October 1914. He worked in iron and steel manufacturing. He died in Philadelphia. Elisabeth assumed her maiden name, returned to Britain and was living at Maxtoke, Woodland Drive, East Horsley, Surrey at the time of her death there. They had eight children:
    - Muriel Edith Onions (1887–1965).
    - Kathleen Daisy Onions (1888–1982).
    - Florence Eleanor Onions (1893).
    - Forrest Proffitt Onions (1896–1974).
    - Arnold Proffitt Onions (1898–1986).
    - Doris Edith Onions (1900).
    - Eileen Onions (1902–52).
    - Mildred Onions (1903).
- George Henry 'Harry' Onions (8th August 1864–1964) was a clerk in an ironworks in 1881. He was an iron manufacturer in 1891, living with his parents at the time of both censuses. He married Annie Alexandra Saunders (c.1861–1932) in 1892 at Prescot, Lancashire. She was born in Liverpool, Lancashire. By 1901 George was a commission agent and they were living on the Mondisfield/Compton Road, Wolverhampton. By 1911 he was an iron and steel merchant and they were living at 7 Richmond Road, Wolverhampton. George changed the family surname to

Webb, his mother's maiden name. Annie died in Birmingham and George at Leamington Spa, Warwickshire. They had three children:
  ◦ Dorothy Onions (1894–1906).
  ◦ George William Alexander Onions (1897–1964) was a bank clerk at London City & Midland Bank Ltd, Temple Row, Birmingham from 1913. He enlisted at Stafford in 2/1st Staffordshire Yeomanry (3321) on 7th December 1914, described as a 6' tall bank clerk. He was living at 7 Richmond Road, Wolverhampton. He transferred to 1/1st Staffordshire Yeomanry on 14th June 1915 and embarked at Southampton for the Mediterranean Expeditionary Force on 27th October, disembarking at Alexandria on 10th November. He changed his name to Webb by deed poll on 10th July 1916. He attended a course at Zeitoun 28th–30th October and was awarded the good conduct badge on 8th November. George was admitted to 22nd Mounted Brigade Field Ambulance at Fayum with septic sores on 21st November, transferred to the General Hospital, Fayum on 30th November, to the Citadel Military Hospital, Cairo on 1st December and to the Convalescent Hospital, Abbassia on 19th December. Granted class 2 proficiency pay on 7th December. He was attached to 18th Squadron, Machine Gun Corps, 22nd Mounted Brigade at Romani on 8th January 1917. He was discharged to the Base Depot on 16th January, transferred to the Machine Gun Corps (Cavalry) (96040) on 27th February and was posted to 18th Squadron. On 19th May he was admitted to a field ambulance, transferred to 31st General Hospital, Port Said on 28th May with onychia (inflammation of the nail folds) and rejoined his unit on 18th June. He was admitted to 78th General Hospital, Alexandria on 7th November with diarrhoea. George transferred to RFC Aboukir for a cadre course on 4th January 1918 and was commissioned in the RAF on 13th May as an observer officer. He served with No.47 Squadron from 6th June. He was in hospital 18th–30th September and transferred to 16 Wing on 16th October. A medical board at Matlock, Derbyshire on 11th December found him unfit for General Service, unfit for Home Service for four weeks, but fit for light duty. He transferred to the Unemployed List on 25th February 1919. George married Kathleen Miriam Fleming (born 1902) in 1925 at Wolverhampton, Staffordshire. They were living at 11 Alexandra Terrace, Marlborough, Wiltshire at the time of his death at the Radcliffe Infirmary, Oxford. George and Kathleen had two sons.
  ◦ Rhoda Onions (1900–89).

His maternal grandmother, Elizabeth 'Eliza' Ridd (c.1822–12th December 1878), was born at Challacombe, Devon. She married William Skemp (c.1820–49) (registered as Scamp) in 1844 at Barnstaple, Devon. He was born at Braunton, Devon and was a mercer, textile merchant, living with his siblings at Cheltenham, Gloucestershire in 1841. William and Eliza moved to Shoreditch, London and had three children:

- William Henry Skemp (born 1845) born at Bideford, Devon, was assisting his father in 1861. He married Emma Bastard (1846–9th December 1923) at Torrington, Devon in 1868, where she was born. He was a draper and a Baptist teacher and they were living at 79 High Street, Bilston in 1870, when he was declared bankrupt and his business was liquidated. William and Emma moved to America c.1872/73. Emma returned to England with her two sons and was living with her widowed father at 35 South Street, Great Torrington in 1881, assisting him in his fishing tackle business. William is assumed to have remained in America and died between 1891 and 1901. Emma was still living at 35 South Street in 1901, running her fishing tackle business. By 1911 she was living with her brother, John Bastard, a bank cashier, and his family at 4 Headland Park, Plymouth, Devon. Her son, Charles, an unemployed bookkeeper was with her. She was living at 10 Collings Park, Plymouth at the time of her death there. William and Emma had four children:
  - William Henry Skemp (1870–72).
  - John Robert Skemp (1871–72).
  - Charles Edward Skemp (1874–1956) was born in Chicago, Illinois.
  - Robert Victor Skemp (1876–1905) was born in Wisconsin.
- Charles Widlake Skemp (1847–1930) emigrated to America in 1861 and settled in Buffalo, Erie Co, New York. He joining the US Army and rose to the rank of sergeant in the infantry. Charles married Bridget Love (May 1848–1st May 1913), born in Ireland, in Buffalo in 1870. They were living in Buffalo in 1900 and 1910 and he was a bookkeeper. Bridget is buried in Holy Cross Cemetery, Lackawanna, Erie Co. In 1925 Charles was living at Buffalo, with his unmarried daughter acting as housekeeper. He is buried in Forest Lawn Cemetery, Buffalo. They had a daughter, Elizabeth 'Eliza' Mary Skemp c.1879.
- George Robert Skemp (1850–51) was born at Shoreditch, London.

William died of cholera at St Leonard, London during the pandemic in 1849. In 1851 Eliza was a milliner and a widow, living with her two sons, William and Charles, at 86 Kingsland Road, Shoreditch. Eliza Skemp married William's brother and George's maternal grandfather, Robert Skemp (also seen as Scamp) (24th April 1825–13th June 1905), born at North Tamerton, Cornwall, in 1853 at Shoreditch. Robert was a hosier and lace man and Baptist preacher in 1871, when they were living at 12 High Street, Bilston, near Wolverhampton, Staffordshire. In addition to Amy they had three other children, all born at Wolverhampton:

- Eliza Emily Skemp (1854–21st January 1911) was an assistant in a lace shop in 1871. She married Samuel George Lovatt (1853–27th January 1908) in 1879. Samuel was a traveller and clerk to a provision merchant in 1881 and they were living at 30 Cambridge Street, Bilston. By 1891 they were living at 34 Gaolgate Street, Stafford. They had four children – Samuel Robert Lovatt (1881–1954), Amy Susan Lovatt (1885–1938), Elsie Skemp Lovatt (1888–1936) and Eunice Lovatt (1891–1964).

- Robert Skemp (3rd January 1858–8th April 1922) married Kate Sumner (1854–20th June 1932), born at Southwell, Nottinghamshire, in 1880. He was a cashier in 1881 and they were living at 5 Court, 4 House, High Street, Darlaston, Staffordshire. They emigrated to the USA in 1887 and settled at Scottdale, Westmoreland Co, Pennsylvania. His father, Robert, joined them there in 1897. Robert junior was superintendent of the American Sheet and Tin Plate Co in 1900. They had four children – Robert Skemp 1881, Arthur John Skemp 1884, Leo Norman Skemp 1887 and Harold Skemp 1890.
- Elizabeth Harriet Skemp (1860–25th March 1929) married Ebenezer Frederick Attwood (22nd February 1862–7th November 1907) in 1888. He was a clerk in a gas office in 1901 and they were living at 9 New Garden Street, Stafford. They emigrated to America and settled at Scottdale, Westmoreland Co, Pennsylvania before 1907, where he was a roll turner. He died at Scottdale and she at Washington DC. They had three children – Harold Attwood 1890, Lorna Winifred Attwood 1892 and Kathleen Martha Attwood 1898.

George was educated at West Monmouthshire Grammar School, Pontypool, Monmouthshire and by 1901 was an analytical chemist's assistant at Abersychan, Monmouthshire. He was employed at Tirpentwys Colliery to train as a mining engineer and was involved in an accident on 1st October 1902, in which eight miners were killed when the winding cable broke as they were ascending an upcast pit. George left mining and opened his own steel merchant and manufacturer's agency. He emigrated to Australia in 1904 for health reasons.

West Monmouthshire Grammar School was funded by the charitable donations of William Jones, who died in 1615. He bequeathed money to the Worshipful Company of Haberdashers for the foundation of a grammar school in Monmouth. However, it was not until the end of the 19th century that Monmouth School was encouraged to build a sister school for west Monmouthshire. Pontypool was chosen for the school on six acres of land donated by John Capel Hanbury. The foundation stone was laid in 1896 for what was then named Jones' West Monmouth School. The official opening by 1st Viscount Tredegar was in 1898. The School started with seventy boarders and thirty dayboys and gradually expanded. It became a county grammar school under Monmouthshire County Council in 1954 and the last boarders left in 1958. In 1982 the School became a comprehensive and amalgamated with three secondary modern schools at Twmpath, Trevethin and the Wern. Further expansions have taken place since and there are currently almost 800 pupils. Amongst the School's famous alumni are:

- Sir Anthony Hopkins (born 1937), actor, director and producer.
- Arthur Edwin Stevens CBE (1905–95), designer of the world's first wearable electronic hearing aid.
- Mako Vunipola (born 1991), England rugby union player.
- Ieuan Thomas (born 1974), Great Britain 400m runner.

Abersychan, Monmouthshire, birthplace of Labour politician Roy Jenkins (1920–2003). The village expanded rapidly in the 19th century due to the discovery of ironstone and the construction of the British Iron Company works there.

The sinking of two shafts at Tirpentwys Colliery began in 1878 and the first coal was raised in 1881. Ownership passed from Darby and Norris in 1884 to the Tirpentwys Colliery Co and some years later to Tirpentwys Black Vein Steam Coal & Coke Co, which operated the colliery until nationalisation in 1947. By 1896 there were 821 men employed there, rising to 1,682 by 1923. The mine closed in 1969.

George married Florence McFarlane Donaldson (30th October 1884–8th May 1970), born at Hutchesontown, Glasgow, Lanarkshire, Scotland, at St Paul's, Brisbane, Queensland, Australia on 31st August 1907. They returned to Britain, arriving on 15th November 1907 and he was described as a commercial traveller. They lived initially in Scotland, where he was an iron and steel merchant in 1911. They moved to Edgbaston, Birmingham, Warwickshire before moving to Cranford Avenue, Sale, Cheshire by 1915. They had a son, George Zac Onions (2nd November 1909–3rd April 1932), born at Giffnock, Renfrewshire and died at 4 Hagley Court, Hagley Road, Edgbaston, Birmingham.

Florence's parents, Alexander Donaldson and Christina MacFarlane (died 1 September 1948), married in Paisley, Scotland in 1881. They emigrated to Australia before 1887. In addition to Florence they also had Agnes Mary Donaldson (1887–1953) born at Brisbane. She married Herbert Frederick Smith (1874–1952), born at Wollongong, New South Wales, there in 1914. They had a daughter in 1916. They both died at Moreton Street, New Farm, Brisbane.

George enlisted in 3rd (King's Own) Hussars at Sale, Cheshire on 5th September 1914 (21378) and went to France on 18th October 1915. He was in Dublin, Ireland with 9th Reserve Regiment of Cavalry during the 1916 Easter Rising. He was appointed officer cadet and was commissioned in The Rifle Brigade on 26th September 1916. George spent a weekend in London without

George and Florence.

leave and was involved in a disturbance in a restaurant. As a result he was court-martialled and cashiered on 22nd December.

George enlisted in 1st Devonshire on 14th April 1917 and went to France on 17th April. He was evacuated to hospital in England in May and did not return to duty in France until March 1918. Promoted lance corporal. **Awarded the VC for his actions south of Achiet-le-Petit, near Bapaume, France on 22nd August 1918, LG 14th December 1918.** Later that day he was evacuated to a hospital in Liverpool, Lancashire. The VC was presented by the King in the ballroom at Buckingham Palace on 13th February 1919. George was demobilised on 14th February 1919. He was commissioned for one day (17th August 1919) into The Rifle Brigade (Service Battalions) in recognition of his valuable services. He was allowed to wear the uniform on appropriate occasions.

On 22nd February 1919 George was honoured with a civic reception at Sale Town Hall in front of a crowd of several thousand people. He was presented with a gold watch, a cheque for £185 (£100 in one source) and a framed address from Sale District Council. Florence received a brooch displaying the crest of her husband's regiment in gold. George attended two VC reunions – the VC Garden Party at Buckingham Palace on 26th June 1920 and the VC Dinner at the Royal Gallery of the House of Lords, London on 9th November 1929. At the latter event he met the other two of the 'Savoury Pie' trio of West Country Regiment VCs – Veale and Sage.

George enlisted in the Auxiliary Division of the Royal Irish Constabulary on 16th June 1921 (82855) and served in C Company. He was discharged on demobilisation on 13th January 1922. He is understood to have worked for two London firms but lost both positions through neglect. He was appointed the Bristol and district salesman for Messrs Berkel and Parnell in 1925 and was also manager of a firm of ironmasters and merchants in the Birmingham area and the publicity agent for the Colliery Guardian Company, London, a trade journal. He and Florence lived in Northumberland, at 16 Salisbury Terrace, Weston-Super-Mare, Somerset in 1923,

Sale Town Hall (David Dixon).

George Onions receiving a framed address on the steps of Sale Town Hall. His wife, Florence, is seated to the left of the table.

Theodore Veale (11th November 1892–6th November 1980) was awarded the VC for his actions east of High Wood, France on 20th July 1916, while serving with 8th Devonshire. He appears in the third book in this series, *Victoria Crosses on the Western Front: Somme 1916*.

Thomas Henry Sage (8th December 1882–20th July 1945) was awarded the VC for his actions at Tower Hamlets Spur, east of Ypres, Belgium on 4th October 1917, while serving with 8th Somerset Light Infantry. He appears in the fifth book in this series, *Victoria Crosses on the Western Front: Third Ypres 1917*.

Recruiting for the Auxiliaries began in July 1920 and the Division had grown to 1,900 strong by November 1921. Although part of the Royal Irish Constabulary, the Division operated independently in rural areas in companies about one hundred strong. They were heavily armed and highly mobile, under the command of Brigadier General FP Crozier. George Onions was one of three VCs to serve in the Auxiliaries, the others being James Leach and James Johnson. The Division was not suited for counterinsurgency and was poorly trained. With an ill-defined role, it gained a reputation for drunkenness, ill discipline and brutality. It was disbanded in 1922.

at 43 Ryland Road, Edgbaston in June 1925, and at 4 Hagley Court, Hagley Road, Edgbaston, where she died.

On 6th May 1925 George cashed a cheque for £5 in the grocer's shop owned by Frederick George Scutt, of 218 Cheltenham Road, Bristol. He told the manager, Edmund George Lamb, of 157 Cheltenham Road, that he had been transferred to the Birmingham district but had run short of money. The cheque was payable at Lloyds Bank, Birmingham but was returned marked 'no account'. George was arrested by the Birmingham Police and transported to Bristol by Sergeant Williams. He was found guilty of fraud on 25th June and ordered to repay £2/10/- by 1st July and the remainder within two months. He was also bound over by the magistrates, Alderman W Whitefield and Mr JH Maggs, to be of good conduct for two years.

George helped form a National Defence Company of 200 war veterans in Birmingham in 1936. He was commissioned as a captain in the National Defence Corps in Birmingham on 12th July 1939. The Company was absorbed into the Regular Army on the outbreak of war as 11th (Home Defence) Battalion, Royal Warwickshire Regiment. George was appointed captain in the Royal Warwickshire Regiment, TA Reserve on 24th August 1939 and acting major on 8th December. He resigned on 1st April 1941 due to ill health but was appointed major on 19th May 1942 in the South Staffordshire Zone, Home Guard.

Dudley Road Hospital, where George died in April 1944.

George was involved in a motoring accident and was admitted to Dudley Road Hospital, Birmingham, where he died a few weeks later on 2nd April 1944, having suffered a heart attack. He is buried in Quinton Cemetery, Halesowen Road, Birmingham (Sect 6, Grave 7364). The grave fell into disrepair and was

Bilston War Memorial.

George Onions' refurbished grave in Quinton Cemetery (Memorials to Valour).

refurbished by stonemason Mark Brady, of Stoneset, Birmingham, at no cost for the sixtieth anniversary of George's death in April 2014. He is also commemorated on a Department for Communities and Local Government commemorative paving stone, dedicated at Bilston War Memorial, Bilston, West Midlands on 22nd August 2018.

In addition to the VC he was awarded the 1914–15 Star, British War Medal 1914–20, Victory Medal 1914–19 and George VI Coronation Medal 1937. The VC is held by The Keep Military Museum, Barrack Road, Dorchester, Dorset.

51396 LANCE SERGEANT EDWARD BENN SMITH
1/5th Battalion, The Lancashire Fusiliers

Edward 'Ned' Smith was born on 10th November 1898 at 1 North Quay, Maryport, Cumberland. His father, Charles Henry Smith (16th February 1869–1945), born at Tupsley, Herefordshire, married Martha née Benn (27th April 1874–22nd September 1950), born at Maryport, Cumberland, in 1893 at Cockermouth, Cumberland. They were boarding with her father in 1901. By 1911 he was a fisherman and they were living at 1 North Quay, Maryport. They were still there in 1939. Charles served during the Great War in the Royal Naval Reserve in the Dardanelles. Martha's family served the Maryport lifeboat for two generations. She was living at 12 South Quay, Maryport at the time of her death. Ned had nine siblings:

- John Benn Smith (5th November 1896–February 1992) was an errand boy in a bookshop in 1911. He married Ada Winifred Clark (1900–38) in 1920 at Cockermouth and they had two children:
    ○ Ada Winifred Smith (1920–93) married William John Morrison Thompson (1917–40) in 1940. They lived at 10 Mill Street, Maryport. William was

Maryport around the time that Ned Smith was born there.

Ned's parents married in Cockermouth.

MV *Fishpool* (4,950 tons) was built in 1940. On 14th November 1940 she was sailing from the Tyne to Vancouver in ballast when she was hit by seven incendiary bombs southwest of Rockall. Twenty-five crewmen were killed, the ship was abandoned and one lifeboat with fifteen aboard was never seen again. *Fishpool* was taken in tow and repaired. On 9th May 1941, at Barrow-in-Furness, she was damaged by a parachute mine, which killed two crewmen. Finally on 26th July 1943, while discharging ammunition and aviation spirit at Syracuse, she was sunk in an air raid. Twenty-three crewmen and five DEMS gunners were killed. There were eighteen survivors.

serving as a Merchant Navy cook (160785) aboard MV *Fishpool* (4,950 tons), when she was bombed on 11th November 1940. He was one of twenty-five crewmen who were killed and is buried in Rothesay Cemetery, Buteshire, Scotland. Ada married James Cullen in 1942 and they had two children.

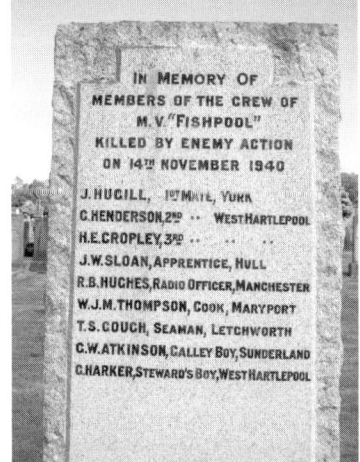

The *Fishpool* memorial in Rothesay Cemetery (Scottish War Graves Project).

- Audrey Smith (born 1931) married Ronald Brereton (1929–92) in 1954. They had two children.

John married Hilda Higgins (26th April 1910–August 2005) in 1945.
- Sarah Annie Smith (born 1902).
- Emma Smith (born 1903).
- Martha Annie Smith (29th April 1905–1979) married John Costin Ivison (23rd June 1902–27th January 1985) in 1924. Martha was living with her daughter at 7 South Quay, Maryport in 1939. John was not with her and was probably away serving with the Royal Naval Reserve (A11508). He was living at Nether Croft, Finsthwaite, Ulverston, Cumbria at the time of his death. They had two children:
  - Charles Henry Ivison (born 1925) was a Merchant Navy seaman during the Second World War. He married Jane S Bailey (born 1926) in 1948.
  - Margaret Coulthard Ivison (born 1927) married James Barlow (born 1913) in 1952. They had a daughter, Ann Barlow, in 1953.
- Jane Grubb Smith (born 6th September 1908) married Joseph William Rafferty (3rd October 1904–1988), a rope splicer below ground, in 1925. They had a daughter, Edith Rafferty (born 1926), who was living with her maternal grandparents in 1939. Edith married Henry Herbert Luckhurst (1914–93) in 1952. He served as a lance sergeant in the Royal Army Pay Corps during the

Second World War (825116) and was taken prisoner by the Japanese. He became a civil servant in Kenya and in 1955 returned from Beira, Mozambique. Edith and Henry had two children. Jane and Joseph divorced, possibly before 1939, when she was a waitress at the Golden Lion Hotel, Maryport and he was living with his future second wife, Ethel May Pattinson (1910–86), at 4 Bells Lane, Workington, Cumberland. Ethel had a son, Joseph Pattinson (born 1936), whose surname had changed to Rafferty by 1939. Joseph and Ethel married in 1947. Jane married Thomas Anderson in 1947.

- Lilian Smith (12th July 1910–December 2002) married Arthur White (14th May 1906–June 1984) in 1928. He was a locomotive shunter at in iron works in 1939 and they were living at 10 Hyde Street, Workington. They had three children:
  - Arthur White (1928–90).
  - Charles E White (1932–2009).
  - Doreen Jean White (1938–2008) married Donald M Broatch (born 1937) in 1959. He was living with his parents at 10 The Oval, Salterbeck, Workington in 1939. Donald and Doreen lived at Timperley, Cheshire. They had two sons.
- Isabel Smith (18th November 1911–1965) was a confectioner cake maker in 1939 living at 175 John Street, Workington. She died unmarried.
- Charles Henry Smith (29th November 1913–1978) married Winifred Dixon Robinson (22nd November 1910–1973) in 1937. He was a public works contractor in 1939 and they were living at 4 New Crown Yard, Maryport. Charles was a customs officer by 1950. They are understood to have had a son, John Smith, in 1944.
- Muriel W Smith (born 1920) married William Thompson in 1945. They had two daughters – Susan I Thompson 1948 and Christine Thompson 1950).

Ned's paternal grandfather is unknown. His grandmother, Emma Smith (c.1852–1907), was born at Tupsley, Herefordshire. She was living with her paternal grandparents, John Smith, a farmer and nurseryman, and his wife Elizabeth, at Hampton Deane, Tupsley in 1861. By 1871 she was living with her widowed grandfather at Littley Cottage, Hampton Road, Tupsley.

His maternal grandfather, John Benn (13th July 1840–21st September 1906), a seaman/fisherman, married Sarah Ann née Little (1846–98) on 27th October 1868 at St Peter's Parish Church, Camerton, near Maryport. She was a servant at the time. Sarah had a daughter, Eleanor Benn Little (1867–1935), who was a domestic servant in 1891 at the Queens Head Inn, 10 Senhouse Street, Crosscanonby. Eleanor had two children – Sarah Eleanor 'Millie' Little 1885 and Robert L Little 1889. She married Hugh Arthur Seeds (c.1862–1932), a boiler riveter in a blast furnace, in 1891. He was born in Ireland according to the 1901 Census and at Workington, Cumberland in the 1911 Census. They were living at 29 Warren Street, Middlesbrough, Yorkshire in 1891 and at 51 Fleetham Street, Middlesbrough in 1911. They had a son, John

Ned's maternal grandparents were married at St Peter's Church, Camerton. The church is on a bend of the River Derwent, surrounded on three sides by the river and on the west by farmland. The only access is across fields. There has been a church there since the 11th century and it was rebuilt in 1694 and 1796. The tower and spire were added in 1855 and the building was restored in 1885 and 1892.

Most of the burials in Malbork Commonwealth War Cemetery are of men who died while prisoners of war in nearby camps. After the war graves were moved from local burial grounds and concentrated at Malbork. There are 232 Second World War and thirteen First World War burials that were moved from Gdansk (Danzig) Garrison Cemetery in 1960.

Benn Seeds, in 1892. Meanwhile John and Sarah were living at 3A North Quay, Crosscanonby, Cumberland in 1881 and at 4 Strand Street, Crosscanonby, near Maryport in 1891. He was living at 1 North Quay, Netherall, Maryport in 1901, by when he was a market gardener. He died at West Newton, Cumberland. In addition to Martha they had three other children:

- Thomas Benn (1871–1936) married Jane Douglas (6th November 1875–1959) in May 1896 at Wigton, Cumberland. They had four children – Sarah Ann Benn 1899, John Benn 1902, Thomas Benn 1904 and Dorothy Benn 1910.
- Betsy Benn (10th March 1878–12th February 1955) married John Henry Timney (24th July 1875–1956), a dock labourer, on 20th August 1896 at St Mary's Church, Maryport. They were living at 3 Furnace Terrace, Furnace Road, Maryport in 1911. They had five children – John Edward Marsh Timney 1897, Sarah Ann Timney 1901, Thomas Timney 1903, Mary Timney 1905, William H Timney 1917 and George Benn Timney 1919. George served as a private (5253104) in 7th Worcestershire and was taken prisoner in the retreat to Dunkirk. He died on 26th June 1944 (Malbork Commonwealth War Cemetery, Poland – 9 A 11).
- Mary Isabella Benn (1882–1913) was a general domestic servant at 18 North Street, Netherhall, Cumberland in 1901. She married William Ferguson (1878–1933) in 1905. In 1911 she was living at 6 Dean Street, Middlesbrough, Yorkshire while her husband was in Canada. Her death was probably caused by complications

following the birth of her daughter Mary. They had three children – William Ferguson 1906, John Ferguson 1907 and Mary I Ferguson 1913.

Ned was educated at the National School, Maryport, Cumberland and then worked at Oughterside Colliery, near Maryport. He enlisted in the South Wales Borderers (2963) on 11th December 1915 and transferred to the Reserves. On 4th May 1917 he joined the Lancashire Fusiliers (42192 later 51396) and went to France on 10th December. He was posted to 1/5th Lancashire Fusiliers and was subsequently promoted corporal and acting lance sergeant.

Awarded the Distinguished Conduct Medal for his actions on 10th August 1918 in the area of Touvent Farm and Staff Copse, southeast of Hébuterne, in which he led a daring attack on a superior enemy force. On returning from a patrol he noticed about forty enemy troops coming out of their lines to take up night outpost positions. With his party of only four he waited and ambushed them, inflicting heavy casualties and scattering them in the process. He then skilfully extracted his force without loss, **showing greatest enterprise and marked ability to command, LG 30th October 1918. Awarded the VC for his actions east of Serre, France on 22nd–23rd August 1918, LG 22nd October 1918.** The VC was presented by the King in the ballroom at Buckingham Palace on 9th November 1918. When he returned to Maryport after the investiture he received a hero's welcome and was presented with a long case clock, a silver tea set, £200 in War Bonds, a gold watch with chain, a gold brooch and a Meerschaum pipe. He was escorted to his home by members of the Royal Defence Corps.

Ned was promoted sergeant and was offered a commission but he declined. He remained in the Army after the war and transferred to the Cameron Highlanders

The Distinguished Conduct Medal was instituted on 4th December 1854 for warrant officers and below for 'distinguished, gallant and good conduct in the field'. It ranked second only to the Victoria Cross and equated to the Distinguished Service Order for officers when awarded for gallantry. It was the first official decoration awarded by the British to recognise acts of individual gallantry in the Army. During the First World War there was concern that the number of medals being awarded would devalue it. As a result the Military Medal was instituted on 25th March 1916, as a lesser award for bravery. Nevertheless 24,591 DCMs were awarded during the First World War plus 472 Bars and nine second Bars. In 1942 other ranks of the Royal Navy and Royal Air Force also became eligible. In 1993 the DCM was discontinued after a major review of the honours system, which removed distinctions of rank in respect of awards for bravery. With the Conspicuous Gallantry Medal and the Distinguished Service Order when awarded for gallantry, it was replaced by the Conspicuous Gallantry Cross as the second highest award for gallantry for all ranks of all services.

Regimental Sergeant Major Edward Benn Smith VC DCM.

(33838) on 5th May 1919, but later transferred to 1st Lancashire Fusiliers (69891) at Blackdown. He was appointed drum major in 1920 and company sergeant major in 1924. In 1926 he was posted to Malaya as a sergeant major instructor with the Federated Malay States Volunteer Regiment at Ipoh, Perak. He returned to Britain in 1930 and was appointed RSM 1st Lancashire Fusiliers on 29th July 1932. He served with the Battalion at Colchester and in China at Shanghai and Tientsin. Ned retired in May 1938 and joined the Corps of Commissionaires in London.

Ned attended two VC reunions – the VC Garden Party at Buckingham Palace on 26th June 1920 and the VC Dinner at the Royal Gallery of the House of Lords, London on 9th November 1929.

On 10th October 1938 Ned was recalled and was granted a short-service commission in 2nd Lancashire Fusiliers as a lieutenant (quartermaster) (107894) on 1st September 1939. He went to France with the Battalion as part of the BEF in January 1940. Ned died at No.5 Casualty Clearing Station as a result of a self-inflicted gunshot wound in the QM store at Bucquoy on 12th January 1940, very close to where his VC action took place (Beuvry Communal Cemetery Extension – 1 B 7). Only Major Smith, Captain Gregory, Second Lieutenants Marsh and Fulton, eight sergeants and a platoon were permitted to attend from the Battalion. Ned is commemorated in a number of places in Maryport, Cumbria:

- War Memorial, Netherhall Corner.
- A Department for Communities and Local Government commemorative paving stone was dedicated at Maryport Harbour, South Quay on 22nd August 2018.
- War Memorial at St Mary's Church and a plaque within the church.

In addition to the VC and DCM he was awarded the British War Medal 1914–20, Victory Medal 1914–19, 1939–45 Star, War Medal 1939–45, George V Silver Jubilee Medal 1935, George VI Coronation Medal 1937 and the Army Long Service & Good Conduct Medal. The medals were left to the Regiment. However, one of his siblings requested that they be returned to the family in the 1950s. The Regiment was unable to produce any documentary evidence of ownership and the medals

Ned Smith's grave in Beuvry Communal Cemetery Extension.

The Army Long Service and Good Conduct Medal, instituted in 1830, was replaced by the Medal for Long Service and Good Conduct (Military) in 1930. It was initially awarded to soldiers after twenty-one years service in the infantry or twenty-four in the cavalry. In 1870 the qualifying period was reduced to eighteen years of irreproachable service. A recipient subsequently awarded the Meritorious Service Medal had to stop wearing the Army Long Service and Good Conduct Medal. In 1916 a new ribbon edged with white bands was introduced to distinguish it from the Victoria Cross.

were handed over. The VC and DCM were sold by Sotheby's for £7,000 on 23rd November 1977 and at Spink's, London to Lord Ashcroft for £19,000 on 12th March 1996. The VC is held by the Michael Ashcroft Trust, the holding institution for the Lord Ashcroft Victoria Cross Collection, and is displayed in the Imperial War Museum's Lord Ashcroft Gallery.

LIEUTENANT COLONEL RICHARD ANNESLEY WEST
North Irish Horse, attached 6th Battalion, Tank Corps

Richard West was born on 26th September 1878 at 1 Oxford Street, Cheltenham, Gloucestershire. He was known as Alec in the family. His father, Augustus George West (19th January 1841–30th June 1911), was born at Annamoe Glebe, Co Wicklow, Ireland. He was educated at St Columba's College and Rossall and was commissioned in 76th Hindoostan Regiment on 9th November 1858. He was promoted lieutenant on 3rd August 1861 and resigned his commission on 15th May 1866. Augustus studied at the Royal Agricultural College, Cirencester,  Gloucestershire in 1866 and settled at White Park, Co Fermanagh, Ireland. He also had residences at Balix and Llog Cloghfin, Co Tyrone. Augustus married Sara née Eyre (7th May 1837–21st December 1914) on 31st July 1867 at Kingstown, Dublin. She was born at Eyre Court, Glebe, Co Galway, Ireland. Augustus died at White Park and Sara at Lisnaskea, Co Fermanagh. Richard had six siblings:

- Erskine Eyre West (19th May 1868–24th February 1950), born at 32 Landsdowne Road, Dublin, Ireland, was educated at Monkton Combe and Trinity College, Cambridge. He entered King's Inns, Dublin at Easter 1891 and was called to

the Bar in 1895. Erskine was commissioned as a captain in the Londonderry Royal Garrison Artillery (Southern Division RGA) on 17th September 1892 and resigned in March 1904. He was appointed Deputy Registrar to the Court of the Irish Land Commission on 17th September 1897. Erskine married Annette Aileen Maude Huddart (13th April 1875–12th February 1954), born at Pembroke Road, Dublin, on 3rd August 1899 at St Stephen's, Westbourne Park, London. They had two children:
- Augustus Cuthbert Erskine West (1900–68), born at Kingstown, Dublin, married Mabella Lyall Reynolds (1903–99), born at Stockport, Cheshire, in 1927 at Kingston-upon-Thames, Surrey. Augustus was commissioned in 4/10th Baluch Regiment on 16th July 1920. Promoted captain on 16th July 1927. On 9th September 1936 he was appointed Assistant Commandant, Eastern Frontier Rifles, Bengal Battalion, Dacca, attached to the Dum Dum Detachment. He transferred to the Special Unemployed List on 1st April 1937 and ceased to be liable to recall on 29th July 1950. He reached the rank of lieutenant colonel in the Indian Army. He was living at 23 Pashley Road, Eastbourne, Sussex at the time of his death. Mabella died in Birmingham, Warwickshire.
- Dudley Somerset Erskine West (1904–91) was born at 16 Westbourne Gardens, Bayswater, London. He trained at the Royal Military College, Sandhurst and was commissioned in the Cheshire Regiment on 27th August 1924 (30705). He was aboard Polish MS *Chrobry* off the coast of Norway on 15th May 1940 when she was bombed. The senior officer of 1st Irish Guards plus five of his officers and four other ranks were killed. The order to abandon ship was given, Dudley assumed command and organised the evacuation. After all the boats were utilised he waited for a destroyer to approach and organised ropes between the two ships to allow the remaining personnel to clamber to safety. He was awarded the MC (LG 27th September 1940). Promoted major 27th August 1941 and lieutenant colonel 28th October 1947. Awarded the OBE (LG 1st January 1951). Appointed temporary colonel on 4th January 1952 and transferred to the Reserve of Officers on 1st January 1955 with the honorary rank of colonel. He ceased to belong to the Reserve on 24th June 1959. Dudley was living at 19 Chester Close, Queen's Ride, Barnes, London at the time of his death, leaving effects valued at £896,789 (£1.9M in 2018).

- Adeline Elisabeth West (24th October 1869–27th February 1951), born at Marietta, Co Dublin, was a spinster living at The Lodge, Gibsons Hill, Streatham, London at the time of her death at The British Home and Hospital for Incurables, Streatham.
- Augustus William West (5th May 1871–13th December 1957), born at Altadore, Co Dublin, was educated at Monkton Combe and the Royal Agricultural College, Cirencester 1889–91. He was appointed Assistant Land Commissioner for Ireland

MS *Chrobry*, a passenger ship built for the Poland – South America Line in 1939 in Denmark, was on her maiden passenger voyage to South America when war broke out. She was converted in Britain to a troop transport and made one transatlantic voyage before being used during the Norwegian campaign. En route from Tieldsundet to Bodo she was attacked by German dive-bombers in Vestfjorden. The ship was set on fire and ammunition exploded. Several army personnel were killed. The destroyer HMS *Wolverine* took off 700 survivors, while the sloop HMS *Stork* drove off other German aircraft before taking off the remaining survivors. *Chrobry* was scuttled by aircraft from the aircraft carrier HMS *Ark Royal* on 16th May (Adam Werka).

1899–1903. Augustus married Frances Madeline Jane Thomson née Hanmer (24th October 1872–4th August 1920), born in Queensland, Australia, on 14th November 1900 at Framfield, Sussex. She was the widow of Lieutenant Colonel George Leonard Thomson, 35th Foot. They had two children:
- Denys Maida Hanmer West (1901–66), born at Newtown Hill, Leixlip, Co Kildare, married Richard St John Jefferyes Colthurst (1887–1955) in 1927 at Kensington, London. Richard had married Cecily Charlotte Cholmondeley (1886–1958), born at Kensington, London, in 1911 at Wem, Shropshire. The marriage ended in divorce. Denys and Richard had two sons.
- Joan Valerie Hanmer West (1902–80), born at Newtown Hill, married John Charles Henry in 1927 at Eton, Buckinghamshire. They had two children. She was living in Cardiganshire in 1939. The marriage ended in divorce in 1943. He was known to have lived at Lodge Park, Straffan, Co Kildare.

Augustus married Hazel Valerie Laverton née West (died 3rd September 1954) in 1926 at St George, Hanover Square, London. She was the widow of Major Herbert Curling Laverton, Black Watch (1875–1923).
- Dudley Alexander West (13th July 1874–26th June 1904), born at Altadore, Co Dublin, was educated at Combe Down and the Royal Agricultural College, Cirencester 1894–96. He was appointed Executive Commissioner of the Chamber of Mines for Rhodesia and served in the South African War 1899–1902. Dudley was appointed FRGS in May 1904. He never married and died of yellow fever at Vera Cruz, Mexico.
- Sarah Elmina West (13 February 1877–19th September 1954), born at 1 Oxford Street, Cheltenham, never married.

- Georgiana Geraldine de Blaisy West (22nd June 1880–13th November 1961) was a spinster living at 33 Wyndham Crescent, Woodley, Berkshire at the time of her death there.

Richard's paternal grandfather, Reverend William James West (9th June 1809–22nd October 1859), born at Harcourt Street, Dublin, was educated at Trinity College, Dublin (BA 1830, MA 1832). He was ordained at Raphoe, Co Donegal on 23rd February 1834 and was admitted to priest's orders at Ferns, Co Wexford on 5th October 1834. William was Rector of Delgany, Co Wicklow 1847–59 and Rural Dean of Bray. He married Elmina née Erskine (16th April 1811–30th November 1886), born at Sydney Place, Bath, Somerset, on 3rd August 1838 at St Mary's, Bryanston Square, London. They lived at Ederney, Co Fermanagh and Balix and Legcloghfin, Co Tyrone. He died at Delgany, Co Wicklow and she at Galtrim House, Bray, Co Wicklow. In addition to Augustus they had eight other children:

Harcourt Street, Dublin, where Richard's paternal grandfather was born in 1809.

Trinity College Dublin dates back to 1592. In the 18th century it was regarded as a Protestant establishment. Catholics were allowed to apply for admission from 1793, but it was not until 1873 that religious tests were abolished. Irish Catholic bishops imposed a ban on Catholics entering Trinity College, which was not rescinded until 1970. Women were admitted as full members in 1904. Following independence, Trinity College had a cool relationship with the new Irish state, but thrives today with student numbers doubling by the 1990s. In 1991 Thomas Noel Mitchell became the first Roman Catholic elected Provost of Trinity College.

- William Alexander Erskine West (West-Erskine from 1872) (12th September 1839–22nd October 1892), born at Annamoe Glebe, Co Wicklow, was educated at Christ Church, Oxford and emigrated to South Australia. He was member for Mount Barker in the South Australian House of Assembly 1872–75 and for Encounter Bay 1878–81. He was Commissioner of Public Works in Sir James Penn Boucaut's government June 1875–February 1876 and was elected to the South Australian Legislative Council in May 1885. He retired in 1891, returned to Britain and died at St Anne's Hill, Co Cork.

Christ Church Delgany, where Richard's paternal grandfather, Reverend William James West, was the Rector 1847–59. The church was built in 1789.

Richard's paternal grandparents married at St Mary's, Bryanston Square, London. The church, built in 1823–24, is known colloquially as 'St Mary's Church London', being the most central Anglican church named St Mary's in inner London.

- Henry Matthew West (27th December 1842–4th February 1913), born at Annamoe Glebe, was a clerk in Holy Orders. He married Helen Mary Dunlop (15th February 1852–8th March 1933), born at Monasterboice, Co Louth, on 8th May 1874 at St George's, Dublin. They were living at Folly Court, Staverton, Wokingham, Berkshire at the time of his death there, leaving effects valued at £61,544/8/6 (£6.7M in 2019). She lived at Staverton, Murdoch Road, near Wokingham and subsequently died there. Henry and Helen had nine children – William Robert West 1875, Alexander Henry Dunlop West 1877, Annie Elmina Blanche West 1877, Harry Erskine West 1879, Helen Susan Rachel West 1884, Jessie Georgiana Dorothy West 1884, Charles Skeffington West 1886, Eileen Myrtle West 1891 and Kathleen Violet West 1891. Charles Skeffington West was

Richard's paternal grandmother, Elmina Erskine, was born at Sydney Place, Bath, built between 1795 and 1808. Queen Charlotte lived at No.93 in 1817 and William IV at No.103.

commissioned as a lieutenant in the RNVR on 28th August 1914. He served at Antwerp with the Hawke Battalion in October and was promoted lieutenant commander on 24th December. On 28th January 1915 he transferred to the Collingwood Battalion at Blandford, Dorset as second in command. He joined the Mediterranean Expeditionary Force on 7th June. Two days later he was slightly wounded by a gun shot to the left hand and arm and was admitted to 15th General Hospital. He transferred to the Convalescent Depot on 25th June, embarked on HMT *Manitou* on 28th June and transferred to the Howe Battalion on 4th July. Charles was appointed CO 14th November–2nd December and 16th January–22nd February 1916. He was then granted leave in Britain and rejoined the unit on 17th May. MID, LG 1st November 1916. Appointed CO 22nd November–2nd December and was granted leave to Britain 3rd–15th January 1917. He was second in command from 26th February. Awarded the DSO (LG 17th April 1917) for rendering invaluable service by most ably guiding and placing companies in their battle positions within 400 yards of the enemy. He worked continuously under heavy shellfire and was largely responsible for the success of the operations. Appointed CO 11th March–5th April and was MID (LG 15th May 1917). Appointed CO 21st June and acting commander on 10th July. He was granted leave in Britain 27th August–6th September and was again second in command 15th November–15th December. MID, LG 11th December 1917. Appointed CO 18th December and was killed in action on 30th December 1917 (Metz-en-Couture Communal Cemetery British Extension, France – II F 6)

- Alexander Erskine West (13th June 1844–9th August 1871), born at Annamoe Glebe, married Katherine Darley (18th August 1847–26th June 1896), born in Van Diemen's Land (Tasmania), on 1st October 1867 at Bray, Co Wicklow. He died at Carlingford, Co Louth and she at The Hermitage, Portchester Gate, London.

William Alexander Erskine West-Erskine emigrated to South Australia and became a politician.

Richard's cousin, Charles Skeffington West, is buried in Metz-en-Couture Communal Cemetery British Extension. Also buried there is George Henry Tatham Paton VC, whose story is related in the sixth book in this series, *Victoria Crosses on the Western Front: Cambrai to the German Spring Offensive November 1917 – March 1918.*

- Elmina Eliza West (29th April 1846–19th August 1866), born at Annamoe Glebe, died at Mount Herbert, Bray, Co Wicklow.
- Frederick John West (10th August 1848–1st September 1895), born at Delgany, married Laura Mary Swinden (died 14th February 1914) in 1876 at Gilbert, South Australia. They had a son, William Alfred Augustus West, the following year. Frederick died at Glenelg, South Australia and Laura at Adelaide.
- Arthur Fitzgerald West (13th May 1850–6th February 1851).
- Alfred Edward West (13th August 1851–9th September 1919), born at Delgany, married Florence Levey (12th May 1855–17th September 1936), born in Québec, Canada, on 24th May 1877 at St George, Hanover Square, London. They were living at Kilcroney, Bray, Co Wicklow at the time of his death at Navan, Co Meath, leaving effects valued at £35,607/0/3 (£1.9M in 2018). She was living at Mount Pleasant, Vallée des Vaux, Jersey, Channel Islands at the time of her death there. They had four children – Cyril Charles West 1878, Hazel Valerie West 1881, Harold Richard Alfrey West 1884 and Aubrey Fenton West 1888.
- Amelia Louisa West (30th August 1853–24th April 1875) was born at Delgany and died in Rome, Italy.

His maternal grandfather, Reverend Canon Richard Booth Eyre MA (30th October 1798–26th July 1884), born at Clonfert, Co Galway, Ireland, was Rector of Eyrecourt, Co Galway. He married Sarah née Persse (c.1806–13th November 1841), born at Roxborough, Co Galway, on 18th August 1829. In addition to Sarah they had six other children, all born at Clonfert:

- Robert Dudley Eyre (23rd March 1831–26th August 1920) sailed for New Zealand aboard the clipper *Empress*, departing Ireland on 3rd February 1865 and arriving at Auckland on 15th May. He married Matilda Norton (c.1845–1929) in 1868. They had three children – Richard Booth Dudley Eyre 1867, Sydney Seymour Eyre 1875 and Egmont Annesley Eyre 1878.
- Anne 'Nannie' Eyre (born c.1832) married Thomas Eyre on 12th April 1854.
- Elizabeth Jane Eyre (c.1834–19th October 1897) married Maurice Griffin Dennis in 1858. They had six children – Agnes Persse Eyre 1855, Emma Eyre 1857, Thomas Arthur Eyre 1859, Herbert Hedges Eyre 1860, Sarah Persse Eyre 1862 and Dudley Richard Eyre 1868.
- Richard Annesley Eyre (c.1835–3rd April 1876) married Mary Dorothy Churton (1838–19th September 1923), born at Threapwood, Flintshire, on 23rd September 1869 at Bishop House, Auckland, New Zealand.
- Maria Helena Eyre (c.1836–c.1906) married Henry Albert Mathew Drought (born c.1811). They had seven children – Albert Eyre Drought, Edgar Bristow Drought, James Justinian Drought, Percy James Drought, Richard Eustace Annesley Drought, Robert Henry Persse Drought and Sarah J Drought. James Justinian Drought served in East Africa 1895, Nandi 1895–96 and the South African War

1899–1902. He raised the Londiani Defence Force on 4th August 1914 to protect viaducts and other important points on the railway between Molo and Lumbwa, Kenya. He was appointed Commandant next day and Commandant No.5 Section Railway Defence on 7th August. Commissioned as a lieutenant on the General List on 2nd October, later revised to 5th August. James resigned to raise Ross's Scouts as second in command, paymaster and quartermaster on 27th October. He was appointed acting OC on 24th December and the unit was absorbed by the East African Mounted Rifles. He was appointed OC Lake Troop and Intelligence Officer, East Lake Area on 15th January 1915. He raised and commanded the Skin Corps of native irregular scouts and equipped the unit from German sources. In April 1915 his Troop was attached to the Intelligence Department responsible for the border from Lake Victoria to the Masai Escarpment as well as all intelligence work for the East Lake District to Mwanza. Promoted captain on 1st September and was appointed OC Armed Scouts in October. James was mentioned in Lieutenant General The Hon JC Smuts', C-in-C East African Force, Despatch dated 8th May 1916. In June 1916 he planned and took part in the capture of Ukerewe Island and the rice crop. Following this the Skin Corps and Armed Scouts were paid by the East Lake Border Police as a reward for their service. Awarded the MC, LG 26th June 1916. Promoted captain East Lake Border Police on 4th October 1917. He relinquished command on 18th October and transferred to the Unattached List. Appointed acting Assistant Provost Marshal Base on 22nd February 1918. From 16th May he was also acting Assistant Provost Marshal Force and Camp Commandant GHQ. Awarded the Belgian Croix de Chevalier de l'Ordre de Leopold on 25th June. Temporary captain as Assistant Provost Marshal Base, Dar-es-Salaam and graded as staff captain on 25th July. Appointed Assistant Provost Marshal, East African Force as temporary major 23rd October 1918–18th April 1919. He was wounded three times and relinquished his commission on 20th April 1919, retaining the rank of captain. He was living at Droughtville, Londiani, Kenya Colony in April 1921.
- Catherine Frances Eyre (c.1838–21st December 1914).

Richard married Honora Louisa Madeline Buston (c.1820–5th September 1888), born at Clonfert, in 1842. She died in Co Galway. Richard died at Rathdown, Dublin. Richard and Honora had three children:

- Florence Geraldine Eyre (born c.1845).
- Madeline Esther Eyre (15th March 1848–29th March 1913) married John Hope (c.1851–10th April 1911) on 6th December 1876 at Portumna, Ireland. He died at his home at Kilpoole House, Wicklow. They had four children – Richard Ralph Eyre-Hope 1878, Florence Eyre-Hope 1879, Ethel Madelene Eyre-Hope 1881 and Ludlow William Eyre-Hope 1887.

- Hastings Augustus Eyre (2nd October 1854–31st December 1920) was commissioned from the Militia on 17th March 1877 in 100th Foot and 9th Foot on 15 September. Promoted lieutenant 13th September 1879 in the Norfolk Regiment. Qualified as an Instructor of Musketry. Promoted captain 10th January 1883, restored and honorary captain 13th May 1885 and employed as a Paymaster with the Army Pay Department from the same date. Honorary major 13th May 1895 and substantive 16th February 1899. Staff Paymaster 14th February 1900, promoted lieutenant colonel and stationed at Devizes, Wiltshire from 14th February 1905. Appointed 1st Class Assistant Accountant, Army Accounts Department on 1st May 1905 and Accountant 9th July 1906. He retired on 2nd October 1911. Hastings married Kathleen 'Kate' Frances Walsh (c.1857–24th December 1931) on 3rd June 1882 at St Mary Le Bow, London. He was living at Askham, Seabrook Road, Hythe, Kent at the time of his death there. Kate was still living there at the time of her death at Grey House, Sevenoaks, Kent. They had three children:
  - John Lionel Eyre (born 1883).
  - Richard Philip Hastings Eyre (1888–1982) served in the ranks and was mobilised with the TF for 206 days before being commissioned in the Army Service Corps on 2nd March 1915. Promoted temporary lieutenant on 21st June and temporary captain on 16th September. He was appointed adjutant 1st July 1918–13th November 1919. He served in Greek Macedonia, Serbia, Bulgaria, European Turkey and the Islands of the Aegean from 29th August 1916 until 11th November 1918 (MID, LG 21st July 1917 and 5th January 1919). Awarded the MBE, LG 3rd June 1919. He was employed in the War Office from 26th November 1921 and as a staff captain there from 1st January 1925. Promoted captain 15th September 1926, serving at Aldershot, and brevet major 1st January 1929. He was appointed adjutant 21st January 1929–20th January 1932. He was the Aldershot Command Barrack Officer and last appears in the Army List in 1935. Re-employed in a special employment from 1st August 1941. Richard married Daphne Brierley (30th March 1906–14th November 1969), born at Wimbledon, Surrey, in 1933 at Kensington, London. They were living at Gays Cottage, Winsford, Minehead, Somerset at the time of her death there. He died at The Beacon Hotel, Victoria Hill Road, Fleet, Hampshire.
  - Nora Kathleen Eyre (1893–1968).

Richard was educated at Channel View School, Clevedon, Somerset, at Monkton Combe School, Bath, Somerset and at Uckfield Agricultural and Horticultural College, Sussex. He enlisted as a trooper in 45th (Irish Hunt) Company, Imperial Yeomanry and served in South Africa during the Second Boer War January 1900–March 1901. He was in action at Cape Colony, Rhodesia, Belmont 23rd November 1899, Modder River 28th November 1899, Orange Free State, Wepener 9th–

Monkton Combe School was founded in 1868 by Reverend Francis Pocock and a junior school was established in 1888. The current purpose-built premises date from 1907. A pre-prep school was added in 1929. In 1992 the School became fully co-educational, merging with Clarendon School for Girls, Bedford. The school has a strong evangelical Christian heritage. Amongst its famous alumni are:

- Bernard Cornwell OBE (born 1944), historical novelist.
- Major General John Frost CB DSO & Bar MC DL (1912–93), who commanded the small parachute force on the Bruneval Raid in February 1942 and 2nd Battalion, The Parachute Regiment at Arnhem bridge in September 1944.
- Sir Richard Peirse (1892–1970), C-in-C Bomber Command.
- Sir Richard Stilgoe (born 1943), songwriter and musician.

25th April 1900 and Transvaal. In July 1901 he transferred to 2nd Kitchener's Fighting Scouts. He was promoted corporal and was commissioned as a lieutenant in November 1901. Richard was appointed superintendent with the Transvaal Repatriation Department until 31st March 1904. After the war he remained in South Africa farming and later training racehorses for the Duke of Westminster. He was appointed lieutenant and Assistant Adjutant, Transvaal Horse Artillery Volunteers January 1904–1st July 1910. He transferred to the Transvaal Reserve of Officers in 1912.

Richard West married Maude Ethel Cushing (20th February 1884–16th May 1973), born at Kentish Town, London, on 16th July 1909 at Pretoria, Transvaal, South Africa. She was a music vocalist in 1901, living with her mother. She became a musical comedy actress with the stage name Maude Aston. They met when she was on tour in South Africa. He fell in love with her across the footlights in Durban and asked her to marry him. She turned him down but told him that she would be ending her tour in Cape Town. He rode across the Cape to meet her and she accepted his proposal. They lived at Albert Street, Rosettenville, near Johannesburg, Transvaal. When Richard enlisted in 1914 they were living at The Grove, Cabra, Dublin, Ireland. She was living at 1 Hobart Place, Eaton Square, London in September 1918, later at Kingsleigh, Marine View, Hove, Sussex and at 14 Trafalgar Square, Chelsea, London in 1920. She was living at Lower Rew Farmhouse, Martinstown, Dorchester, Dorset at the time of her death. Richard and Maude had a daughter:

- Gertrude Annesley 'Anne' West (17th November 1918–23rd September 2004), born at Hove, Sussex, was a vocalist and married Major Donald Stapleton Carden BA (6th October 1914–16th June 1984), Royal Leicestershire Regiment, born at Bromley, Kent, on 6th August 1938 at Cuckfield, Sussex. Donald was commissioned (General List) on 19th March 1937 (70489) with seniority from 30th January 1936. He was MID for distinguished service in the Middle East December 1940–February 1941 (LG 8th July 1941). He was promoted captain 30th January 1944, major 30th January 1949, lieutenant colonel 16th February 1958 and colonel 12th May 1963. Donald was awarded the CBE (LG 1st January 1969) and retired on 12th August 1971. The marriage ended in divorce in 1946. Donald married Heather Monimia Morgan Chandler (born 1923) in 1947 at Wharfedale, Yorkshire. He was living at Small Down House, Chesterblade, Shepton Mallet, Somerset at the time of his death there. Donald and Heather had four children – Susan Mary Monimia Carden 1948, Averil Prudence Carden 1950, Catriona Caroline Carden 1951 and Timothy John Reginald Carden 1955. Gertrude married Colonel Percy Vyvyan Lovell Payne (22nd December 1900–25th February 1993), born at Nottingham, on 21st April 1948 at Chelsea, London. Percy was commissioned from the Royal Military College, Sandhurst in the Royal Munster Fusiliers on 16th July 1920 and transferred to the Wiltshire Regiment on 2nd August 1922. He was promoted lieutenant on 16th July 1922 and was appointed ADC to GOC Bombay District on 1st October 1924. Promoted war substantive major and temporary lieutenant colonel on 2nd January 1943. MID for gallant service in the Middle East (LG 13th January 1944). Appointed acting colonel on 9th May 1945. Promoted major 1st January 1949 (6987) and transferred to the Reserve of Officers (last in the Army List August–October 1948) until reaching the age limit on 17th November 1951. He was granted the honorary rank of colonel. Percy had married Bertha Rosina Janetta Vester (1908–94) in 1938 at Jerusalem, Palestine, where she was born. He was Publicity Manager of the Shell Company in Egypt at the time. They had a daughter, Djemila Lovell Payne, in 1939, who married John Ambrose Cope (born 1937) in 1969 and they had two daughters. He was Conservative MP for South Gloucestershire 1974–83 and for Northavon 1983–97. He held various parliamentary and government appointments – Assistant Whip 1979–81, Lord Commissioner of the Treasury 1981–83, Treasurer of Her Majesty's Household 1983–97, Deputy Chief Whip 1983–87, Minister of State for Employment 1987–89, Privy Counsellor 1988, Minister of State for Northern Ireland 1989–90, Paymaster-General 1992–94 and Conservative Chief Whip in the House of Lords 2001–07. Knight Bachelor 1991 and created Baron Cope of Berkeley on 4th October 1997. Percy and Bertha's marriage ended in divorce. Gertrude and Percy had two children – Katherine L Payne 1950 and Simon Payne. Gertrude and Percy were living at Lower Rew Farmhouse, Martinstown, Dorchester, Dorset in 1958 and he later died there. Gertrude died in Surrey.

Maude's father, Henry William Cushing (12th April 1842–12th April 1899) was an engineering draughtsman. He married Mary Pearson (1842–72) on 25th August 1863 at St Pancras, London. They had two children – William Henry Cushing 1866 and Albert Walter Cushing 1869. Henry married Emily née Day (c.1848–3rd December 1912), a vocalist born at St Marylebone, London, on 12th April 1873 at St Mary's, Battersea, London. They were living at Nunwell, 53 Eglantine Road, Wandsworth, London in 1891, where Henry subsequently died. Emily was living at 48 Rectory Road, Barnes, Surrey in 1911 and died there the following year. In addition to Maude they had four other children:

* Gertrude Emily Louise Cushing (14th November 1879–4th March 1959) was a pianoforte teacher in 1911, living with her mother. She married John Cullinan (born 29th September 1881 or 14th March 1880) on 2nd October 1913 at Colaba, Bombay, India. He was appointed a conductor in the Indian Army Ordnance Corps on 7th May 1922 and was serving at Army HQ in 1929. He was appointed assistant commissioner with the rank of lieutenant on 27th March 1929 and major (commissaries) on 15th May 1932, while serving at Army HQ (Master General of the Ordnance School). He was granted twelve months leave outside India from 13th March 1935 and had retired by 1939, when they were living at

Richard's wife, Maude Ethel Cushing, a musical comedy actress with the stage name Maude Aston, was the aunt of Peter Wilton Cushing OBE (1913–94), famous for his roles in Hammer Productions horror films and for playing Sherlock Holmes and Dr Who. He also appeared in the first *Star Wars* film.

Peter Cushing.

The house on the right is 53 Eglantine Road, Wandsworth, Maude Cushing's family home.

St Mary's Church, the oldest church in Battersea, is Grade 1 listed. There has been a church on the site since c.800 and the present building was completed in 1777. The artist and poet William Blake married Catherine Boucher there in 1782. The artist Joseph Mallord William Turner (1775–1851), known as William Turner, painted the Thames from the vestry window. Bendict Arnold (1741–1801), an American general during the American Revolutionary War before defecting to the British in 1780, is buried in the crypt. The Church also has links with the explorer, Robert Falcon Scott (John Gay).

Merrestwood, Worthing, Sussex. She died at Herondale Nursing Home, 21 Aymer Road, Hove, Sussex.

- George Edward Cushing (1st July 1881–1st November 1956) married Nellie Maria King (6th March 1882–22nd March 1961), born at St Saviour, London, on 3rd July 1907 at Emmanuel Congregational Church, Camberwell, London. He was a quantity surveyor in 1911 and they were living at 46 Rectory Road, Barnes, Surrey. They were living with their son, David, at Cherry Tree Cottage, Dorking, Surrey in 1939 and at Rustington, Brockham Lane, Betchworth, Surrey at the time of his death there. She was still living there at the time of her death at Redhill County Hospital, Surrey. They had two sons – David Henry Cushing (1910–87) and Peter Wilton Cushing OBE (1913–94), the actor known particularly for his roles in Hammer Productions horror films.
- Sydney Percival Cushing (6th July–25th September 1885).
- Ernest Charles Cushing (29th June 1889–8th November 1947), an insurance clerk, married Ada Katherine Shelley (1889–21st April 1942), born at Brentford, Middlesex, in 1912 at Horsham, Surrey. He transferred from a secondment to 100th Provisional Battalion (attached 6th Provisional Cyclist Company, Kelsale, Suffolk, Eastern Command) and was restored to 9th London and transferred to 25th London, Richmond Park Camp, Roehampton in June 1916. Appointed acting

captain, assistant commandant and adjutant of 247th Divisional Employment Company 15th June 1918–26th March 1919. He disembarked at Folkestone on 7th April and was disembodied on 8th April 1919. His address at that time was Broadview, Slinfold, Sussex. They were living at Green Corner, 48 Longdown Lane, North Ewell, Surrey at the time of her death there. They had two sons:
 ○ Antony Henry Shelley Cushing (born 1917), born at Horsham, Sussex, served as a lieutenant with an Indian Army Emergency Commission on 23rd September 1941 and was promoted temporary captain on 28th September 1942.
 ○ Bernard Rutherford Cushing (1920–42), born at Richmond, Surrey, was commissioned on 5th April 1941 in 46th (The Liverpool Welsh) Royal Tank Regiment (180767) and died on active service between 22nd and 24th July 1942 (El Alamein Cemetery, Egypt – XXI D 24).

Ernest married Letitia Emily Stacey (25th November 1895–1978), born at Croydon, Surrey, in 1944 in Surrey. She was an insurance clerk living at 5 Edgar Road, Coulsdon, Surrey at the time of the 1939 Census. They were living at 11 Normandy Lane, Angmering-on-Sea, Sussex at the time of his death there. She died at Worthing.

Richard returned to Britain before the Great War. He enlisted in the North Irish Horse (1015) in Belfast, Ireland on 20th August 1914, described as 6′ tall, weighing 175 lbs, with blue eyes, brown hair and his religious denomination was Church of England. His Medal Index Card shows that he went to France on 21st August, which seems incredibly quick, even in an emergency. His service record suggests that he served at Home and was discharged at York on 22nd September on being gazetted as a lieutenant in the North Irish Horse (Special Reserve) with seniority from 11th August 1914. He went to France, probably with C Squadron (GHQ Troops). **Mentioned in Field Marshal Sir John French's Despatch of 8th October 1914, LG 19th October, 20th October and 9th December 1914.** On 13th June 1915, Richard was appointed temporary major and attached to 1/1st North Somerset Yeomanry. He was appointed honorary major on 10th July and temporary captain on 13th September. On 16th September he was admitted to 6th Cavalry Field Ambulance with influenza, transferred to the Allied Forces Base Hospital on 27th September and was evacuated to Britain on HMHS *Brighton* the following day. He embarked on 8th November, disembarked next day, joined 5th General Base Depot, Rouen on 10th November and rejoined the unit on 13th November. Promoted captain on 18th November and was appointed temporary major 9th March 1916–8th September 1917. **Awarded the DSO for his actions at Monchy-le-Preux, France on 11th April 1917. His squadron was sent forward to reinforce the right flank of the brigade under very heavy shell and machine gun fire. By his excellent example, rapid grasp of the situation and skilful disposition of his squadron, he did much to avert** an impending German counterattack, LG 1st January 1918. Mentioned in Field Marshal Sir Douglas Haig's Despatch of 7th November 1917, LG 11th December 1917.

Richard left 1/1st North Somerset Yeomanry on 23rd December 1917 and was seconded to 6th Battalion Tank Corps on 2nd January 1918 to command C Company. He was appointed acting major while commanding a company on 18th January. Granted leave in Britain 27th January–12th February. He was admitted to 2/1st West Riding Field Ambulance with pyrexia of unknown origin on 13th June and transferred next day to 8th General Hospital, Rouen. He rejoined the unit on 23rd June and was granted leave to Britain 9th–27th July.

Awarded the MC for his actions at Guillaucourt on 8th August 1918 in command of a company of light tanks. He had two horses shot from under him during the day but he and his orderly killed five of the enemy and took seven prisoners. On 10th August he rendered great services to the cavalry by his personal reconnaissance of the ground in front of Le Quesnel. During this advance he was able to point out many targets to his tanks that they would not otherwise have seen. Later in the day, under heavy machine gun fire, he rallied the crews of disabled tanks and withdrew them with great skill after dark, LG 7th November 1918. He was appointed second in command on 9th August and was wounded but remained at duty next day.

Awarded a Bar to the DSO, LG 7th November 1918. The citation for this award is almost the same as for the VC and was awarded for actions on the same date. Unusually, it appears that he received two awards for the same action. **Awarded the VC for his actions at Courcelles and Vaulx Vraucourt, France on 21st August and 2nd September 1918, LG 30th October 1918.** Richard was appointed acting lieutenant colonel on 22nd August and assumed command of the Battalion. **Mentioned in Field Marshal Sir Douglas Haig's Despatch of 8th November 1918, LG 20th December 1918.** He was killed during his VC action at Vaulx Vraucourt, France on 2nd September 1918. He is buried in Mory Abbey Military Cemetery – III G 4. He left effects valued at £1,687/6/11. Richard is commemorated in a number of other places:

Richard West's grave in Mory Abbey Military Cemetery

* Six Scimitar reconnaissance vehicles in A Squadron, 1st Royal Tank Regiment, were named after recipients of the Victoria Cross – HRB Foote, PJ Gardner, C Robertson, CH Sewell, RWL Wain and RA West.

- Tank Corps Museum, Bovington, Dorset:
    - An 8″ German howitzer presented in his honour.
    - Named on the Honours Board.
- Ireland
    - Family headstone in Colebrooke Churchyard, Co Fermanagh.
    - War Memorials:
        St Ronan's Church, Colebrooke.
        Enniskillen, Co Fermanagh.
        Main Street, Brookeborough, Co Fermanagh.
        Carrickfergus, Co Antrim.
        Hibernian United Services Club (now National Museum), Collins Barracks, Dublin.
    - Victoria Cross Memorial, Ennikillen Castle.
    - North Irish Horse Memorial in Belfast City Hall.

The West family grave in Colebrooke Churchyard.

Enniskillen War Memorial (Rowey).

Blue plaque on Richard West's birthplace at 1 Oxford Street, Cheltenham (Blue Plaque Places).

The Castle of Good Hope, Cape Town, where the South African VC memorial plaque is located.

- Cheltenham, Gloucestershire:
  - Blue plaque dedicated at his birthplace at 1 Oxford Street, in 2009.
  - A Department for Communities and Local Government commemorative paving stone was dedicated at Cheltenham War Memorial, The Promenade on 2nd September 2018.
- War Memorial, Monkton Coombe School, Somerset.
- Ring of Remembrance (L'Anneau de la Mémoire), Ablain-Saint-Nazaire, Pas-de-Calais, France.
- Named on one of eleven plaques honouring 175 men from overseas awarded the VC for the Great War. The plaques were unveiled by the Senior Minister of State at the Foreign & Commonwealth Office and Minister for Faith and Communities, Baroness Warsi, at a reception at Lancaster House, London on 26th June 2014 attended by The Duke of Kent and relatives of the VC recipients. The South African plaque is mounted at the Castle of Good Hope, Cape Town.

The Queen's South Africa Medal was instituted in 1900 for military personnel, civilian officials and war correspondents, who served during the Second Boer War from 11th October 1899 to 31st May 1902. Approximately 178,000 were awarded. There are twenty-six clasps.

The VC, DSO & Bar and MC were presented to his widow by the King in the ballroom of Buckingham Palace on 15th February 1919. Maude was living at 14 Trafalgar Square, Chelsea, London in 1920. She was living at Lower Rew Farmhouse, Martinstown, Dorchester, Dorset at the time of her death.

In addition to the VC, DSO & Bar and MC, he was awarded the Queen's South Africa Medal 1899–1902 with three clasps (Cape Colony, Orange Free State & Transvaal), King's South Africa Medal 1901–02

The King's South Africa Medal was awarded to British, Dominion and Colonial military personnel who served in the Second Boer War. They had to be in the theatre on or after 1st January 1902 and had completed eighteen months service in the conflict prior to 1st June 1902, not necessarily continuously. The medal was never awarded singly, but was always paired with the Queen's South Africa Medal. Two clasps were awarded and the qualifying criteria meant that most Medals were awarded with both but there were exceptions. Nursing sisters qualified for the medal but not the clasps and 587 were awarded. By 1902 most Dominion contingents had returned home. As a result only 154 Medals were awarded to Canadians and about 200 to New Zealanders, including six nurses.

with two clasps (South Africa 1901 & South Africa 1902), 1914 Star with Mons clasp, British War Medal 1914–20 and Victory Medal 1914–19 with Mentioned-in-Despatches Oakleaf. The VC was held on loan by the Tank Corps Museum, Bovington, Dorset but was withdrawn by a relative and sold privately in June 2002 to Lord Ashcroft. The VC is held by the Michael Ashcroft Trust, the holding institution for the Lord Ashcroft Victoria Cross Collection and is displayed in the Imperial War Museum's Lord Ashcroft Gallery. His VC group was one of fifty exhibited by the Michael Ashcroft Trust, in association with Spink, at 69 Southampton Row, London 16th–25th April 2008. The Michael Ashcroft Trust hosted an exhibition of eighteen VC groups, including Richard's, from Lord Ashcroft's collection at the Rugby Football Union Museum, Twickenham, London 16th–20th September 2008. The exhibition was held in conjunction with a charity match for 'Help for Heroes' between 'England Old Uns' and 'The Rest of the World Old Uns' on 20th September 2008.

Sources

The following institutions, individuals and publications were consulted:

Regimental Museums

RHQ The Royal Scots, Edinburgh; Lancashire County and Regimental Museum, Preston; Lancashire HQ Royal Regiment of Fusiliers; The Tank Museum; RHQ Devonshire and Dorset Regiment, Exeter.

Individuals

Doug and Richard Arman, Gaye Ashford, Maj (Ret'd) Marcus Beak, Norman Best, David Fletcher, Tony Grant, DJ Huggins, Alan Jordan, Steve Lee, Alasdair Macintyre, Robert Mansell, Colin Martin, Bill Mullen, Iain Stewart, Vic Tambling, Glenys Taylor, Gemma Wade, Jackie Wood.

Schools and Universities

Oratia District School, Auckland, New Zealand; Taunton College, Southampton.

Divisional Histories

Iron Division, The History of the 3rd Division. R McNish. Allen 1976.
The Fifth Division in the Great War. Brig Gen A H Hussey and Maj D S Inman. Nisbet 1920.
History of the 17th (Northern) Division. A H Atheridge. University Press 1929.
The Royal Naval Division. D Jerrold. Hutchinson 1923. (63rd Division).

Regimental/Unit Histories

Royal Navy
    Gallant Deeds. Compiler Vice Admiral W H D Boyle. Gieves, Portsmouth 1919.

The Royal Scots
    The Royal Scots 1914–19. Maj J Ewing. Oliver & Boyd 1925. Two volumes.

The Devonshire Regiment
 The Devonshire Regiment 1914–18. Compiler C T Atkinson. Eland Bros 1926.
 The Bloody Eleventh: History of the Devonshire Regiment Volume III: 1914–1969. WJP Aggett. Devon and Dorset Regiment 1995.

The Lancashire Fusiliers
 The History of the Lancashire Fusiliers 1914–18, Volumes I and II. Maj Gen J C Latter. Gale & Polden 1949.
 The Lancashire Fusiliers Annual. No 26–1916 and No 28–1918. Editor Major B Smyth. Sackville Press 1917 and 1919

Australian Imperial Force
 Official History of Australia in the War of 1914–1918, Volume IV – The Australian Imperial Force in France, 1917. 11th Edition 1941.
 They Dared Mightily. Lionel Wigmore, Jeff Williams & Anthony Staunton 1963 & 1986.

New Zealand
 The New Zealand Division 1916–1919. A Popular History Based on Official Records. Col H Stewart CMG DSO MC. Whitcombe & Tombs Ltd, Auckland 1921.

General Works

A Bibliography of Regimental Histories of the British Army. Compiler A S White. Society for Army Historical Research 1965.
A Military Atlas of the First World War. A Banks & A Palmer. Purnell 1975.
The Soldier's War 1914–18. P Liddle. Blandford Press.
Into Battle 1914–18. E Parker. Longmans 1964.
The Times History of the Great War.
Topography of Armageddon, A British Trench Map Atlas of the Western Front 1914–18. P Chasseaud. Mapbooks 1991.
Before Endeavours Fade. R E B Coombs. Battle of Britain Prints 1976.
British Regiments 1914–18. Brig E A James. Samson 1978.

Biographical/Autobiographical

The Dictionary of National Biography 1901–85. Various volumes. Oxford University Press.
The Cross of Sacrifice, Officers Who Died in the Service of the British, Indian and East African Regiments and Corps 1914–19. S D and D B Jarvis. Roberts Medals 1993.
Australian Dictionary of Biography.
Whitaker's Peerage, Baronetage, Knightage & Companionage 1915.

Our Heroes – Containing Photographs with Biographical Notes of Officers of Irish Regiments and of Irish Officers of British Regiments who have fallen or who have been mentioned for distinguished conduct from August 1914 to July 1916. Printed as supplements to Irish Life from 1914 to 1916.

The Bond of Sacrifice, A Biographical Record of all British Officers Who Fell in the Great War. Volume I Aug–Dec 1915, Volume II Jan–Jun 1915. Editor Col L A Clutterbuck. Pulman 1916 and 1919.

The Roll of Honour Parts 1–5, A Biographical Record of Members of His Majesty's Naval and Military Forces who fell in the Great War 1914–18. Marquis de Ruvigny. Standard Art Book Co 1917–19.

The Dictionary of Edwardian Biography – various volumes. Printed 1904–08, reprinted 1985–87 Peter Bell Edinburgh.

Specific Works on the Victoria Cross

The Register of the Victoria Cross. This England 1981 and 1988.

The Story of the Victoria Cross 1856–1963. Brig Sir J Smyth. Frederick Muller 1963.

The Evolution of the Victoria Cross, A Study in Administrative History. M J Crook. Midas 1975.

The Victoria Cross and the George Cross. IWM 1970.

The Victoria Cross, The Empire's Roll of Valour. Lt Col R Stewart. Hutchinson 1928.

The Victoria Cross 1856–1920. Sir O'Moore Creagh and E M Humphris. Standard Art Book Company, London 1920.

Victoria Cross – Awards to Irish Servicemen. B Clark. Published in The Irish Sword summer 1986.

Heart of a Dragon, VC's of Wales and the Welsh Regiments 1914–82. W Alister Williams. Bridge Books 2006.

Devotion to Duty, Tributes to a Region's VCs. James W Bancroft. Aim High 1990.

VC Locator. D Pillinger and A Staunton. Highland Press, Queanbeyan, New South Wales, Australia 1991.

Black Country VCs. Barry Harris. Black Country Society 1985.

The VC Roll of Honour. J W Bancroft. Aim High 1989.

A Bibliography of the Victoria Cross. W James McDonald. W J Mcdonald, Nova Scotia 1994.

Canon Lummis VC Files held in the National Army Museum, Chelsea.

Recipients of the Victoria Cross in the Care of the Commonwealth War Graves Commission. CWGC 1997.

Victoria Cross Heroes. Michael Ashcroft. Headline Review 2006

Monuments to Courage. David Harvey. 1999.

Beyond the Five Points – Masonic Winners of The Victoria Cross and The George Cross. Phillip May GC, edited by Richard Cowley. Twin Pillars Books, Northamptonshire 2001.

Irish Winners of the Victoria Cross. Richard Doherty & David Truesdale. Four Courts Press, Dublin, Ireland 2000.

A Breed Apart. Richard Leake. Great Northern Publishing 2008.

Other Honours and Awards

The Distinguished Service Order 1886–1923 (in 2 volumes). Sir O'Moore Creagh and E M Humphris. J B Hayward 1978 (originally published 1924).
Orders and Medals Society Journal (various articles).
The Old Contemptibles Honours and Awards. First published 1915. Reprinted by J B Hayward & Son 1971.

Official Publications and Sources

History of the Great War, Order of Battle of Divisions. Compiler Maj A F Becke. HMSO.
History of the Great War, Military Operations, France and Belgium. Compiler Brig Gen Sir J E Edmonds. HMSO. Published in 14 volumes of text, with 7 map volumes and 2 separate Appendices between 1923 and 1948.
Navy Lists.
Army Lists – including Graduation Lists and Record of War Service.
Air Force Lists.
Home Guard Lists 1942–44.
Indian Army Lists 1897–1940.
India List 1923–40.
Location of Hospitals and Casualty Clearing Stations, BEF 1914–19. Ministry of Pensions 1923.
London Gazettes
Census returns, particularly for 1881, 1891 and 1901.
Australian service records in the National Archives of Australia.
Service records in Archives New Zealand.
Officers and Soldiers Died in the Great War.

National Archives

Unit War Diaries under WO 95
Military maps under WO 297.
Medal Cards and Medal Rolls under WO 329 and ADM 171.
Soldier's Service Records under WO 97, 363 and 364.
RN Officers' Records under ADM 196.
Army Officers' Records under WO 25, 76, 339 and 374.
RAF Officers' Records under Air 76.
Births, Marriages and Deaths records.

Reference Publications

Who's Who and Who Was Who.
The Times 1914 onwards.

The Daily Telegraph 1914 onwards.
Kelly's Handbook to the Titled, Landed and Official Classes.
Burke's Peerage.

Internet Websites

History of the Victoria Cross – www2.prestel.co.uk/stewart
Commonwealth War Graves Commission – www.yard.ccta.gov.uk/cwgc
Scotland's People – http://scotlandspeople.gov.uk
Free Births, Marriages and Deaths – www.freebmd.com
Memorials to Valour – http://www.memorialstovalour.co.uk

Periodicals

This England magazine – various editions.
Coin and Medal News – various editions.
Journal of The Victoria Cross Society.
Gun Fire – A Journal of First World War History. Edited by AJ Peacock, but no longer published.
Stand To! – journal of the Western Front Association.

Useful Information
(Some details may be affected by Brexit)

Accommodation – there is a wide variety of accommodation available in France. Search on-line for your requirements. There are also numerous campsites, but many close for the winter from late September.

Clothing and Kit – consider taking:

    Waterproofs.
    Headwear and gloves.
    Walking shoes/boots.
    Shades and sunscreen.
    Binoculars and camera.
    Snacks and drinks.

Customs/Behaviour – local people are generally tolerant of battlefield visitors but please respect their property and address them respectfully. The French are less inclined to switch to English than other Europeans. If you try some basic French it will be appreciated.

Driving – rules of the road are similar to UK, apart from having to drive on the right. If in doubt about priorities, give way to the right, particularly in France. In many areas you have to give way to vehicles coming in from the right, even from apparently minor roads onto major routes. Obey laws and road signs – police impose harsh on-the-spot fines. Penalties for drinking and driving are heavy and the legal limit is lower than UK (50mg rather than 80mg). Most autoroutes in France are toll roads. In rural areas the speed limit is 80kph but in many places the old 90kph signs remain. The red-framed name board at the entrance to a village or town automatically imposes a 50kph speed limit.

    <u>Fuel</u> – petrol stations are usually only open 24 hours on major routes and larger supermarkets. Payment by credit cards in automatic tellers is increasingly becoming the norm. The cheapest fuel is at hypermarkets.

    <u>Mandatory Requirements</u> – if taking your own car you need:
        Full driving licence (an International Driving Permit may also be required post-Brexit).
        Vehicle registration document.
        Comprehensive motor insurance valid in Europe (Green Card).

European breakdown and recovery cover.
Letter of authorisation from the owner if the vehicle is not yours.
Spare set of bulbs, headlight beam adjusters, warning triangle, GB sticker, high visibility vest and breathalyzer. Requirements do vary, so check before departing. An emission quality sticker is required if driving in Paris or certain other cities.

Emergency – keep details required in an emergency separate from wallet or handbag:
Photocopy passport, insurance documents and EHIC (see Health below).
Mobile phone details.
Credit/debit card numbers and cancellation telephone contacts.
Travel insurance company contact number.
Who to contact in an emergency.

Ferries – the closest ports are Boulogne, Calais and Dunkirk. The Shuttle is quicker, but usually more expensive.

Health

European/Global Health Insurance Card – entitles the holder to medical treatment at local rates. Existing EHICs remain valid until their expiry date. Apply online for the GHIC at https://www.ghic.org.uk/Internet/startApplication.do. It is issued free and is valid for five years. You are only covered if you have the GHIC with you when you go for treatment.

Travel Insurance – you are also strongly advised to have full travel insurance. If you receive treatment get a statement by the doctor (*feuille de soins*) and a receipt to make a claim on return.

Personal Medical Kit – treating minor ailments saves time and money. Pack sufficient prescription medicine for the trip.

Chemist (*Pharmacie*) – look for the green cross. They provide some treatment and if unable to help will direct you to a doctor. Most open 0900–1900, except Sunday. Out of hours services (*pharmacie de garde*) are advertised in Pharmacie windows.

Doctor and Dentist – hotel receptions have details of local practices. Beware private doctors/hospitals, as extra charges cannot be reclaimed – the French national health service is known as *conventionné*.

Rabies – contact with infected animals is very rare but if bitten by any animal get the wound examined professionally <u>immediately</u>.

Money

ATMs – at most banks and post offices with instructions in English. Check your card can be used in France and what charges apply. Some banks limit how much can be withdrawn. Let your bank know you will be away, as some block cards if transactions take place unexpectedly.

Credit/Debit Cards – major cards are usually accepted, but some have different names – Visa is Carte Bleue and Mastercard is Eurocard.

Exchange – beware 0% commission, as the rate may be poor. The Post Office takes back unused currency at the same rate, which may or may not be advantageous. Since the Euro, currency exchange facilities are scarce.

Local Taxes – if you buy high value items you can reclaim tax. Get the forms completed by the shop, have them stamped by Customs, post them to the shop and they will refund about 12%. Brexit may change this.

Passport – a valid passport is required.

Post – postcard stamps are often available from vendors, newsagents and tabacs.

Public Holidays – just about everything closes and banks can close early the day before. Transport may be affected, but tourist attractions in high season are unlikely to be. The following dates/days are public holidays:

1 January
Easter Monday
1 May
8 May
Ascension Day
Whit Monday
14 July
15 August
1 & 11 November
25 December

In France many businesses and restaurants close for the majority of August.

Radio – if you want to pick up the news from home try BBC Radio 4 on 198 kHz long wave. BBC Five Live on 909 kHz medium wave can sometimes be received. There are numerous internet options for keeping up with the news.

Shops – in large towns and tourist areas they tend to open all day. In more remote places they may close for lunch. Some bakers open Sunday a.m. and during the week take later lunch breaks. In general shops do not open on Sundays and those that do have limited hours.

Telephone

<u>To UK</u> – 0044, delete initial 0 then dial the rest of the number.

<u>Local Calls</u> – dial the full number even if within the same zone.

<u>Mobiles</u> – check yours will work in France and the charges.

<u>Emergencies</u> – dial 112 for medical, fire and police anywhere in Europe from any landline, pay phone or mobile. Calls are free

<u>British Embassy (Paris)</u> – 01 44 51 31 00.

Time Zone – one hour ahead of UK.

Tipping – a small tip is expected by cloakroom and lavatory attendants and porters. Not required in restaurants, when a service charge is included.

Toilets – the best are in museums and the main tourist attractions. Towns usually have public toilets where markets are held; some are coin operated. Otherwise on the battlefields facilities are sparse. Finding a local café may be the best option, although they are closing as rapidly as British pubs.

Index

Notes:
1. Not every person or location is included. Most family members named in the Biographies are not.
2. Armed forces units, establishments, etc. are grouped under the respective country, except for Britain's, which appear under the three services – British Army, Royal Air Force and Royal Navy. Royal Naval Division units appear under British Army for convenience.
3. Newfoundland appears under Canada although not part of it at the time.
4. Cathedrals, Cemeteries/Crematoria, Churches, Commonwealth War Graves Commission, Hospitals, Schools and Universities appear under those group headings.
5. All orders, medals and decorations appear under Orders.
6. Belgium, Britain, France and Germany are not indexed in the accounts of the VC actions as there are too many mentions.

Abbassia, 88
Abbeville, 48
Aberdeen, 134, 143
Aberdeen Line, 88, 108
Abersychan, 139, 152–3
Ablain-Saint-Nazaire, 137, 179
Ablainzeville, 1
Aborigines, 96
Achiet-le-Grand, 6–8, 26–9, 54
Achiet-le-Petit, 7–8, 12, 14–15, 154
Adamson, Lawrence, 124
Adelaide, 169
Aegean, 171
Africa, 106, 121
Aikman VC, Frederick, 136
Air Raid Precautions, 140–1
Albany, WA, 76, 104
Albany Creek, Qld, 91
Albert, 1, 3, 7, 9, 14, 26, 28, 39–40
Alberta, 140–2
Alderbury, 49
Aldershot, 47, 53, 135, 171
Aldridge, 149
Aleppo, 101
Alexandria, Egypt, 53, 78, 99, 101, 104, 120–2, 150
Allenby, Gen Sir Edmund, 101
Alrewas, 84, 93, 115, 130
Altadore, 164–5
Alton, 47, 135, 141
Alvediston, 45, 49–50
American Revolutionary War, 175
American Sheet & Tin Plate Co, 152
Amesbury, 50

Ancre, 3, 12, 14, 27, 37
Andover, 111, 140
Angmering-on-Sea, 176
Angus VC, William, 136
Annamoe Glebe, 163, 166–9
Anson aircraft, 142
Antrim, Co, 84, 97, 178
Antwerp, 168
ANZAC, 122
Anzac & Cove, 53, 80
Anzac Day, 122
Apiata VC, Cpl Willie, 82
Arabs, 81
Arcy Woods, 17, 25
Arizona, 75
Armadale, 101
Armentières, 79
Arnhem, 172
Arnhem Land, 96
Arnold, Bendict, 175
Arras, 1, 7, 9, 14, 21, 28
Arsenal FC, 146
Arundell, Sir Matthew, 50
Ashington, 132
Asia, 118
Associated Chambers of Commerce of Australia, 109
Aston, 46, 64, 147
Aston Villa FC, 146
Atlantic, 120
Atlantic Transport Line, 53
Auckland, 74, 76, 110, 169
Augustinians, 94

Index

Australia/n, 62–3, 76, 83–5, 87–9, 93–4, 97–8, 100, 104, 108, 110–11, 113–16, 118–21, 123, 126, 129–30, 132, 152–3, 165
Australian armed forces, 92, 103, 114
   Australian Army, 89, 100, 109, 124, 127
      AIF HQ, 100–101, 105–106, 111
      Australian Corps, 17, 26, 32, 111
      Australian HQ Egypt, 101
      Australian Imperial Force, 86–7, 95, 97, 99–100, 104, 109, 110, 113, 122, 124
      Chief of the General Staff, 90, 114
      Citizen Military Forces, 112
      Coast Defence, 112
      Inspector General, 89–90
      Southern Command, 112
      Corps,
         Volunteer Defence Corps, 90, 114
      Divisions,
         1st Australian, 17, 22, 26, 104
         2nd Australian, 41–2
         3rd Australian, 12, 26, 41–2
         4th Australian, 17
         5th Australian, 17, 22, 42
      Brigades,
         1st, 22–3, 25–6
         1st Light Horse, 81
         2nd, 17, 22–3, 25
         3rd, 22, 26, 87, 121
         3rd Training, 101–102, 111
         4th, 17, 19–20
         6th, 42
         8th, 42
         9th, 44
         10th, 42
         11th, 41–2, 44
         14th, 22
         15th, 22
         Overseas Training, 106
      Cavalry,
         18th Australian Light Horse, 119
         Australian Light Horse, 90
      Engineers/Royal Australian Engineers, 110, 112
         19th Chief Engineer Works, 114
         21st Construction Sqn, 114
      Infantry Regiments/Battalions, 113
         1st, 22, 26
         2nd Training, 101, 104
         3rd Garrison, 112
         4th, 22–3, 26
         5th, 22–3, 25, 101
         6th, 21–5, 104
         6th Bn, Royal Melbourne Regt, 111
         6th Regt (Militia), 95
         7th, 22–3, 25, 102
         7th Depot, 86
         8th, 17, 22–5, 94, 104–105, 112–13
         9th Garrison, 100
         10th, 26
         10th Training, 85
         11th, 117
         12th Training, 122
         13th, 19–20
         13th Training, 122
         15th Training, 96, 101
         16th, 17, 19–20, 115, 119, 122
         23rd Depot, 104
         24th, 111, 125
         24/39th, 124
         34th, 44
         40th, 85, 86
         41st, 41–4, 85, 88
         43rd, 43–4
         44th, 44
         47th, 101
         48th Kooyong, 110
         57th, 95–6
         59th, 26, 101, 123
         66th, 101
         Militia, 109
         Victorian Rifles, 103–104
      Medical,
         1st Australian Dermatological Hospital, Bulford, 88
         1st Australian Field Ambulance, 104
         1st Australian General Hospital, 89, 106–107, 121
         1st Auxiliary Hospital, 121
         2nd Australian Stationary Hospital, Mudros, 77–8
         3rd Australian General Hospital, 101
         4th Australian Field Ambulance, 121–2
         6th Australian Field Ambulance, 89
         5th Australian General Hospital, 101
         9th Australian Field Ambulance, 86
         2/9th Australian General Hospital, 125
         14th Australian General Hospital, 101
         16th Australian General Hospital, 101
         47th Australian Camp Hospital, 125
         113th Australian Convalescent Depot, 125
         Base Hospital, Fremantle, 123, 128
         No.1 Australian Corps Recovery Camp, 125
      Other units,
         1st Australian Division Base Depot, 105
         1st Australian Division Reinforcement Camp, 105
         1st Division Artillery, 99
         1st Division Signal Coy, 99
         1st Military District, 89

2nd Division Signal Coy, 99
3rd Australian Division Base Depot, 86, 88–9
3rd Australian Division Training School, 126
3rd Division Signal Coy, 99
3rd Military District, 100, 102, 111
4th Australian Division Base Depot, 122
5th Australian Division Base Depot, 96
6th Military District, 86
7th Signal Regt, 93
10th Brigade Light Trench Mortar Bty, 86
17TH Works Coy, 87
62nd Depot, 117
101st Wireless Regt, 93
AIF Depot, Tidworth, 122
Australian Base Depot, Rouelles, 86
Australian Corps Signal Coy, 100
Australian Infantry Base Depot, 122
Australian School of Musketry, Tidworth, 122
Base Depot, Étaples, 104
Central Army Records Office, 89
General Details Depot, Melbourne, 113
New Guinea Deployment Depot, 125
New Guinea Force Training School, 125
No.2 Command Depot, Weymouth, 89, 102
No.3 Group, Codford, 86
No.4 Command Depot, Hurdcott, 89
No.4 Officers Training School, 104
No.5 Group, 101
No.7 Officers Training School, 104
Perham Down Depot, 105
Recruit Depot Battalion, 102
Senior Cadets, 95, 102
Small Arms School, Bonegilla, 125
Z Force, 118
Royal Australian Air Force, 95, 102, 116–17
1 Aircraft Depot, Laverton, Vic, 102
1st Wing AFC, 111
2 Australian Flying Sqn, 110
3 Squadron AFC, 110–11
5 Medical Receiving Station, 95
7 Training Sqn, 111
Central Depot, NSW, 102
Central Flying School, 110
Medical Branch, 95
Royal Australian Navy,
HMAT A7 *Medic*, 96
HMAT A9 *Shropshire*, 101
HMAT A10 *Karroo*, 99
HMAT A11 *Ascanius*, 121
HMAT A18 *Wiltshire*, 104
HMAT A38 *Ulysses*, 110

HMAT A40 *Ceramic*, 101, 120
HMAT A48 *Seeang*, 85
HMAT A54 *Runic*, 123
HMAT A64 *Demosthenes*, 88
HMAT A71 *Nestor*, 100
No.1 Hospital Ship *Karoola*, 97
Australian Capital Territory, 91, 93, 114, 129, 131
Australian Cricket Team, 124
Australian Federation of Broadcasting Stations, 109
Australian Government,
Ministry of Defence, 112
Australian Governor General, 89
Australian National Travel Association, 109
Australian Official History, 20
Australian United Steam Navigation Co, 119
Auxiliary Fire Service, 64
Avonmouth, 53, 106
Axbridge, 123, 127
Axford VC, TL, 128–9
Ayr, 55–8, 60
Ayrshire, 55–7, 72, 110

Badcoe VC, Peter, 93
Baghdad, 141
Balaclava, Vic, 98, 100
Balix, 163, 166
Ballina, 94, 97
Ballymena, 97
Bames Ness, 143
Bandiana Army Camp, 114, 130
Bankrupcy Acts, 57
Bapaume, 9, 33, 36–7, 40, 81, 154
Barclay Curle & Co, 106
Barford, 64
Barnes, 164, 174–5
Barnstaple, 150
Baron Cope of Berkeley, 173
Baroness Warsi, 82, 92, 114, 130, 179
Barrow, Lt Arthur, 111
Barrow-in-Furness, 158
Barton upon Irwell, 140
Basford, 145
Basingstoke, 141
Basra/h, 141
Bass Strait, 103
Bastiaan, Ross, 125–7, 130
Bath, 48–9, 56, 166–7, 171
Battersea, 174
Battle, 127
Baveno, 57
Bay of Plenty, 73
Bayswater, 164
Beaconsfield, Tas, 85–6
Beak, Cdr Daniel VC, 1, 7–8, 41, 45–62
Beaucourt-sur-Ancre, 52

Index

Beaudesert, Qld, 87, 89–91
Beaulencourt, 37
Beaumetz, 122
Beaumont Hamel, 70
Beauregard Dovecot, 3–5, 27
Bedford, 144
Bedfordshire, 58, 144
Behagnies, 9, 28, 31
Beharry VC, Sgt Johnson, 84, 93, 115, 130
Beira, 159
Belfast & City Hall, 53, 84, 88, 108, 120–1, 123, 178
Belgium, 83, 89, 93, 96, 115, 130, 155
Bell, Miss May, 71
Belmont, 171
Bendigo, Vic, 94–5, 102, 109–10
Bendigo, Bishop of, 96
Bennett, Lt Gen Henry, 104
Bennett, Lt Gen Sir Phillip, 114
Berkhamstead, 143
Berkshire, 56, 58, 60, 166–7
Berlin Airlift, 144
Bermondsey, 47, 98
Berwick St John, 49
Berwick, Vic, 107
Betchworth, 175
Bethnal Green, 98
Beugnâtre, 37
Bideford, 151
Biefvillers, 27, 32–3, 35–7
Bihaucourt, 3, 9, 27, 35
Bilbao, 144
Bilston, 66–8, 138–9, 146–7, 149, 151, 156–7
Bindoon, 116
Bingham, 74
Birdwood, Gen, 88
Birkenhead, 110
Birmingham, 46, 63–8, 71, 110, 126, 139, 141, 147–8, 150, 153–4, 156–7, 164
  Police, 156
Bisdee, 75
Black Death, 50
Black Rock, 95, 99
Blackboy Hill & Camp, 119
Blackburn VC, Arthur, 107
Blake, William, 175
Blamey, Gen, 113
Blandford Forum, 46, 168
Bodmin, 117
Bodo, 165
Boer/South African Wars, 90, 92, 99, 165, 169, 171, 179
Boiry-Becquerelle, 30
Bombay, 141, 174
Bonegilla, 124
Bonham's & Goodman's, 93

Bordon, 141
Borella VC, A, 128–9
Borneo, 56
Boscombe, 89
Bothwell, 147
Boucaut, Sir James, 166
Boucher, Catherine, 175
Bougainville, 126
Boulogne, 56, 89, 105, 122, 144
Boulton, Matthew, 146
Bournemouth, 148
Bovington, 178, 180
Bower Chalke, 50
Box Hill, Vic, 108, 110–11
Boyelles, 30–1
Branksome Park, 148
Braunton, 150
Bray, 166, 168–9
Bray-sur-Somme, 42, 89
Braybrook, 126
Brazil, 120
Breach, Maj George, 138
Breaking the Road for the Rest, 113
Brentford, 175
Brewarrina, 86
Bridgend, 127
Bridgnorth, 65
Brierley Hill, 67
Brighton & Beach, Vic, 100, 107
Brisbane, 87–91, 99, 119, 125, 153
Bristol, 47, 50, 55, 127, 154, 156
Britain, Battle of, 61
British Army (for Indian units *see* Indian Army),
  Army List, 57, 140, 149, 171, 173
  Army Reserves, 127, 148, 161, 164
    Class Z, 128
    Reserve of Officers, 164, 173
    Special Reserve, 134, 176
    Territorial Army Reserve, 156
    Transvaal Reserve of Officers, 172
  Field Forces,
    British Expeditionary Force, 1, 17, 41, 162
    East African Expeditionary Force, 170
    Mediterranean Expeditionary Force, 150, 168
  General List, 170
  Militia, 171
  Regular Army, 156
  Retired List, 59
  Territorial Force, 48, 147, 171
  Armies,
    First, 1, 32, 37, 41, 62
    Second, 1
    Third, 1–3, 12, 17, 26, 31–2, 37, 41, 58
    Fourth, 1, 12–14, 17, 31–2, 37, 41, 105
    Eighth, 62

Army Corps,
  III, 12, 32, 42, 48
  IV, 1, 3, 8–9, 14, 26–8, 32, 37, 40–1
  V, 1, 3, 26, 32, 37, 40–1
  VI, 1, 8–10, 26, 28, 30–2, 37, 41
  VII, 57
  XVII, 41
  Cavalry, 41
  Desert Mounted, 90, 101
Commands,
  Aldershot, 171
  British Army of the Rhine, 58
  Eastern, 58, 175
  Malta, 59
  Middle East, 59
  Scottish, 135
  Strategic, 56
Corps,
  Army Cyclist, 69
  Army Pay Department, 171
  Army Service, 47–8, 171
  National Defence, 156
  Royal Army Ordnance Corps, 46, 140
  Royal Army Pay, 158
  Royal Defence, 161
  Royal Electrical & Mechanical Engineers, 46
Districts/Areas,
  Bombay, 173
  East Central, 58
  Lowland, 138
Divisions,
  1st, 58
  1st Cavalry, 9, 32
  2nd, 8–9, 11, 28, 31
  2nd Cavalry, 32
  3rd, 5, 9, 17, 28, 30–1
  5th, 3, 5, 7–8, 12, 14, 27, 32–3, 40–1
  7th, 49
  12th, 12, 14
  17th, 32, 37
  18th, 12
  21st, 32, 37, 40
  32nd, 17, 20, 25, 41–2
  37th, 3, 5, 27, 31–32, 36, 40–1
  38th, 37
  42nd, 1, 3, 14, 16, 26–7, 32, 40
  47th, 12, 14
  50th, 59
  52nd, 30, 31
  56th, 30, 31
  58th, 42–4
  59th, 30
  63rd (Royal Naval), 1, 3, 5–8, 32, 37, 40, 45
  Guards, 8–9, 28, 30–1
  Highland, 58
  Irish, 58
  Scottish, 134
Brigades,
  1st Tank, 3
  2nd Guards, 9, 28, 30–1
  2nd Tank, 1, 8, 11
  3rd Tank, 26
  5th, 9
  6th, 31
  8th, 9–12, 17, 28, 31
  9th, 9, 28, 31
  12th, 59
  13th, 27, 33
  14th, 42
  15th, 14, 27
  22nd Mounted, 150
  50th, 37, 39
  51st, 37, 40
  52nd, 37–9
  63rd, 28, 36
  64th, 32
  68th, 58
  76th, 28–9
  95th, 12, 14, 27
  96th, 17, 19, 42
  97th, 17, 19–20, 22, 25
  99th, 9, 31
  111th, 28
  112th, 28
  114th, 37, 39
  125th, 1, 3, 5
  127th, 3
  151st, 59
  156th, 30
  167th, 30
  168th, 30
  188th, 5–8, 40
  189th, 1, 5–8, 40
  190th, 5, 7–8, 40
  Lowland, 134
Cavalry,
  3rd (King's Own) Hussars, 153
  7th Dragoon Guards, 139
  9th Reserve Regt, 153
  12th Royal Lancers, 12
  Imperial Yeomanry,
    45th (Irish Hunt) Coy, 171
  North Irish Horse, 1, 163, 176, 178
  North Somerset Yeomanry,
    1/1st North Somerset Yeomanry, 176–7
  Scottish Horse, 99
  Staffordshire Yeomanry,
    1/1st Staffordshire Yeomanry, 150
    2/1st Staffordshire Yeomanry, 150

Index

Infantry,
    1st Foot, 134
    9th Foot, 171
    35th Foot, 165
    92nd Regiment, 56
    100th Foot, 171
    Anson Battalion (RND), 7, 8, 51, 54
    Argyll & Sutherland Highlanders,
        4th Argyll & Sutherland Highlanders, 56
        10th Argyll & Sutherland Highlanders, 17, 20
    Bedfordshire,
        4th Bedfordshire, 8
    Benbow Battalion (RND), 51
    Black Watch, 165
    Cameron Highlanders, 161
        3rd (Reserve) Cameron Highlanders, 58
    Cheshire, 164
    Collingwood Battalion (RND), 168
    Devonshire, 144
        1st Devonshire, 14, 16, 154
        3rd Devonshire, 144
        8th Devonshire, 155
        9th Devonshire, 144
    Dorsetshire,
        3rd Dorset, 141
    Drake Battalion (RND), 1 6–8, 40–1, 45, 51–4, 60
    Duke of Cornwall's Light Infantry, 69
        1st Duke of Cornwall's Light Infantry (Pioneers), 14
    Duke of Wellington's, *see* West Riding
    East African Mounted Rifles, 170
    East Surrey,
        1st East Surrey, 14, 16
    Gloucestershire,
        12th Gloucestershire, 14, 16, 27
    Gordon Highlanders,
        3rd Gordon Highlanders, 57
        8th Gordon Highlanders, 57
        10th Gordon Highlanders, 56
    Grenadier Guards,
        3rd Grenadier Guards, 28, 30
    Hampshire/Royal Hampshire, 46, 140
        10th Hampshire, 140
    Hawke Battalion (RND), 6–8, 40, 168
    Herefordshire,
        1st Hertfordshire, 48
    Highland Light Infantry, 55, 134
        2nd Highland Light Infantry, 31, 58
        1/5th Highland Light Infantry, 81
        7th & 1/7th Highland Light Infantry, 80–1
    Home Guard, 156
        South Staffordshire Zone, 156
    Hood Battalion (RND), 6–8, 40, 53
    Howe Battalion (RND), 51, 168
    Irish Guards,
        1st Irish Guards, 57, 164
        2nd Irish Guards, 97
    King's (Liverpool), 59
        1st King's, 59
    King's Own Scottish Borderers,
        2nd King's Own Scottish Borderers, 33
    King's Own Yorkshire Light Infantry,
        2nd King's Own Yorkshire Light Infantry, 20
    King's Royal Rifle Corps, 56
    King's Shropshire Light Infantry,
        7th King's Shropshire Light Infantry, 11–12, 28–9
    Lancashire Fusiliers, 161
        1st Lancashire Fusiliers, 162
        2nd Lancashire Fusiliers, 162
        1/5th Lancashire Fusiliers, 1, 3, 5, 157, 161
        1/7th Lancashire Fusiliers, 3–5
        1/8th Lancashire Fusiliers, 3, 5
        10th Lancashire Fusiliers, 37–40, 63, 70
        16th Lancashire Fusiliers, 19–20
    London,
        9th London (Queen Victoria's Rifles), 175
        25th London, 175
        1/28th London, 8
    Manchester,
        10th Manchester, 40
        12th Manchester, 38–9
    Norfolk, 171
    Oxfordshire & Buckinghamshire Light Infantry, 147
    Parachute,
        2nd Battalion, 172
    Renfrew Militia, 56
    Rifle Brigade, 65, 153–154
    Royal Fusiliers,
        7th Royal Fusiliers, 8
        23rd Royal Fusiliers, 78
    Royal Green Jackets, 56
    Royal Highland Fusiliers, 55
    Royal Irish Regiment,
        2nd Royal Irish Regiment, 8
    Royal Leicestershire, 173
    Royal Munster Fusiliers, 173
    Royal Regiment of Scotland,
        1st Battalion, 137
        2nd Battalion, 134
    Royal Scots, 138
        2nd Royal Scots, 11, 12, 17, 28–31, 131, 135
        3rd Royal Scots, 135
        11th Royal Scots, 135
        12th Royal Scots, 134

Royal Scots Fusiliers, 55
   1st Royal Scots Fusiliers, 11, 28, 55
   6th Royal Scots Fusiliers, 55
Royal Warwickshire, 65, 156
   11th (Home Defence) Royal Warwickshire, 156
Scots Guards, 30
Somerset Light Infantry,
   8th Somerset Light Infantry, 155
South Lancashire,
   1st South Lancashire, 59
South Staffordshire,
   1st Volunteer Battalion, South Staffordshire, 67
   1/6th South Staffordshire, 66–7
South Wales Borderers, 161
Suffolk,
   1st Reserve Garrison Bn, Suffolk, 56
West Riding (Duke of Wellington's),
   9th West Riding, 38–40
Wiltshire, 127, 173
Worcestershire,
   7th Worcestershire, 160
   10th Worcestershire, 70
Machine Gun Corps, 48
   7th Battalion MGC, 49
   17th Battalion MGC, 39
   18th Sqn MGC, 150
   42nd Battalion MGC, 3
   63rd Battalion MGC, 6
   Machine Gun Corps (Cavalry), 150
Miscellaneous units,
   2nd Kitchener's Fighting Scouts, 172
   5th General Base Depot, 176
   6th Infantry Base Depot, 144
   6th Provisional Cyclist Coy, 175
   24th Divisional Train, 47–8
   27th Division Grenade School, 140
   73rd Brigade Supply Section, 47
   100th Provisional Battalion, 175
   201st Coy ASC MT, 148
   247th Divisional Employment Coy, 176
   A Depot Supply Coy, 48
   Armed Scouts, 170
   Army Accounts Department, 171
   ASC Cadet School/Unit, 148
   ASC Remounts, 127
   Base Horse Transport Depot, 48
   Crystal Palace Dispersal Centre, 55
   East Lake Border Police, 170
   Infantry Base, Cherbourg, 58
   Infantry Base Depot, 140
   Lines of Communications Area, 48
   Londiani Defence Force, 170
      No.5 Section Railway Defence, 170
   Military Accounts Department, 141
   National Defence Coys, 156
   No.1 Base Depot, 140
   No.1 Dispersal Unit, Fovant, 48
   No.2 Dispersal Unit, Crystal Palace, 144
   No.2 Transfer Centre, 78
   Receiving Depot, Wareham, 48
   Ross's Scouts, 170
   Scottish Command Depot, 135
   Shirehampton Remount Depot, 127
   Skin Corps, 170
   VII Corps Reinforcement Camp, 57
   XXII Corps Reinforcement Camp, 74
Royal Army Medical Corps/Army Medical Services,
   1st Auxiliary Hospital, 121
   1 Convalescent Depot, Boulogne, 89
   1st Field Ambulance, 135
   1/1st South Midland Casualty Clearing Station, 122
   1st & 2/1st Southern General Hospital, 78
   2/1st West Riding Field Ambulance, 177
   2nd General Hospital, Le Havre, 105
   2nd Western General Hospital, Manchester, 105
   3rd Convalescent Depot, 48
   3rd London General Hospital, Wandsworth, 106–107
   5 Casualty Clearing Station, 162
   5th Southern General Hospital, Portsmouth, 140
   6th Cavalry Field Ambulance, 176
   6th General Hospital, Rouen, 89
   7th General Hospital, St Omer, 86
   7th Stationary Hospital, 104–105
   8th General Hospital, Rouen, 122, 177
   8th Stationary Hospital, Wimereux, 122
   10 Casualty Clearing Station, 89, 104
   12th Stationary Hospital, 48
   14th General Hospital, Wimereux, 89
   15th General Hospital, Alexandria, 168
   17 Casualty Clearing Station, 86
   20th Stationary Hospital, 140
   21st Field Ambulance, 49
   22nd Mounted Brigade Field Ambulance, 150
   25 Casualty Clearing Station, 121
   27th Field Ambulance, 135
   28 Ambulance Train, 122
   28th Field Ambulance, 135
   28th General Hospital, 140
   29th Field Ambulance, 135
   31st General Hospital, 150
   37 Casualty Clearing Station, 89
   39 Casualty Clearing Station, 49
   39th General Hospital, Le Havre, 122

Index

41 Casualty Clearing Station, 105
50 Casualty Clearing Station, 48
56th General Hospital, 57
63rd General Hospital, 140
64 Casualty Clearing Station, 135
74th Field Ambulance, 48
78th General Hospital, 150
Allied Forces Base Hospital, 176
British Red Cross Convalescent Hospital, Montaza, 101
Citadel Military Hospital, Cairo, 150
Convalescent Hospital, Abbassia, 150
Egyptian Army Hospital, Port de Koubbeh, Cairo, 78
Fargo Military Hospital, Larkhill, 88
Fort Pitt Military Hospital, 135
General Hospital, Fayum, 150
Military Hospital, Birmingham, 149
Military Hospital, Boscombe, 89
Military Hospital, Devonport, 144
Military Hospital, Inverness, 56
Military Hospital, Mullingar, 135
No.1 Convalescent Depot, Perham Down, 122
Norfolk War Hospital, 122
Parkhouse Military Hospital, Tidworth, 88
Queen Alexandra Hospital, Cosham, 89
Royal Artillery, 127
  3rd Midland Brigade RFA, 147
  8th Reserve Battery RFA, 127
  16th Brigade RHA, 25
  51st Heavy Artillery Group, 111
  82nd Brigade RFA, 147
  242nd Brigade RFA, 65
  Artillery Training School, 147
  Londonderry Royal Garrison Artillery, 164
  No.2 Depot RFA, 127
  Royal Field Artillery, 26
  Royal Garrison Artillery, 26
  Southern Division RGA, 164
  Transvaal Horse Artillery Volunteers, 172
  XII Corps Ammunition Column RFA, 140
  XXVI Army Brigade RFA, 32
  XC Brigade RGA, 32
Royal Engineers,
  248th Field Company, 6
Royal Flying Corps, 57, 140, 148
  3 Sqn, 110
  16 Sqn, 110
  44 Reserve Sqn, 110
  49 Reserve Sqn, 110
  69 Sqn, 110–11
  RFC Aboukir, 150
  School of Aerial Gunnery, Turnberry, 110
  School of Military Aeronautics, Reading, 148

Tank Corps, 12, 48, 163
  1st RTR, 177
  3rd (Light) Battalion, 5, 7
  6th (Light) Battalion, 1, 8–9, 11–12, 163, 177
  7th Battalion, 5, 7, 27–8, 32
  10th Battalion, 5, 7, 17, 27
  12th Battalion, 8–9, 11, 28
  13th Battalion, 22
  15th Battalion, 8–9, 11
  17th Armoured Car Bn, 8
  46th (The Liverpool Welsh) RTR, 176
  No.1 Gun Carrier Coy, 8
  No.3 Tank Supply Coy, 8 9
  Reserve Unit, Swanage, 48
  Training establishments/units,
  24 Tank Corps Officer Cadet Battalion, 48
  First Army Artillery School, 111
  Inns of Court OTC, 143
  No.1 Cadet Battalion, Bisley, 48
  No.2 School of Instruction, 144
  No.10 Officer Cadet Battalion, Gailes, 140
  Royal Military Academy, Woolwich, 58
  Royal Military College, Sandhurst, 57–8, 164, 173
  Second Army School, 105
  Staff College, Camberley, 56, 58
British Columbia, 147
British Cyclo-Cross Association, 70
British Government Departments/Ministries, 53
  Admiralty, 88, 104
  Communities & Local Government, 71, 83, 93, 115, 130, 137, 157, 162, 179
  Employment, 173
  Faith & Communities, 82, 92, 114, 130, 179
  Foreign & Commonwealth Office/Secretary, 82, 92, 114, 130, 179
  House of Lords, 60, 173
  Ministry of Defence, 134
  Northern Ireland, 173
  Privy Council, 173
  Treasury, 173
  War Office/Department, 58, 70, 79, 134, 141, 171
British Iron Co, 153
Broadmeadows Camp, 102, 104, 119
Brockenhurst, 78–9
Brodie, Lt Col WL VC, 31
Broken Hill Propriety Ltd, 109
Bromfield, 145
Bromley, 173
Bromley VC, Maj Cuthbert, 80
Bromsgrove, 64
Brookeborough, 178
Brown, Capt Arthur, 111
Brown VC, WE, 128

Brownlee, Gerry, 82
Bruce, PM Stanley, 103
Bruneval Raid, 172
Buckingham Palace, 60, 81, 106, 123, 136, 154, 161, 179
Buckinghamshire, 165
Bucquoy, 33, 162
Buffalo, NY, 151
Bulford & Camp, 74, 88
Bulgaria, 171
Bullecourt, 105, 122
Buller District, NZ, 73
Bunker Hill Co, 75
Bunning brothers, 118
Burma, 61
Bury, 46, 71
Busbie, 57–8
Buteshire, 158

Cabarlah, 93
Cabra, 172
Cadder, 148
Caerleon, 147
Caernarvonshire, 149
Cairns, 103
Cairo, 101, 121
Calais, 57
Calcutta, 56
Caldwell VC, Thomas, 136
California, 75, 98
Callington, 128
Calne, 50
Camberwell, 47, 97, 175
Cambridgeshire, 46
Cambuslang, 131–4, 136–7
Camden, 148
Cameron, PM David, 84, 93, 115, 130
Cameron VC, Donald, 136
Camiers, 49
Camp Pell, Melbourne, 113
Campbell, ACT, 91, 93, 114, 129, 131
Camplin, John, 77
Canada/ian, 83, 93, 115, 126, 130, 140–1, 143, 145, 147–8, 160, 169, 179
Canadian Armed Forces,
  Canadian Army,
    Canadian Army Corps, 32
    Canadian First Army, 59
    Cavalry,
      19th Alberta Dragoons, 142
    Medical/ Royal Canadian Army Medical Corps,
      2nd Canadian General Hospital, 48
    Royal Military College, Kingston, 58
  Royal Canadian Air Force, 142
    3 Personnel Reception Centre, 143
    12 Training School, 142
    412 Sqn RCAF, 143
    Central Flying School, 142
    No.1 Auxiliary Manning Depot, 142
    No.1 General Reconnaissance School, 143
    No.1 Manning Depot, 142
    No.3 Training Command, 142
    No.8 Service Flying Training School, 142
    No.11 Elementary Flying Training School, 142
    RCAF Station Moncton, 142
    RCAF Station Rockcliffe, 142
    Special Reserve, 142
Canberra, 130
Canning River, 116–17
Cap-de-la-Madeline, Ont, 142
Cape Colony, 147, 171, 179
Cape Town, 108, 120, 123, 172, 178–9
Cardiganshire, 165
Cardwell Reforms, 55, 134
Carisbrooke, 144
Carless, CSM FJ, 5
Carlingford, 168
Carloforte Bay, 77
Carlton Club, 56
Carmichael VC, John, 136
Carnegie, Vic, 102
Caroline Bay, 82–3
Carrickfergus, 178
Carroll VC, J, 129
Cartwright VC, G, 128–9
Casey, Gov Gen Richard, 103
Castle of Good Hope, 178–9
Castlemaine, 101
Cathedrals,
  Glasgow, 136–37
  Salisbury, 50
  St Paul's, 52
Caulfield, 95–6, 99–100, 102
Cawley, Sgt H, 5
Cemeteries & Crematoria,
  Ayr Cemetery, 56, 58, 60
  Brighton Lawn Cemetery, Melbourne, 113–14
  Brookwood Cemetery, Woking, 60
  Burscough Bridge Churchyard, Ormskirk, 143
  Cathcart Cemetery, 84
  Colebrooke Churchyard, Co Fermanagh, 178
  Forest Lawn Cemetery, Buffalo, 151
  Hawkhead Cemetery, Paisley, 136
  Holy Cross Cemetery, Lackawanna, 151
  Karori Cemetery, Wellington, NZ, 82–3
  Kensal Green Cemetery, 57

Knockbreda Cemetery, Belfast, 84
Linn Cemetery, Glasgow, 84
Mount Thompson Crematorium, Brisbane, 91
Pinaroo Cemetery, Albany Creek, 91–2
Quinton Cemetery, Birmingham, 71, 156
Rothsay Cemetery, 158
Springvale Botanical Cemetery & Crematorium, Melbourne, 114, 123, 129–30
Thornaby-on-Tees Cemetery, 143
Westburn Cemetery, Cambuslang, 136–7
Challacombe, 150
Chamberlain, Anne, 68
Chamberlain, Neville, 68
Channel Islands, 144, 169
Chapeau de Gendarme, 44
Chapelle Blanche, 29
Charford, 50
Chauval, Lt Gen Sir Harry, 89–90
Chelsea 141, 172–3, 179
Cheltenham, 60, 150, 163, 165, 178–9
Cherbourg, 58
Cheshire, 110, 139–40, 144–5, 153, 159, 164
Chester, 139
Chicago, 65, 151
Chichester, 128
Childers, 111
Childers Reforms, 55
China, 83, 93, 115, 130, 162
Chipping Sodbury, 45, 47
Cholderton, 50
Christian Brothers, 115–17
Christian Salveson Whaling Co, 123
Chuignes, 17, 25, 105
Chuignolles, 17, 26
Church Crookham, 64
Church Missionary Society, 96
Churches,
    Abbey Church, Paisley, 133–4
    All Saints, St Kilda, Vic, 95, 98–9
    Ann Street Presbyterian, Brisbane, 91
    Bearwood Baptist, 71
    Cathedral Church of St Philip's, Birmingham, 148
    Christ Church, Darwin, 96,
    Christ Church, Delgany, 167
    Collins Street Independent, Melbourne, 125–6
    Edgbaston Parish, 141
    Emmanuel Congregational, Camberwell, 175
    Holy Trinity, Balaclava, Vic, 98, 100
    Old Parish Church (Auld Kirk), Kirkport, 55
    St Bartholomew's, Ottawa, 142
    St Charles RC Chapel, Cambuslang, 131–3
    St George's, Dublin, 167
    St John's, Wolverhampton, 63
    St Margaret's RC, Johnstone, 131, 134
    St Mary, Alderbury, 49
    St Mary Le Bow, London, 171
    St Mary's, Battersea, 174–5
    St Mary's, Bearwood, 71
    St Mary's, Bryanston Square, London, 166–7
    St Mary's, Caulfield, 113–14
    St Mary's, Handsworth, Staffs, 146
    St Mary's, Maryport, 160, 162
    St Matthew's, Bethnal Green, 98
    St Michael's Uniting, Melbourne, 125
    St Paul's, Brisbane, 153
    St Peter's, Camerton, 159–60
    St Peter's, Harborne, 68
    St Ronan's, Colebrooke, 178
    St Stephen's, Westbourne Park, London, 164
    St Thomas, Dudley, 69
    Smethwick Baptist, 69
    Wood Street Chapel, Bilston, 138, 147
    Wycliffe Anglican, Surrey Hills, Melbourne, 129
Churchill, PM Winston, 55
Churt, 57
Chute, 50
Cia Naviera del Atlantico, 76
Civil Commissioner, Baghdad, 141
Clamp VC, William, 136
Clapham, 99
Claremont, Tas, 85
Claremont, WA, 116
Cleopatra's Needle, 63
Clevedon, 171
Clifton, 98
Cloncaird Castle, 55–8
Clonfert, 169–70
Clontarf & Boys' Orphage, 116–18
Clyde, 123
Clydebank, 104
Clydeside, 77
Coburg, Vic, 110
Cockermouth, 157
Codford & Camp, 74, 78, 86, 101, 122
Codlin moth, 103
Codsall, 67
Coffee Redoubt, 12
Cojeul, 26
Colchester, 147, 162
Colebrooke, 178
Colley, Sgt Harold VC, 37–9, 63–71
Colliery Guardian Co, 154
Collingridge, Russell, 82
Collins Barracks, Dublin, 178
Commercial Bank Zambia, 46
Commonwealth Games, 124

Commonwealth/Imperial War Graves
  Commission,
  Adanac Military Cemetery, 81–2
  Beuvry Communal Cemetery Extension, 162
  Bienvillers Military Cemetery, 12
  Cambrai Louveral Memorial, 97
  Chatham Naval Memorial, 80
  Chunuk Bair Memorial, 80
  El Alamein War Cemetery, 176
  Étretat Churchyard Extension, 147
  Gdansk (Danzig) Garrison Cemetery, 160
  Giavera British Cemetery, 49
  Heath Cemetery, Harbonnières, 23
  Helles Memorial, 80
  La Clytte Military Cemetery, 65
  Lone Pine Memorial, 80
  Mailly Wood Cemetery, 70
  Malbork Commonwealth War Cemetery, 160
  Messines Ridge (New Zealand) Memorial, 106, 108
  Metz-en-Couture Communal Cemetery British Extension, 168
  Mirano Communal Cemetery Extension, 49
  Mory Abbey Military Cemetery, 177
  Plymouth Naval Memorial, 80
  Port Moresby (Bomana) War Cemetery, 124, 126
  Portsmouth Naval Memorial, 80
  Quarry Copse Cemetery, 29
  Ramleh War Cemetery & Memorial, 81
  The Huts Cemetery, 96
  Torokina War Cemetery, 126
  Tourlaville Communal Cemetery Extension, 58
  Twelve Tree Copse Cemetery, Krithia, 80
  Varennes Military Cemetery, 16
  Vis-en-Artois Memorial, 46
  Vraucourt Copse Cemetery, 136
Compagnie Maritime Belge, 119
Conon-Doyle, Arthur, 65–6
Conservative Party, 173
Conway, 149
Cook, Capt James, 87
Cork, 115
Cork, Co, 166
Cornwall, 63, 117, 128, 151
Cornwell, Bernard, 172
Corps of Commissionaires, 162
Corsham, 132
Coseley, 146
Cosham, 89
Coulsdon, 128, 176
Courcelette, 32, 40
Courcelles-le-Comte, 9–12, 29, 136–7, 177
Coventry, 65
Cox, Maj Gen Sir Herbert, 101
Cranbourne Chase, 50

Crete, 53
Crewe, 65
Cromwell, Oliver, 94
Crosscanonby, 159–60
Crossmolina, 94–5, 97
Croydon, 46–7, 64, 176
Croydon, Vic, 95
Crozier, Brig Gen FP, 155
Crystal Palace, 51–2, 144
Cuckfield, 173
Cumberland, 143, 157, 159–61
Cumbria, 158, 162
Cunard Line, 77, 120
Curlu, 43
Currey VC, WM, 128–9
Cushing, Maude Ethel, 172, 174–5
Cushing, Peter, 174–5
Cutler VC, Sir Roden, 92, 115, 130

Dacca, 164
Dakar, 123
Dallmellington, 72
Dalmuir, 108
Dalziel VC, H, 128–9
Dar-es-Salaam, 170
Darby, Lt Harold, 24
Dardanelles, 80, 157
Darebin Creek, 99
Darlaston, 152
Darwin, NT, 96
De L'Isle VC, Lord, 108, 129
Deakin, PM Alfred, 103
Delgany, 166–9, 169
Deloraine, Tas, 86
Denmark, 83, 93, 115, 130, 165
Dennistoun, 80
Densham & Sherlock, 103
Depression, 128
Deputy Lieutenant, 57, 172
Derbyshire, 150
Derwent, River, 160
Devizes, 171
Devonport, 74, 85, 110, 144
Devonport, Tas, 86
Devonshire, 88, 96–8, 101, 150–1
Dewart, Joseph, 82
Dickebusch, 54
Dieppe, 61
Discharged Servicemen's Employment Board, 109
Disraeli, Benjamin, 85
Domesday Book, 49
Dominion Press, 107
Doncaster, 143, 146
Donegal, Co, 166
Donhead St Mary, 46–7

Index 201

Dookie, Vic, 98–9
Dorchester, 157, 172–3, 179
Dorking, 175
Dorsetshire, 46, 89, 111, 148, 157, 168, 172–3, 178–80
Dover, 79
Downham, 46
Downie, Ken, 84
Dr Who, 174
Drocourt, 37
Droughtville, 170
Dublin, 123, 153, 163–4, 166, 170, 172
Dublin, Co, 164–5, 178
Dudley, 66, 69
Dugshai, 56
Duke of Gloucester, 108
Duke of Kent, 82, 92, 114, 130, 179
Duke of Westminster, 172
Duke of York, 90, 108, 129
Dum Dum, 164
Dumbarton, 119
Dunedin, 83
Dunkirk, 55, 160
Durban, 145, 172
Durham, 46
Durrington, 85, 147
Dwyer VC, JJ, 128–9
Dyce, 143

Eades, Pte Henry, 14, 16
Eaglesham, 79
Earl of Beaconsfield (Benjamin Disraeli), 85
East Africa, 169
East Albury, NSW, 92, 115
East Horsley, 149
East Lake Area/District, 170
East Renfrewshire, 84
Eastbourne, 47, 164
Easter Rising, 153
Eastern Railway, 118
Eaucourt l'Abbaye, 36–8, 40
Ecoust-St-Mein, 37
Ederney, 166
Edgbaston, 139, 153, 156
Edict of Nantes, 94
Edinburgh & Castle, 55–6, 100, 137–9
Edmonton, 47
Edmonton, Alta, 141–2
Egypt, 76, 78, 83, 88, 93, 99–101, 104, 109, 115, 120–2, 130, 173
El Jalil, 81
Elbe, 106
Elderslie, 133
Elford, Herbert, 120
Elliot VC, Rev'd Keith, 82

Elmore, 99
Elsternwick, 94–6, 98, 103
Elstow, 144
Eltham, 148
Ely, 46
Encounter Bay, 166
English Channel, 113
Enniskillen & Castle, 178
Erie Co, 151
Ervillers, 9, 28, 31
Essex, 46, 56, 132, 135, 143–4
Étaples, 88, 96, 104–105
Eton, 165
Étretat, 147
Evesham, 148
Exeter, 98
Export Credit Insurance Corp of Rhodesia, 46
Eye, 148
Eyrecourt, 169

Fairfield Shipbuilding & Engineering Co, 76
Fargny, Mill & Wood, 42–4
Farnborough, 64
Farnham, 57
Fayum, 150
Federal Steam Navigation Co, 104
Federated Malay States Volunteer Regiment, 162
Fermanagh, Co, 163, 166, 178
Ferns, 166
Field Punishment No.2, 86, 88
Finsthwaite, 158
Fisher, CSM J, 5
Fishguard, 105
Fleet, 171
Fleet Finch 2 aircraft, 142
Flers, 37
Flinders Island, 103
Flintshire, 169
Florida, 65
Foch, Marshal Ferdinand, 41
Folkestone, 56, 88, 176
Foo Fighters, 85
Football Association, 146
Foote VC, JW, 177
Forsyth, Sgt Samuel VC, 32, 34–6, 71–84
Foucaucourt, 42
Fovant, 48
Framerville, 17, 23
France, 83, 93, 96, 100–101, 104–105, 107, 110–11, 115, 122, 128, 130, 134–7, 144, 147, 153–5, 161–2, 176–7, 179
Fraser, PM Malcolm, 103
Fraser, Sgt, 135
Freeman, Harry, 146
Freemasons, 57, 108

Berwick Lodge, 108
Bolton Memorial Lodge, 108
Old Melbournians Lodge, 108
Fremantle, 116, 118–19
French Armies,
  First, 1
  Sixth, 1
  Tenth, 1, 17
French, FM Sir John, 176
French Revolution, 55
Freyberg, Bernard VC, 52
Frilsham, 58
Froissy Beacon, 17, 22, 26
Frost, Maj Gen John, 172
Fulton, 2Lt, 162

G Thompson & Co, 88
Gallipoli, 52–3, 77–80, 90, 99, 120–1, 129
Galway, Co, 163, 169–70
Gardner VC, PJ, 177
Gardner VC, William, 136
Garenne Wood, 26
Garratt, Lt Charles, 19–20
Gartcosh, 147–8
Gaston, RSM TW, 23
Gates, Capt, 53
Gavrelle, 53
Genoa, 76
German/y, 81, 83, 93, 111, 115, 130
German armed forces, 170
  Army, 1
  Air Force/Luftwaffe, 59, 165
    Jagdgeschwader 1, 111
    Jasta 11, 111
  Navy,
    U–138, 123
    U–515, 120
    UB–48, 77
    UB–68, 77
    UC–23, 53
German East Africa, 106
German Spring Offensives, 113
German West Africa, 106
Gibraltar, 25
Giffnock, 153
Glamorgan, 127
Glasgow, 58, 76, 79–80, 106, 131–4, 136–8, 153
Glebe, 163
Glencorse Barracks, 134
Glenelg, 169
Glenhuntly, 110
Gloucestershire, 45, 47, 98, 111–12, 150, 163, 179
Goldsbrough, Mort & Co, 99
Gomiécourt, 12, 17, 26, 28–9

Goold-Adams, Sir Hamilton, 89
Goondiwindi, 125
Gordon, LCpl Bernard VC, 41, 43–4, 85–93, 129
Gordon, Capt Alick, 135–6
Gourock, 123
Govan, 76
Grandcourt, 32
Great Barrier Island, 104
Great Exhibition, 52
Great Torrington, 151
Great Western Railway, 16, 105
Greece, 76
Greek Macedonia, 171
Greenhalgh, Cpl C, 5
Gregory, Capt, 162
Grévillers, 27, 32–6, 81
Grieve VC, Robert, 124, 129
Griffin, J&R Ltd, 69
Grimsby, 139
Groote Eylandt, 96
Gueudecourt, 37
Guillaucourt, 177

Hackney, 118
Haig, FM Sir Douglas, 1, 17, 41, 54, 69, 177
Hale, 145
Halifax, Nova Scotia, 143
Hally Copse, 31
Hamel, 89
Hamelincourt, 26, 30
Hamilton, 136–7
Hamilton VC, John B, 136
Hamilton VC, JP, 128
Hammer Film Productions, 174–5
Hampshire, 45–7, 50, 56–8, 61, 64, 78–9, 89, 111, 122, 135, 140–1, 143–5, 171
Handsworth, Staffs, 146–8
Hanwell, 47
Harbonnières, 17
Harborne, 148–9
Harland & Wolff, 53, 88, 108, 123
Harlaxton, 110
Hartshorn, Alta, 141
Hastings, 127
Hawke's Bay, 74, 75
Hawthorn, Vic, 98, 108, 110, 123
Headley, 45
Heath Town, 64
Hébuterne, 161
Helena Vale, WA, 119
Heliopolis & Camp, 121
Hellenic-Mediterranean Line, 76
Helouan, 121
Help for Heroes, 180

Heninel, 26
Henley-on-Thames, 145
Henry George Foundation, 109
Herefordshire, 110, 157, 159
Herleville & Wood, 17, 21–2, 25, 105
Hertford, 47
Hertfordshire, 47
Hervey Bay, 90
Hewson, Pte F, 5
High Wood, 39–41, 155
Hill, Benny, 51
Hindenburg Line, 40–1, 100
Hobart, Tas, 92–3
Holt, PM Harold, 124
Honywill, Capt Albert, 16
Hopkins, Sir Anthony, 152
Hornchurch, 46, 78
Horsham, 64, 141, 175–6
Hospitals,
  Belfast City, 84
  British Home & Hospital for Incurables, Streatham, 164
  Children's Memorial Hospital, Chicago, 65
  Corinan Private Hospital, Murrumbeena, 100
  County Hospital, Lowestoft, 46
  Dudley Road, Birmingham, 156
  Fremantle Lunatic Asylum, 118
  Hollywood Private, Perth, WA, 130
  Hospital for the Insane, Claremont, WA, 115–16
  Luton, 58
  Manchester Royal Infirmary, 105
  Melbourne Hospital, Vic, 108
  Poor Law Infirmary, Birmingham, 78
  Portrack General, Stockton, 46
  Princess Margaret's, Swindon, 60
  Radcliffe Infirmary, Oxford, 150
  Redhill County Hospital, 175
  Repatriation General Hospital, Heidelberg, Melbourne, 129
  Repatriation Hospital, Caulfield, 106
  Roebourne, WA, 118
  Royal West Sussex, 128
  Shirehampton, 128
  Tidewell Hospital, Sarasota, 65
  Wells Mental Hospital, 49
Hove, 172–3, 175
Howell VC, GJ, 128, 129
Howell-Price, Richmond, 136
Huguenots, 94
Hurdcott & Camp, 89, 96, 111
Hutchesontown, 153
HV McKay Massey Harris Propriety Ltd, 126
HV McKay Propriety Ltd, 126
HV MacKay Sunshine Harvester, 128
Hythe, 171

Idaho, 74
Ilford, 143
Illinois, 65, 151
Imbros, 121
India, 56, 58–9, 83, 86, 93, 115, 130, 174
Indian Army, 164
  Army Headquarters Dehli, 174
  Bombay District, 173
  Indian Army Emergency Commission, 176
  Indian Army List, 57
  Indian Army Ordnance Corps, 174
  Indian Army Reserve, 57
  Infantry,
    4/10th Baluch Regt, 164
    76th Hindoostan Regt, 163
    Eastern Frontier Rifles, 164
      Bengal Battalion, 164
  Ordnance School, 174
  Special Unemployed List, 164
Indonesia, 95
Industrial Development Corp of Rhodesia, 46
Industrial Revolution, 146
Ingram VC, GM, 128–9
Inkerman, 133
Ipoh, 162
Iraq, 61, 83, 93, 115, 130
Ireland, 94, 97, 105, 115, 117, 123, 133–5, 151, 153, 159, 163, 166, 169–70, 172, 178
Irish Land Commission, 164
Irles, 16, 26–7, 32, 34
Iron Shipbuilding Co, 120
Irvine, 140
Islay, 123
Isle of Wight, 64, 144
Islington, 147
Israel, 81
Italy, 57, 76–7, 111, 140, 169

Jackson, Thomas, 82
Jackson VC, W, 129
Jaffa, 81
Japan/ese, 61, 83, 87, 93, 97, 115, 118–19, 130, 159
Jarrah Timber & Trading Co, 103
Jasper, 141
Java & Battle of, 87, 119
Jellicoe, John, 75
Jenkins, Roy, 153
Jenner, Edward, 45
Jersey, 144, 169
Jersey cows, 89
Jerusalem, 173
Jews, 81
Johannesburg, 63, 144, 172
John Brown & Co, 77, 104–105
Johnson, Ian, 124

Johnson VC, James, 155
Johnston, Capt George, 23
Johnstone, 131, 134
Jones, William, 152
Joynt, Lt William VC, 17, 21, 23–5, 94–115, 128–9
Jubbulpore, 59

Kallista, 95, 108
Kamloops, 147
Keating, Lt Gen Tim, 82
Keelung, 119
Kells, 74
Kelsale, 175
Kemmel, Mount, 1
Kemsley, Sir Alfred, 108–109
Kendal, 143
Kenna VC, Edward, 92, 115, 130
Kenny VC, TJB, 128–9
Kensington, 46, 52, 147, 165, 171
Kent, 88, 144, 171, 173
Kentish Town, 172
Kenya, 159, 170
Ketley, 66
Kew, Vic, 100
Khyber Pass, 59
Kilbarchan, 131, 133–4
Kildare, Co, 165
King Edward I, 133
King George V, 54, 79, 81, 106, 123, 136, 154, 161, 179
King George VI, 58–9, 90, 108, 129
King George's Sound, 76
King Robert I (Scotland), 133
King Robert II (Scotland), 133
King Robert III (Scotland), 133
King William I (Conqueror), 98
King William IV, 167
King's Inns, Dublin, 163
King's Norton, 64–5, 68, 149
Kingston-upon-Hull, 132
Kingston-upon-Thames, 164
Kingstown, 163–4
Kipling, Rudyard, 50
Kirkcudbrightshire, 74
Kirkmichael, 55
Kirori Galvanising Co, 73
Kitchener, FM Lord Herbert, 104
Kobe, 119

La Boisselle, 32, 70
Lackawanna, 151
Lady Islington, 79
Lagnicourt, 32
Lake Victoria, 170
Lambeth, 52

Lambourn, 56, 60
Lanarkshire, 58, 71, 74, 80, 131–2, 136–8, 147–8, 153
Lancashire, 46, 48, 71–2, 127, 139–40, 143–4, 149, 154
Lancaster House, London, 82, 92, 114, 129, 179
Lancing, 47
Landi Kotal, 59
Lapin Wood, 25
Lauder VC, David, 136
Launceston, 85–7
Laverton, 102
Le Barque, 40
Le Hamel, 111
Le Havre, 48, 86, 105, 122
Le Quesnel, 177
Le Sars, 37, 40
Le Transloy, 35
Lea, Sgt J, 5
Leach VC, James, 155
League of National Security, 109
Leamington Spa, 150
Ledbury, 110
Lee, 148
Leeds, 140
Legacy Club, Melbourne, 107, 109
Legcloghfin, 166
Leixlip, 165
Leighterton, 111
Lemnos, 78, 120–1
Levis Cup Trial, 70
Lewes Prison, 88
Leyton Marsh, 132
Liberal Party, 148
Lihons, 18
Lihu Farm, 18
Lincoln, 110
Lincolnshire, 110, 139
Lindfield, 95
Liner Requisition Scheme, 123
Linton, 82
Linwood, 131–2, 134, 137
Liquor Trade Defence Union, 109
Lisnaskea, 163
Liss, 56
Liverpool, 72, 120–1, 141, 145, 149, 154
Llantwit Fardre, 127
Llog Cloghfin, 163
Lloyds Bank, 148, 156
Locon, 135
Logeast Wood, 1, 6–9
Londiani, 170
London, 46–7, 51–3, 55–6, 60, 63, 79, 88, 91–2, 97–9, 102, 105–106, 108, 113–14, 118, 126,

128–30, 141, 143–4, 147–51, 154, 162, 164–5, 167–9, 171–5, 179–80
    Greater London Council, 107
London & Glasgow Engineering, 120
London City & Midland Bank Ltd, 150
Long Wood, 26
Longueval, 135
Loos, 56
Lord Ashcroft Victoria Cross Collection, 61, 163, 180
Lord Michael Ashcroft, 61, 84, 163, 180
Lorna Doone, 138
Lothingland, 46
Loupart & Wood, 1, 32–3, 35–6, 40–1, 81
Louth, Co, 167, 168
Lowerson VC, AD, 128–9
Lowestoft, 46
Lozenge (Hill 140), 3–4
Ludlow, 145
Lumbwa, 170
Lyall VC, Graham, 136
Lydda, 81
Lykiardopulo, GM, 76
Lyon, Sgt Edward, 143
Lyons, J & Co, 66

Mackay, 103
MacKay VC, David, 136
MacKenzie, Sir Thomas, 79
Macleod, Vic, 114
Mactier, Katie, 124
Madagascar, 61
Madame Wood, 17–19, 122
Maggs, JH, 156
Makara Beach, 74
Malaya, 162
Malbork, 160
Mallee, 103, 128
Malta, 59, 76, 120
Malvern, Vic, 96, 99
Manawatu-Wanganui, 73
Manchester, 105, 139–40, 144
Manning, 116
Mansfield, Katherine, 75
Mantle, Jack VC, 51
Mareth Line, 59
Maricourt, 42–3
Marietta, 164
Marlborough, 150
Marlborough, NZ, 72
Marly Woods, 26
Marquess of Tullabadine, 99
Marseille, 52, 100–101, 104, 120, 122
Marsh, 2Lt, 162
Martha's Vineyard, 50

Martinpuich, 37–40, 70
Martinstown, 172–3, 179
Marylebone, 47
Maryport, 157–62
Masai Escarpwent, 170
Massey Ferguson, 126
Massey Harris, 126
Matlock, 234, 236
Maybole, 56
Mayo, Co, 94–5, 97
McCarthy, Lt Lawrence VC, 17, 19–20, 115–31
McDonald, LCpl, 135
McDougall VC, Stanley, 129
McGinn, Lt Leslie, 24–5
McGregor, William, 146
McIver, Pte Hugh VC, 17, 29–30, 131–8
McKay, Hugh Victor, 126
McMurdo, Sgt Gerald, 35–6
Meath, Co, 169
Meerschaum, 161
Melbourne, 76, 84, 89–90, 94–6, 98–104, 106–12, 114, 119–20, 123–4, 126–9
    Chamber of Commerce, 109
    Metropolitan Town Planning Commission, 109
    Town Hall, 125
Menzies, PM Sir Robert, 124
Merchant Navy/Mercantile Marine, 62, 114, 158
Mesopotamia, 141
Messines, 65
Messrs Berkel & Parnell, 154
Messrs James Dunlop & Co, 134
Mexico, 165
MI6, 107
Michael Ashcroft Trust, 61, 84, 163, 180
Middle East, 104, 121, 173
Middlesbrough, 159–60
Middlesex, 47, 175
Midlothian, 56, 134, 137–9
Millbank, 144
Milne VC, William, 136
Minehead, 171
Miraumont, 1, 3–5, 14–15, 27, 32
Mirlinbarrwarr, 96
Missouri, 57
Mitchell, Lt Col John, 105
Mitchell & Butler, 70
Mitchell, Thomas, 166
Modder River, 171
Molo, 170
Monaghan, Co, 117
Monash, Lt Gen Sir John, 41, 90, 108, 128
Monasterboice, 167
Monchy-le-Preux, 1, 176
Moncton, NB, 142
Monmouth, 152

Monmouthshire, 139, 147, 152
  County Council, 152
Monowai Gold Mining Co, 76
Mons, 17
Mont Albert, 111, 123, 129
Mont St Quentin, 89
Montauban, 42, 135
Montréal, 145, 148
Montreux, 57
Moon VC, RV, 129
Morotai Island, 95
Morval, 32
Mosquito aircraft, 143
Mount Barker, 166
Mount Everest, 62
Mount Felix, 78, 79
Mount Helena, 118
Mount Lawley, 128
Mouquet Farm, 122
Moxley, 139
Moyenneville, 1, 9–10
Mozambique, 159
Mudros, 78, 120
Mullingar, 135
Munday, Spr Eric, 120
Munro-Ferguson, Sir Ronald, 89
Murdoch, William, 146
Murray VC, Henry, 106–107
Museums,
  Australian War Memorial, 53, 92–3, 114, 127, 129–31
  Birmingham Museum & Art Gallery, 63
  Elmbridge, 79
  Fusiliers' Museum Lancashire, Bury, 71
  Imperial War, 52, 61, 84, 163, 180
  National Gallery of Australia, 93
  National Museum of Ireland, 178
  Royal Navy, 61
  Royal Scots, 137, 138
  Rugby Football Union, Twickenham, 180
  Tank Corps, Bovington, 178, 180
  The Keep Military Museum, Dorchester, 157
Mwanza, 170

Nandi, 169
Napier, 82
Natal, 145
National Bank, 102
National Memorial Arboretum, Alrewas, 84, 93, 115, 130
National Trust of Australia, 109
NATO, 145
Naval & Military Club, Melbourne, 109
Navan, 169
Nepal, 83, 93, 115, 130

Neptune Oil Co, 99
Netherhall, 160
Netherlands, 83, 93, 115, 130
Netherlands Bank of South Africa, 46
Netherton, 69
New Brunswick, 142
New Jersey, 148
New South Wales, 86, 88, 92, 95, 99, 101–102, 110, 114, 130, 132, 153
  Department of Public Instruction, 99
New York, 53, 77, 145, 148–9, 151
New Zealand, 71–2, 74–6, 78–9, 82–3, 93, 104, 110, 130, 169, 179
New Zealand armed forces,
  New Zealand Army,
    Division, 3–5, 8, 14, 26–27, 32, 36–7, 40–1
    Brigades,
      1st NZ Brigade, 32–3
      2nd NZ Brigade, 33, 36
      4th Reseve, 74
    Bns/Regts,
      1st NZ Rifle Bde, 27
      1st Wellington, 33–6, 73
      2nd Auckland, 32–4, 36, 71, 81
      2nd Canterbury, 36
      2nd Otago, 36
      2nd Wellington, 35, 74, 106
      3rd Reserve Battalion, 74
      3rd (Reserve) Wellington, 73
      No.1 NZ Entrenching Battalion, 74
      Wellington Regt, 108
  New Zealand Expeditionary Force, 76, 106
  Other units,
    2nd Anzac Entrenching Battalion, 79
    Infantry Base Depot, Hornchurch, 78
    New Zealand Command Depot, 78
    New Zealand Convalescent Hospital, 78
    New Zealand Engineers, 32, 36, 71, 76, 79
    New Zealand Field Ambulance, 78
    New Zealand Infantry & General Base Depot, Étaples, 79
    No.1 New Zealand General Hospital, Brockenhurst, 79
    No.2 New Zealand General Hospital, Mount Felix, 79
    No.2 New Zealand General Hospital, Walton-on-Thames, 78
    New Zealand Stationary Hospital, 86
    New Zealand Walton Hospital, 79
    New Zealand War Contingent Hospital, 79
  Royal New Zealand Navy,
    HMNZT *Maunganui*, 76
    HMNZT *Ulimaroa*, 73
New Zealand High Commission, 79
New Zealand Parliament, 82

Index   207

New Zealand Post, 83
New Zealand Railway, 73
New Zealand War Contingent Association, 79
Newbury, 60
Newcastle upon Tyne, 147
Newfoundland, 83, 93, 115, 130
Newman, Pte Thomas, 24
Newton Colliery, 131, 134
Newton Hallside, 131–4
Newton VC, William, 103
Newtown Hill, 165
Ngukurr, 96
Nicholas, Alfred & George, 124
Niverville, Air Cmdr A, 142
Norfolk, 46
Norman, Greg, 87
Normandy, 59
Norrie, Sir Charles, 83
North Africa, 62
North Bondi, 115, 130
North Carolina, 75
North Dandalup, 118
North Ewell, 176
North Melbourne, 86
North Raglan Barracks, 144
North Tamerton, 151
North West Frontier, 59
Northam, WA, 117–19, 130
Northavon, 173
Northcote, 102
Northern Ireland, 84
Northern Territory, 96
Northumberland, 132, 139, 147
Northwood, 145
Norway, 164
Norwegian Campaign, 165
Norwich, 122
Nottingham, 173
Nottinghamshire, 145, 152
Nova Scotia, 143
Nundah, 91

O'Brien, Sgt, 35
Ocean Steamship Co, 121
Oceanic Line, 88
Odstock, 49
Old Melbournians, 107
Old Monkland, 74
Oldbury, 63, 68
Olympic Games, 124
O'Neill VC, John, 136
Onions, LCpl George VC, 12, 14–16, 138–57
Onoway, 141
Ontario, 141–2
Orange Free State, 171, 179

Orange Order, 57
Orders, Decorations & Medals,
　1914 Star (Mons Star), 180
　1914/15 Star, 61, 71, 84, 93, 131, 138, 157
　1939–45 Star, 61, 162
　Africa Star, 61–2
　Air Force Cross, 144
　Arctic Star, 61
　Army Long Service & Good Conduct Medal, 162–3
　Australia Service Medal 1939–45, 114–15
　British War Medal 1914–20, 61, 71, 84, 93, 115, 130, 138, 157, 162, 180
　Conspicuous Gallantry Cross, 161
　Conspicuous Gallantry Medal, 161
　Croix de Guerre (France), 58, 122, 131
　Distinguished Conduct Medal, 16, 19, 106–107, 139, 161–3
　Distinguished Service Cross, 136
　Distinguished Service Order, 11, 53, 57–8, 61, 83, 104–107, 114, 136, 161, 168, 172, 176–7, 179
　George Cross, 59
　King George V Silver Jubilee Medal 1935, 61–2, 162
　King George VI Coronation Medal 1937, 61, 93, 115, 131, 157, 162
　King's South Africa Medal, 179
　Legion d'Honneur (France), 58
　Medaille Militaire (France), 101
　Medal for Long Service & Good Conduct (Military), 163
　Mentioned in Despatches, 54, 57, 59, 61, 69, 71, 100, 136, 168, 170–1, 173, 176–7, 180
　Meritorious Service Medal, 109, 163
　Military Cross, 11, 16, 24–5, 52–3, 58, 61, 83, 100, 136, 144, 164, 170, 172, 177, 179
　Military Medal, 19, 70–1, 89, 93, 135–6, 138, 161
　Order of Australia, 92–3, 114–15, 127, 131
　Order of Leopold (Belgium), 170
　Order of St Michael & St George, 83, 89–90, 92, 104, 108–109, 115, 128, 131
　Order of St Patrick, 108
　Order of the Bath, 58, 83, 89–90, 104, 108, 128, 172
　Order of the British Empire, 53, 58, 109, 114, 141, 145, 152, 164, 171, 173–4
　Order of the Garter, 108
　Order of the Thistle, 108
　Queen Elizabeth II Coronation Medal 1953, 61–2, 93, 115, 131
　Queen Elizabeth II Silver Jubilee Medal 1977, 115
　Queen's South Africa Medal, 179

Royal Victorian Order, 83, 108
Victory Medal 1914–19, 61, 71, 84, 93, 115, 131, 138, 157, 162, 180
Volunteer Officers' Decoration, 90, 104, 108, 128
War Medal 1939–45, 61–2, 115, 162
Orelton, 145
Orient Line, 119
Orient Steam Navigation Co, 95
Ormskirk, 127, 143
Osaka Shasan Kaisha, 119
Oste Riff, 106
O'Sullivan VC, Capt Gerald, 80
Ottawa, 141–2
Oughterside Colliery, 161
Ouyen, 101
Ovillers, 32
Oxford, 140, 150
Oxfordshire, 145

Pacific, 87
Packham, Chris, 51
Paddington, 149
Paisley, 131, 133, 136, 153
Pakistan, 83, 93, 115, 130
Palestine, 90, 173
Palestine Mandate, 81
Palestine Police Force, 81
Palmerston North, 82
Panama, 76
Pancras, 128
Papua New Guinea, 124, 126
Paris, 89, 100
Park City, 74–6
Pas-de-Calais, 179
Pasadena, 98
Passchendaele, 89
Paton VC, George, 168
Paxton, Joseph, 52
Payne VC, Keith, 92, 115, 130
Peeler VC, W, 129
Peirse, Sir Richard, 172
Pembroke, 147
Pembrokeshire, 147
Penge, 147
Penicuik, 134
Pennsylvania, 75, 149, 152
Perak, 162
Perham Down, 105, 122
Permezel, Capt Eric, 25
Péronne, 105
Perry, Bishop, 113
Pershore, 65
Perth, WA, 103, 116–18, 124, 128, 130
Petersfield, 57–8

Philadelphia, 149
Philippoussis, Mark, 124
Picton, Ont, 142
Piraeus, 76
Pirbright, 48
Plateau Woods North & South, 17, 21–5
Plymouth, 88, 96, 101, 144, 151
Plympton, 97
Pocock, Rev'd Francis, 172
Poland, 160, 164
Poland–South America Line, 165
Ponsford Newman & Benson Ltd, 109
Pontier, 147
Pontypool, 139, 145, 147, 152
Port Melbourne, 88, 103, 120
Port Moresby, 125
Port Said, 101, 121, 150
Portchester, 145
Portsmouth, 46, 56, 141, 145
Portumna, 170
Pozières, 3, 32, 104, 122
Prahan, 99
Prescot, 149
Preston, 127
Pretoria, 172
Prince Edward Island, 143
Prince of Wales (Edward), 79, 108, 128
Prince Phillip, 92, 114, 130
Privy Council, 108
Proyart, 23
Puckapunyal & Camp, 112, 114
Pugin, Messrs Pugin &, 131
Puisieux, 3–5
Pys, 26, 32

Quéant, 32, 37
Québec, 142–3, 145, 169
Queen Charlotte, 167
Queen Elizabeth I, 50
Queen Elizabeth II, 62, 92, 114, 130
Queen Mary, 79
Queen Victoria, 53, 83, 90
Queen Victoria Diamond Jubilee, 90
Queenscliff, 112
Queensland, 87, 89–91, 93, 99, 103, 111, 153, 165
Queensland Heritage Register, 91

Radio Station 3UZ, 109
Rainecourt, 23
Ramla/h, 81
Ramsay, George, 146
Raphoe, 166
Rathdown, 170
Rawcliffe, 47
Rawlinson, Gen Lord Henry, 41, 105

Reading, 148
Realism Ltd, 145
Redditch, 64
Reed, Joseph, 125
Reid VC, William, 136
Renfrewshire, 79, 131–4, 136, 153
Returned & Services League of Australia, 93, 108, 112, 115, 128, 130
Returned Services Association (NZ), 82
Rhodesia, 46, 171
   Chamber of Mines, 165
Richardson VC, Ppr James, 82, 136
Richmond, Vic, 99
Richmond & Park Camp, 175–6
Ridd, Jan, 138
Riencourt-*lès-Bapaume, 37, 40*
Ring of Remembrance, 137, 179
Robbins, Sgt Frederick, 19
Robertson VC, C, 177
Robins, J, 86
Robinson, Pres Mary, 94
Rochford, 56
Rock Ferry, 144
Rockall, 158
Rockhampton, Qld, 103
Rocquigny, 32
Roehampton, 175
Romani, 150
Rome, 49, 169
Romsey, 47
Rondabosch, 147
Ronga Valley, 73
Roper River, 96
Rosalie Bay, 104
Rosanna, 95, 96
Rosettenville, 172
Rosslare, 105
Rouelles, 86, 89
Rouen, 48, 89, 107, 144, 176–7
Rowling, JK, 45
Roxborough, 169
Royal Automobile Club, 149
Royal Air Force, 5, 17, 19, 26, 65, 81, 144, 150, 161
   8 (Coastal) Operation Training Unit, 143
   16 Group, 143
   16 Wing, 150
   47 Sqn, 150
   59 Sqn, 3, 7
   203 Sqn, 19
   Commands,
      Bomber, 61, 172
      Coastal, 143
   Medical Training Depot, 143
   No.7 Group RAF Instructors School, 111
   No.18 Group, 145
   No.19 (Pilots) Advanced Flying Unit, 143
   RAF Dyce, 143
   RAF Ramla, 81
   RAF Thornaby, 143
   Unemployed List, 150
Royal Geographical Society, 165
Royal Household, 173
Royal Irish Constabulary, 94, 154–5
   Auxiliary Division, 154–5
Royal Navy & Royal Marines, 133, 161
   Defensively Equipped Merchant Ships, 158
   Reserves,
      Royal Naval Volunteer Reserve, 45, 51–2, 55, 168
      Royal Naval Reserve, 157–8
   Royal Marines
      1st Royal Marine Battalion RMLI, 46
      Cyclist Coy RMLI, 51
   Royal Naval Air Service, 52
   Royal Naval Division, units appear under British Army
   Royal Naval Division Association, 60
   Ships,
      HMHS *Aquitania*, 77–8
      HMHS *Brighton*, 176
      HMHS *Formosa*, 120–21
      HMHS *Gloucester Castle*, 140
      HMHS *Guildford Castle*, 105
      HMHS *Princess Elizabeth*, 122
      HMHS *St Andrew*, 105
      HMS *Ark Royal*, 165
      HMS *London*, 123
      HMS *Manitou*, 168
      HMS *Resolution*, 133
      HMS *Stork*, 165
      HMS *Victory VI*, 52
      HMS *Vivid I*, 133
      HMS *Wolverine*, 165
      HMT *Ascanius*, 121
      HMT *Hyda Pasha*, 120
      HMT *Kingstonian*, 77–8
      HMT *Minnewaska*, 52
      HMT *Thermistocles*, 106
      HT *Berrima*, 101
      HT *Caledonia*, 104
      HT *Ellenga*, 101
      HT *Margha*, 275
      HT Rio Padro, 86
Rutherglen, 80, 132
Ruthven VC, W, 129

Saffron Walden, 143
Sage VC, Thomas, 154–5
St Abb's Head, 143
St Anne's Hill, 166

St Chad, 68
St Denis Wood, 22
St Eleanors, PEI, 143
St George, Hanover Square, London, 165, 169
St Joseph's Orphanage, Subiaco, 115–16
St Kilda, Vic, 96, 98–100, 102, 110, 123–4, 130
St Leger, 31
St Leonard, London, 151
St Louis, 57
St Luke, London, 98
St Martin's Wood, 22–3, 25
St Marylebone, 174
St Nazaire, 61
St Omer, 48
St Pancras, 174
St Pol, 48
St Quentin, 21
St Saviour, 175
Sale, District Council & Town Hall, 153–4
Salisbury, 45, 47, 49–50
Salisbury & Yeovil Railway, 50
Salisbury Plain, 88
Salisbury, Rhodesia, 46
Salonica/ka, 53, 140
Salt Lake City, 74
San Francisco, 76
San Jose, 145
San Pietro Island, 77
Sapignies, 9, 31
Sarasota, 65
Sari Bair, Battle of, 80
Saskatchewan, 141
Saskatoon, 141
Scarborough, 63
Schools,
   Adelaide Shorthand & Business Training Academy, 109
   Aquinas College, Subiaco, 116
   Architectural Association, London, 111
   Bournemouth, 51
   Caulfield Grammar, Melbourne, 95
   Central Higher Grade, Manchester, 105
   Channel View, Clevedon, 171
   Charterhouse, 57
   Cheltenham College, 56–7
   Clifton Terrace, Wellington, NZ, 75–6
   Combe Down, 165
   Day Training College, Manchester, 105
   Dudley Road Council, Smethwick, 69
   Eaglesham, 80
   Garneau High, Edmonton, Alta, 141
   Grange Preparatory, Toorak, 103
   Heversham Grammar, 143
   Howard's Commercial & Correspondence College, Adelaide, 109
   King Edwards High, Birmingham, 148
   Lisgar Collegiate, Ottawa, 141
   Loretto, 57
   Melbourne Grammar, 103
   Monkton Combe, Bath, 163, 164, 171–2, 179
   Moore Park Grammar School, 99
   Nailsworth Public, Adelaide, 109
   National School, Maryport, 161
   Orrong Road Kindergarten, Melbourne, 103
   Rossall, 163
   Royal Agricultural College, Cirencester, 163–5
   Royal Victoria Patriotic, Wandsworth, 107
   St Charles RC, Newton, Glasgow, 134
   St Columba's College, 163
   St Denys, Southampton, 50
   St Kilda Scotch College, Vic, 99
   St Mary's, Southampton, 50
   School of Domestic Economy, Manchester, 105
   Taunton's, 50–1
   The Grange, South Yarra, 95
   Thorndon, Wellington, NZ, 75–6
   Tisbury Boys', 50
   Townsville Grammar, Qld, 87
   Uckfield Agricultural & Horticultural College, 171
   Wadestown, Wellington, NZ, 76, 82
   Wesley College, Melbourne, 124, 126
   West Monmouthshire Grammar School, Pontypool, 152
   Westward Ho, 141
Scotland, 55, 71, 74, 79, 84, 100, 131, 140, 148, 153, 158
   High Steward, 133
Scott, Robert, 175
Scottdale, 152
Scottish Rhodesian Finance Council of Rhodesia, 46
Second World War, 46, 51, 61, 63, 65, 81, 87, 90, 103, 107–108, 116–18, 121, 126, 140, 158–60
Sedd el Bahr, 80
Selly Oak, 64
Sensee River, 26, 28, 31
Serbia, 171
Serre, 1, 161
Seven Network, 93
Sevenoaks, 171
Sewell VC, CH, 177
Seymour & Camp, 112–13, 124
Shanghai, 162
Shaw, Savill & Albion Co, 108, 120
Shell Co, 173
Shepton Mallet, 173
Sherlock Holmes, 174
Ships,
   Clipper *Empress*, 169
   MS *Chrobry*, 164–5

MV *Duntroon*, 125
MV *Fishpool*, 158
PS *La Marguerite*, 48
RMS *Aquitania*, 77
RMS *Ascania*, 141, 143
RMS *Carpathia*, 53
RMS *Empress of Britain*, 145
RMS *Empress of Canada*, 145
RMS *Mauretania*, 145
RMS *Samaria*, 145
RMS *Scythia*, 145
RMS *Titanic*, 53
RMS *Viceroy of India*, 120
SS *Alnwick Castle*, 78
SS *Ascanius*, 121
SS *Aurania*, 145
SS *Ceramic*, 120
SS *Dunattor Castle*, 123
SS *Grantala*, 103
SS *Great Eastern*, 63
SS *Guildford Castle*, 106
SS *Ijn Mogami*, 119
SS *Indarra*, 119
SS *La Marguerite*, 89
SS *Laurentic*, 149
SS *Maunganui*, 76
SS *Menominia*, 99
SS *Minneapolis*, 99
SS *Minnewaska*, 53
SS *Montrose*, 145
SS *New Sevilla*, 123
SS *Orcades*, 91, 113, 129
SS *Princess Victoria*, 88
SS *Rajputana*, 97
SS *Runic*, 123
SS *San Giovannino*, 121
SS *Simla*, 99
SS *Stentor*, 106
SS *Testbank*, 120
SS/TSS *Themistocles*, 100, 108
SS *Van Heutz*, 125
SS *Vita*, 141
SS *Wahehe*, 100, 101
SS *Waimana*, 74
SS *Warwick Castle*, 145
SS *Wiltshire*, 104, 111
SS *Winchester Castle*, 145
Shoeburyness, 135
Shoreditch, 150–1
Shout VC, Alfred, 93
Shrine of Remembrance, Melbourne, 108–109
Shropshire, 66, 70, 133, 145, 165
Sidmouth, 143
Sinai, 90
Sisters of Mercy, 115–16

Sizewell, 148
Slinfold, 176
Sling Camp, Bulford, 74
Smethwick, 63, 66, 68–9, 71
Smethwick Crescent Wheelers Cycling Club, 69–70
Smith, LSgt Edward VC, 1, 3–5, 157–63
Smith, Maj, 162
Smith VC, I, 129
Smuts, Lt Gen JC, 170
Société Générale des Transports Maritimes à *Vapeur*, 120
Society for Physical Research, 66
Soldier Closer Settlement Scheme, 107
Solihull, 64
Somerset, 46–7, 49, 123, 127, 140–1, 154, 166, 171, 173, 179
Somerville, Lt, 135
Somme, Offensive, River & Canal, 1, 14, 17, 22, 25–6, 37, 41–3, 70, 122
Sotheby's, 84, 163
South Africa, 83, 93, 106, 115, 130, 144–5, 147, 172, 178–80
South America, 120, 165
South Atlantic, 120
South Australia, 99, 166, 168–9
    House of Assembly, 166
    Legislative Council, 166
    Public Works, 166
South Carlton, 110
South Farnborough, 140
South Gloucestershire, 173
South Stoneham, 45
South West Africa, 120
South Yarra, 97, 103
Southampton, 45–6, 48–51, 55, 61, 79, 85, 122, 140, 143–5, 150
Southern Hemisphere, 126
Southport, 48
Southsea, 56
Southwell, 152
Southwick, 46
Soviet Union, 113
Spain, 144–5
Special Constabulary Force, 109
Spink & Son, 61, 163, 180
Spittlegate, 110
Spur Wood, 42–4
Sri Lanka, 83, 93, 115, 130
Staff Copse, 161
Stafford, 150–2
Staffordshire, 63–9, 84, 93, 115, 130, 138, 140, 146–52
Stalag VIII–B, 120
Stalybridge, 139–41

Star Wars, 174
Statton VC, Percy, 129
Staverton, 167
Stevens, Arthur, 152
Stewart, Walter, 133
Stilgoe, Sir Richard, 172
Stockport, 164
Stockton-on-Tees, 46
Stokes, Kerry, 93
Stonehouse, John, 51
Stourbridge, 68
Straffan, 165
Streatham, 164
Stubbs VC, Sgt Frank, 80
Subiaco, 116, 123
Subiaco Boys' Orphanage, 115
Suda Bay, 53
Suez, 104
Suffolk, 46, 148, 175
Sullivan VC, AP, 129
Summit, 75
Sun Insurance, 140
Sunda Strait, 119
Sunshine, 126
Sunshine Harvester, 126
Surrey, 47, 57, 60, 64, 78–9, 128, 147, 149, 171, 173–6
Surrey Hills, Vic, 95
Sussex, 46–7, 64, 88, 127–8, 141, 164, 171–3, 175–6
Sutton Coldfield, 147
Sutton Veny, 106–107
Swan, WA, 128
Switzerland, 57
Sydenham, 52
Sydney, Harbour & Bridge, 63, 76, 88, 92–3, 99–100, 110, 114–15, 119, 130, 132
Syndal, 124
Syracuse, 158
Syria, 101

Tangyes Ltd, 63
Tanks,
  Mk IV, 5, 7–9, 11, 32
  Mk V, 7–9, 11
  Whippet, 5, 7–9, 11–12, 32–33
Tara & Usna Hills, 26
Taranaki, 72
Taranto, 140
Tardun, 116
Tasman Sea, 76
Tasmania, 85–7, 92–3, 168
Tasmanian Gold Mining & Quartz Crushing Co, 85
Taunton, Richard, 51
Tauranga Bay, 73
Tel-el-Kebir, 122

Thames & Barrier, 63, 175
Thiepval, 32
Thilloy, 40
Thomas, Ieuan, 152
Thornaby-on-Tees, 143
Threapwood, 169
Tidworth, 96
Tieldsundet, 165
Tientsin, 162
Tilbury, 100
Timaru, 82–3
Timperley, 159
Tirpentwys Colliery, 152–3
Tisbury, 45, 49–50
Tisdall VC, Sub Lt Arthur, 80
To Russia and Back Through Comminist Countries, 113
Tombs, Thomas, 82
Tombstone, 75
Tonyrefail, 127
Torokina, 126
Toronto, 142
Torquay, Qld, 91
Torrington, 151
Touvent Farm, 161
Tower Hamlets Spur, 155
Towner VC, ET, 129
Towns, Robert, 87
Townsville, Qld, 86–7, 125
Trades Council, 64
Transvaal, 172, 179
Transvaal Repatriation Department, 172
Trenches,
  Courtine, 18–20
  Foch, 18–19
  Wurttemburg, 20
Trenton, Ont, 142
Trevethin, 152
Triangle Copse, 12
Tunbridge Wells, 144
Tupsley, 157, 159
Turkey/ish, 80–1, 171
Turnberry, 110
Turner, William, 175
Turrall, Pte Thomas VC, 69–70
Twmpath, 152
Tyne, 158
Tynemouth, 139
Tyrell Downs, 103
Tyrone, Co, 163

Ukerewe Island, 170
Ukraine, 83, 93, 115, 130
Ulverston, 158
Union Castle Mail Steamship Co, 106, 123

Union Steamship Co, 76
United Nations, 94
United Service Publicity, 109
United States of America, 57, 65, 74–5, 83, 93, 98, 115, 126, 130, 143, 148–9, 151–2
United States armed forces, 87, 103
    United States Army, 151
        No.1 (Presbyterian USA) General Hospital, 147
    United States Navy,
        USS *Houston*, 119
        USS *Perth*, 119
Universities,
    Birmingham, 78
    Christ Church, Oxford, 166
    Manchester, 105
    Trinity College, Cambridge, 163
    Trinity College, Dublin, 166
Upper Hutt, 73
Upton, 127
Utah, 74–6

Vacuum Oil Co, 99
Valenciennes, 54
Valetta, 76, 120
Van Diemen's Land, *see* Tasmania
Vancouver, 76, 158
Vaulx-Vraucourt, 1, 177
Vauvillers, 17
Vaux-sur-Somme, 111
Vaux Wood, 44
Veale VC, Theodore, 154–5
Vera Cruz, 165
Vermandovillers, 18, 42, 122, 127, 130
Vestfjorden, 165
Victor Comic, 138,
Victoria, 89, 94–104, 107–12, 114, 123–4, 128, 130
    Heritage Register, 126
    State Electricity Commission, 100
    Town & Country Planning Board, 109
Victoria Barracks, Melbourne, 112
Victoria Cross & George Cross Association & Reunions, 60, 113
Victoria Cross Centenary 1956, 60, 91, 113, 129
Victoria Cross Dinner, House of Lords 1929, 60, 154, 162
Victoria Cross Garden Party, 60, 154, 162
Vimy Ridge, 144
Vintage Motor Cycle Club, 70
Viscount Tredegar, 152
Von Richthofen, Baron Manfred (Red Baron), 111
Vosper Ltd, 141
Vraucourt, 37
Vunipola, Mako, 152

Waimangaroa, 73
Wain VC, RWL, 177
Waipawa, 74
Wakamarina, 72
Wales, 105
Walker, Maj Gen Harold, 104
Wallace, William, 56, 133
Wallsend on Tyne, 139
Walsall, 68, 146
Walton-on-Thames, 79
Walvis Bay, 120
Wandsworth, 107, 174–5
Wanstead, 144
War Bonds, 161
War Service Badge, 66
Wardour Castle, 50
Ware, 47
Warlencourt, 32, 36, 39
Warminster, 107
Warren, Revd Hubert, 96
Warwick, 64
Warwickshire, 46, 63–6, 68, 110, 141, 147, 150, 153, 164
Washington DC, 152
Watt, James, 146
Waverley, NSW, 115, 130
WD Joynt & Co, 107
Wednesbury, 67, 146–7
Wellington, 66
Wellington, NZ, 71–6, 82–3
Wellington Bomber, 65
Welshpool, WA, 118
Wem, 165
Wenger, Arsene, 146
Wenlock, 133
Wepener, 171
Wern, 152
West Bromwich, 65–6, 69, 138, 146, 148
West Coast, NZ, 73
West Ham, 144
West, Lt Col Richard VC, 1, 11–12, 163–80
West Midlands, 71, 157
West Newton, 160
Westbourne Park, 164
Westcliffe-on-Sea, 56
Western Australia, 76, 103, 115, 118–19, 123–24, 130
    Government House, 128
    Legislative Assembly, 128
    Lunacy Department, 116
Western Australia Railways, 118
Western Desert, 59
Westham Camp, 141
Westmeath, Co, 135

Westminster, 106, 144
Westmoreland Co, 152
Weston-super-Mare, 47, 123, 125, 127–8, 154
Wexford, Co, 166
Weyhill, 111
Weymouth, 89, 101, 111, 141
Wharfedale, 173
White, Abraham, 118
White Park, 163
White Star Line, 120, 123
Whitefield, Alderman W, 156
Whitehall, Hants, 145
Whiteheath, 68
Whittle VC, JW, 129
Wicklow, 170
Wicklow, Co, 163, 166, 168–9
Wigton, 160
Willenhall, 68
William Denny & Bros, 119
William Dodgshun & Sons, 95
Williams, Police Sgt, 156
Williton, 46
Wilton, 47, 50, 56
Wiltshire, 45–50, 56, 60, 74, 78, 85–6, 88–9, 96, 101, 105–106, 111, 122, 132, 147, 150, 171
Wimbledon, 124, 171
Wimereux, 89
Wincanton, 140
Winchester, 145

Windsor, Vic, 123
Winsford, 171
Wisconsin, 151
Wodonga, Vic, 114, 130
Woking, 60
Wokingham, 167
Wollongong, 132, 153
Wolverhampton, 63, 66–8, 140, 145, 149–51
Wood, Lt Col Ronald, 12
Woodley, 166
Woods VC, J, 129
Woolwich, Dockyard, 128
Worcester, 69, 106
Worcestershire, 64, 65, 68–70, 127, 148
Workington, 159
Workman, Clark, 121
Worshipful Company of Haberdashers, 152
Worthing, 175–6

Yarm-on-Tees, 143
Yate, 45, 47
Yattendon, 58
York, 176
York, WA, 115, 117, 130
York Town, Tas, 85
Yorkshire, 47, 132, 140, 143, 146, 159–60, 173
Ypres, 54, 96, 105, 155

Zeitoun, 101, 150